21 DAYS
TO A
HAPPIER
FAMILY

21 DAYS TO A HAPPIER FAMILY

Dr JUSTIN COULSON, PhD

ABC
Books

All names in the case studies described in this book
have been changed.

The ABC 'Wave' device is a trademark of the
Australian Broadcasting Corporation and is used
under licence by HarperCollinsPublishers Australia.

First published in Australia in 2016
by HarperCollinsPublishers Australia Pty Limited
ABN 36 009 913 517
harpercollins.com.au

HarperCollins*Publishers*
Level 13, 201 Elizabeth Street, Sydney, NSW 2000, Australia
Unit D1, 63 Apollo Drive, Rosedale, Auckland 0632, New Zealand
A 53, Sector 57, Noida, UP, India
1 London Bridge Street, London, SE1 9GF, United Kingdom
2 Bloor Street East, 20th floor, Toronto, Ontario M4W 1A8, Canada
195 Broadway, New York, NY 10007

National Library of Australia Cataloguing-in-Publication data:

Coulson, Justin, author.
  Title: 21 days to a happier family / by Justin Coulson.
  ISBN: 978 0 7333 3481 8 (paperback)
  Subjects: Parenting – Handbooks, manuals, etc.
  Child rearing – Handbooks, manuals, etc.
  Parent and child.
306.874

Cover design by Christa Moffitt, Christabella Designs
Typeset in Sabon LT Std by Kirby Jones

For families that want to be happier

Contents

Foreword

An epiphany is a funny thing. We have that light-bulb moment. We see something, hear something or think something, and in that instant everything changes for us.

We become motivated. Inspired. Committed to change – to do something different. To be someone new.

But epiphanies tend to be short-lived.

Our patterns of behaving in particular ways are well established, and are therefore hard to break. It takes extraordinary sustained effort to make a commitment stick, particularly once the emotion we felt when we made the commitment or had the epiphany has passed.

But in 2002, I had an epiphany that hit hard. It changed everything. It is the reason you have this book in your hand. It was a moment that began a cascade of actions that became life-altering.

The lasting change did not occur because of one moment of insight. While the insight was a catalyst, it was the way my behaviour changed over the subsequent weeks, months and years that made the epiphany lead to a new life.

How a big mistake created a big change

We all have moments with our children that we wish we could take back. It was one of those moments that acted as a critical pivot point in my life and my family's.

Most parenting books don't start with a confession from the

author. But if you are struggling in your family, I want you to know that I have been there – and I often still am. I've made the mistakes – I do understand.

As a young dad I was struggling. My idea of childrearing was to have cute children who would bring me joy, grow up, go to school, become teenagers and that's that. I had clearly never contemplated the realities of parenting. I knew that other people had challenges with their children, but I guessed those parents had no idea how to say 'no' to their children; that they were complete pushovers.

My expectation was that now and then my children would need to be told to change their behaviour, and my demands would be met. End of story.

With no preparation for parenthood and no idea about what I was doing when the children arrived, it is probably no surprise that my experience failed to match my expectations. Having a baby was a joy at times but dealing with sleepless nights, severe reflux, feeding challenges and the other usual issues left me feeling out of my depth. Using naivety as a shield for my incompetence, I passed all childrearing duties to my wife, Kylie. Fortunately, Kylie was better prepared.

But it was having a toddler that really sent me into a spin. Within months of our first daughter beginning to assert a desire for independent thought and action, I became an angry disciplinarian. I threatened. I yelled. I withdrew privileges (from a toddler!). And I smacked. Regularly.

And I could not be told, by anyone, how I might deal with the situation better.

My toddler had become the enemy and, from my perspective, had to be 'broken', in the same way a cowboy breaks in a horse. Toddlerhood, I decided, had to be defeated, and it was my job to tame my daughter and make sure she understood who was boss.

'You've become very hard, Justin,' my grandmother gently

chided me. And I agreed: 'You've got to be! Otherwise the little rats will run riot all over you.' (Nan was unimpressed with my response.)

My mother-in-law suggested a softer approach. 'She has to learn,' was my instant rebuttal.

My refusal to listen to those with wisdom and experience only highlighted my immaturity. I knew better. But if I did know better, why was I struggling so badly?

My punitive responses to my toddler's challenging behaviour increased. She turned three. The terrible twos migrated with her into a new, harder-to-deal-with age-bracket. As my toddler grew, I expected more of her, but she wasn't getting any easier to manage. And despite being aware that what I was doing wasn't working, I became increasingly convinced that I had to be hard on my daughter to stop those toddler tantrums. After all, if something doesn't work, you should do more of it to get a result, shouldn't you?

One Saturday afternoon, Kylie left our two children with me while she ran a short errand. Our baby, Abbie, was just a couple of months old. Chanel was three years older – to the day. Me, I had been up late the night before and only slept a handful of hours before getting up for work at 5am that Saturday morning. I was exhausted.

Within moments of Kylie leaving, Chanel began to act up. My efforts to calm her, by telling her to 'Stop it now!', were ineffective. Her tantrum escalated. Her fraught emotions were contagious and it didn't take any time at all for me to 'catch' the intensity of them. As her tantrum began to build I matched her upset with my anger.

My first reaction was to threaten her. Then I moved on to punishing my three-year-old by locking her in her room. Next I yelled and threatened because she was kicking the door. She responded with more anger and so I opened the door and dragged her into the living room, where I smacked her. Several times. Hard.

She had to learn a lesson. She had to respect me. I was in charge.

It will come as no surprise to any experienced parent that my 'discipline' brought with it unintended consequences. Chanel became louder. She screamed more, rather than less. She cried. And, for some reason, I had expected something different?

Now I was scared the baby would wake up. My anger increased and my response was furious. I forced Chanel back into her bedroom and threw her onto her bed amid a torrid combination of my venomous threats and her frightened and angry screams, cries and tears. Angry at her, and angry at myself, I held the door handle as she sobbed, kicked and tried to get out of her room. I hated being out of control. And I hated her for making me feel and act this way. Yet something told me that Chanel had not *made* me do anything. In my heart I knew that *I* was responsible for how I had behaved. Not her. She was acting like a toddler. And me? I was having as big a tantrum as she was. Only I was double her height and seven times her weight. I had betrayed her with my anger. But I had also betrayed myself, and I had used her as a justification for my angry behaviour.

As I hung onto that door handle, the light-bulb moment occurred. This is not how a father ought to treat his child. A quote came to mind: 'The only time a father should lay his hands on his children is to bless them.' And I was falling short. My hands were anything but a blessing to my little one. If I was being like this with a three-year-old, how was I going to survive with a 16-year-old? And how would she survive?

When Chanel finally stopped fighting with the door handle and, I guess, helplessly succumbed to her bedroom prison, I walked into the backyard for some air. And some clarity. With my back against the door, I stared at the overgrown former vegetable patch of our rental property and tried to drink in the newfound peace of this quiet, sunny Queensland afternoon. But there was no peace inside me – only guilt-induced emotional pain.

'I am a bad father.'

I knew it. In spite of all of the wonderful interactions I'd had with my daughter, I was getting it wrong *every time* her behaviour became challenging. And I had no idea what to do about it. My impatient responses lacked any semblance of understanding, perspective, compassion or kindness. I was only interested in stopping her from being so damn inconvenient. The only tool I was using was my power to coerce and control, and the power struggles were harming her trust in me. I also knew Kylie was wondering what kind of a person she had married.

I was failing my family.

The epiphany was completed when I heard a tremendous fight happening in a backyard a few doors down. A father was screaming at a toddler, whose tantrum was at full force within moments. It was as though my previous interactions with my daughter were being replayed so that I could witness exactly how my behaviour sounded. And it stung.

The challenge of change

I wish I could say that from that day forward I became a perfect parent but that would be dishonest. Change is a process. And change is hard. It is particularly difficult when we don't even know what to change, or how to change it. Having alternative pathways to travel is critical. If we want to stop doing something, it's much easier to successfully do so if we have something to replace it with. I knew of no alternatives.

I was a 26-year-old radio announcer with barely a high-school education. Since I was 15 I had dreamed of being on-air, and over the ensuing years I had built a successful career with one of the top radio stations in the country. I talked on the radio for several hours each morning, programmed the music for the station, and enjoyed the status and perks that came with the job. I knew my top 40. I knew my celebrity gossip. But I knew nothing about being a parent.

I started reading about parenting and personal leadership. I continued making mistakes, but I was attempting to improve. Change was challenging.

My dissatisfaction with who I was as a person was clashing with some workplace issues I was having, and I began a conversation with Kylie that changed our lives: 'Maybe I should quit my career and go and study psychology at university so I can learn how to be a dad.'

Some unanticipated work challenges made the decision easier and a few short months later I was back at school for the first time in a decade. The career, the status and the income were gone. I was a full-time TAFE student in my mid-late twenties with a wife, two children and a mortgage.

For the next eight-and-a-half years I studied full-time, worked part-time, and began a change process that impacted our lives immeasurably. I completed my undergraduate psychological science degree and earned first-class honours, which was a wonderful surprise for a guy who wondered how he'd made it through high school. I graduated a few years later with a PhD in psychology, wrote my first book, and began to teach parents the things I had taken the best part of a decade to learn.

And while my knowledge and understanding were growing, our family was growing too. We had our third and fourth daughters while I completed my undergraduate degree, our fifth daughter while I earned my PhD, and our sixth daughter three years later.

The change process continued. There were regular setbacks, mistakes and absolute failures. There were days when I laughed scornfully at myself for believing I might be a parenting 'expert' when I couldn't get it right for my own family. But slowly, with sustained effort and a commitment to learning what makes family life happy and healthy, we kept our family together. Kylie and I both grew to become better parents.

Change is a process

Family life is still a process. Both Kylie and I still make our fair share of mistakes. We have plenty of moments we wish we could do all over again – though none nearly as unpleasant as the one that started this incredible journey of learning and change. We make no claims to perfection – as you'll see as you read some of the stories in this book.

A critical insight occurred early on in this process of learning what it takes to be a better parent and have a happier family. It guides the entire premise of this book: *being a better parent is not about our children*. At all. Being a better parent is about *us*. It is about refining our character, and developing our unique, positive attributes. It is about becoming the best person we can be so we can effectively guide and teach our children to be the best people they can be. *We make our family happier by making ourselves better*. As we become more patient and understanding, more grateful and mindful, more focused on teaching than punishing, and more interested in being compassionate and kind, we make ourselves better, our children feel more loved, and our family is happier.

It is my hope that as you read this book you'll have light-bulb moments from start to finish. But more than that, it is my hope these epiphanies will not just last a moment, or a day or week. Rather, it is my hope that they will lead to meaningful, long-term change in your life as an individual, as well as in your family. Within 21 days I would love to get an email from you telling me that your family has become happier because of what you have read and the way you have changed. Here's my email address: info@justincoulson.com. Use it. I'd love to hear from you.

Change is a challenge. Change is a process. But if you're up for it, the change you make may be just what you need to make your family happier.

Justin Coulson, September 2015

Introduction

We are what we repeatedly do.
Excellence, then, is not an act, but a habit.
Aristotle

Emailing a stranger and asking for help with a parenting problem is a relatively unusual thing to do. Most people feel uncomfortable exposing their vulnerabilities, particularly around family relationships. To trawl the internet in search of an 'expert', and then to email that person to seek guidance, is an act of faith. It is typically a measure of last resort, only to be considered after everything else you've tried has failed. I receive such emails from worried, frustrated or stressed-out parents regularly, and they usually sound fairly urgent – sometimes even desperate. And I take these emails seriously.

'I need your help!' said an email from mother-of-four Sonya, who had major concerns. We scheduled a video conference session for coaching and at the appointed time, I dialled in. The webcam showed a man and woman seated in a sparsely furnished modern and immaculate soft, grey study. Sonya was sitting attentively in front of the computer with pen in hand. Her husband, Michael, sat slouched in an office chair some distance from the desk. He wore a black polo shirt and an expression that suggested apathy and defensiveness. His legs were stretched out in front of him, crossed, and his arms were folded across his chest.

Sonya got straight to the point. With a reluctant nod of permission from Michael, she detailed the story of her husband's deteriorating relationship with their 13-year-old daughter, Abbey. Niggling annoyances had been building up, and interactions between father and daughter had become increasingly abrasive and contemptuous. In recent days the tension had mounted to the point where Michael became physically aggressive towards Abbey, pushing her against a wall and slapping her. Abbey had run away, and only returned late the next day. The situation had been tense since, and Sonya was desperate to work out how her family could be happy again. Michael was hurt by his daughter's actions. He was angry at her, embarrassed at his own behaviour, and he believed the problem was less his and more Abbey's.

During the session we talked about their relationships, strategies for developing trust, and where to go from here. As the conversation progressed, Michael became increasingly defensive. In his eyes it was all Abbey's fault, and she was the one who needed to change.

'Michael,' I suggested, 'perhaps our thinking another person is "the problem" makes us "the problem".'

Having this insight was essential for Michael to become open to change. If he could not accept that his refusal to forgive his daughter was stopping progress, and if he would not change the way he was acting towards her, things would stagnate at best, or more likely, spiral downwards.

> Our thinking another person is 'the problem' makes us 'the problem'.

Getting relationships right

We all want happy families. Our lives are happier when our family relationships are strong and positive. We thrive when we feel loved, trusted and appreciated, and we flourish when we feel connected and attuned to those around us. But we languish, struggling, when our relationships are filled with contention and rejection.

While it is true that many things contribute to our happiness, the quality of our relationships is one of *the* central predictors of our overall wellbeing. Contrary to popular belief (and our wildest dreams), striking it rich does not translate into happiness and wellbeing. Having new toys to play with feels nice for a while, but our happiness wanes as the hedonic treadmill keeps on turning and we set our sights on newer, brighter, more exciting doodads. Luxuries, comforts and all of the 'things' we are told we need may provide temporary pleasure but fail to provide the long-term joy and meaning in life that we seek.[1] And the cliché that the most important things in life aren't things holds up to scientific examination and personal experience.

Harvard psychologist Robert Putnam quantified the effect good relationships have on our happiness as follows.

> A marriage can cause an increase in happiness equal to a quadrupling salary. Making a good friend is equal to tripling a salary. Belonging to a club can cause an increase in happiness equivalent to doubling a salary. And going on picnics three times a year is the same as receiving a 10 per cent raise.[2]

Which is the better path for improving your life? Better relationships or a quadrupled salary? We might predict that money matters most, but if we have the money and our relationships aren't working, we will still be unhappy. The ultimate take-home message is short and simple, and has become the mantra of the burgeoning positive psychology movement: other people matter. The way we relate to and interact with those closest to us determines how happy we are.

Making families happy means making change possible

If you're reading this book, you probably want your family to be happier. Maybe your children are in a habit of ignoring your requests and you are desperate for them to *just listen!* Perhaps you find yourself shouting and getting angry at the slightest provocation and you want to get your reactions under control. Or you may be dealing with a teenager who is committed to making decisions that are incongruent with your values, and your relationship is suffering.

I grew up with a saying: 'The definition of insanity is to keep doing the same thing you've always done, but to expect a different outcome.'

And yet that's precisely the insane thing we do so often in family life. The children don't listen, so we yell. When they don't react, we yell louder. When the chores aren't done, or curfews aren't adhered to, or homework isn't completed, we confiscate devices or withdraw privileges. When things don't improve, we become increasingly punitive. Our home descends in a spiral of negativity that saps our spirit and ruptures our relationships.

So change is necessary to make our families happier. But change is hard work. If your family is not happy, it will require sustained effort to make the required changes. And it will likely also mean failure. Lots of failure. And when we fail, we begin the change process again.

Michelle, a client I coached, shared with me the following story about how hard change is.

We had our first session together on a Friday afternoon. You assured me that I would make mistakes and probably fail spectacularly the first few times I tried to do what we spoke about, but I was confident. After our phone conversation I set about preparing to make the afternoon and evening

4

perfect for the family. Dinner was ready early. Activities were set out for the children. The house was tidied. But it all unravelled before my husband had even arrived home. The children were feral. They wouldn't do anything I asked them, and the night got worse and worse until I finally gave up and sent them all to bed, and went to bed myself to read a book.

Failure is a part of parenting but it seems that we feel worst about our failures at those times when we are trying hardest to get things right. Fortunately, with sustained effort, things began to improve for Michelle.

On Sunday I had a big win, though. My husband and I were outside with our three-year-old daughter, Lily, and our 18-month-old son, Ethan. Lily was being difficult and threw some small rocks onto the pathway. I told her it was time to pick them up and put them back where they'd come from, but she refused and started to tantrum. She was really, really upset.

My initial reaction was to be angry with her. I wanted to reprimand her for being disobedient and cranky. But then I remembered that this would probably only upset her more. My husband started to tell her off, but I said, 'Let me handle this one.' I asked if I could hold her, and she came to my arms in spite of the tantrum. I picked her up and we walked inside. It was really hard, but I stayed totally calm and loving towards her. I told her that I understood that she was upset, and that as soon as she calmed down we could talk about things. Lily's tantrum seemed to be easing. It was as though she was responding to my patience. I kept trying to be understanding, and told her I knew she was really sad, and gave another offer of a cuddle. She didn't want one. I reminded her that she could have one as soon as she was calm, and offered one more time before I walked out. This time she came straight to me and we hugged.

While she was in my arms, I told her I could see how sad she was. I asked if she was upset because she had to pick up the rocks. My assumption was that the tantrum was because she didn't want to tidy up her mess. I didn't expect her response.

'No mummy. I'm sad because daddy pulled the special mushrooms out of the grass, and that's where the fairies live, and now they won't have anywhere to live because he ruined their home!'

We hugged some more. Then we walked outside and I explained the problem to my husband. He looked at me, dumbfounded.

'Was that it?' was all he could ask.

Michelle explained to me that she would normally have gone 'old-school' in reaction to Lily's tantrum – she would have been angry and explained that no means no, or said, 'When I tell you to do something, you do it!' Then she would have punished her little girl with time out, and demanded that she 'stop being such a child'. But by carefully and intentionally changing her approach – which took significant effort – Michelle's family became happier. Together they scoured the grass for more mushrooms. When they found them, Lily was assured that the fairies could move in there until the other mushrooms grew back. Then they walked to the path where Lily happily picked up all of the rocks without any problems at all.

There are several important lessons to learn from Michelle's story, including the power of empathy and understanding, and the impact of giving our children a voice – each of which we will explore throughout this book. When we see the world through our children's eyes, we change our parenting and make our families happier. In Michelle's case, she was only able to do these things by stopping herself from going down old, familiar paths. For Michelle to make her family happier, she had to change the way she responded to her daughter. But the change was hard work because it went against her typical, normal reaction. You will note, however, that the change didn't take long. Rather than 21 days, it was probably closer to 21 seconds!

Why change is hard

To change our parenting, we have to change our thinking – which means changing the neural pathways we use in every interaction with our children. And that means quite literally forcing our brain to send messages through pathways that are weak, or unused, or perhaps creating new pathways because the ones we wish to use are presently non-existent.

Out of habit (and ease) our brains want to use the neural pathways that have always been used. These are the strong ones – the ones that are naturally and automatically followed. There is little or no resistance when the well-trodden pathways are used, but it is hard when the brain is forced to use weak pathways or make new ones. In doing so, however, the weak pathways grow stronger and new pathways become accessible. We call this neuroplasticity,[3] which simply means our brains have a large degree of flexibility – they can change. As we force ourselves to do things in new ways, we literally re-wire our brains. We create new pathways with our new actions that, when used enough, become new habits that shape our character.

Think of a piece of wood where you use a tool to create a smooth groove about one centimetre deep that runs straight along its surface. Imagine yourself running your gouging tool easily along the groove. Perhaps you decide you would like to create a new groove, starting in the same place but turning midway along to make a curve. As you commence the turn, the walls of your groove will at first prevent you from making a new pathway, and it will take significant effort – and maybe even specialised tools – to break out of the pre-existing path you have gouged in the wood.

American philosopher, essayist and poet Ralph Waldo Emerson described what happens when we make the effort to change well before science could explain it in neuroanatomical terms when he reportedly said, 'That which we persist in doing becomes easier for us to do. Not that the nature of the thing itself has changed, but that our power to do has increased.'[4]

Creating change in our lives wears us out, however, both in our brain and in our body. And when we get worn out, we are likely to revert to our old habits via our old, well-used neural pathways. In times of stress, your worst practised habit becomes your default.

Do you remember the time you made a commitment that you would stop shouting at the children, only to raise your voice in your very next interaction with them? Or perhaps you decided your family would definitely be happier if you spent Sunday afternoons together, only to find that commitments kept popping up, or family members were unwilling to participate in your plans?

In his book, *Willpower*,[5] celebrated psychological scientist Roy Baumeister uses the HALT acronym – Hungry, Angry, Lonely or Tired – to suggest when our commitment to change is most likely to fail. I would add 'Stressed' and 'Sick' to that list, and there are times when change is made all the more difficult because we are experiencing multiple items from that list.

Then there's that other H that gets in the way of change – the one that stands for habit. If you've ever tried to give up chocolate or sweets, improve your fitness or even make the smallest adjustment to the way your family works, you will know that kicking your old habits and replacing them with new ones requires enormous ongoing focus and effort. Making the changes we want to make in our families will be tough at times – especially when our family members also have their own habits they may or may not want to change.

How habits harm our chance at change

One of my favourite workshop activities occurs at the end of many of my presentations. I invite everyone to stand up and pair up with someone nearby. I ask each pair to take a close look at the appearance of their partner, and then turn back to back. While each pair facing away from each other, I invite them to change three things about their appearance – without removing any major clothing articles! Once they've made the three changes I invite them to face one another again and identify what's different. There is a lot of laughter as people comment on dishevelled hair, untucked shirts or folded sleeves. We repeat the process a second time, usually to a chorus of groans. Each pair goes back to back and makes a further three changes. Making the initial three changes is enough for some people, and the extra effort to change even more seems too much. For others, making additional change is near impossible. They may only be wearing a dress and a pair of shoes. Often they don't even have any jewellery.

Once the second series of three changes is completed, everyone turns to face their partner again to identify the ever-stranger adjustments in appearance. At the completion of this second phase I ask each pair to turn back to back *again* and make three further changes. This is the third time they have to do this, and usually the audience looks at me with exasperation. The more vocal participants often complain loudly enough for me to hear that 'This is getting ridiculous!' or 'Not again!' or even 'You've got to be kidding me!' Everyone laughs – and sighs with relief – when at this point I stop the activity and invite them to take their seats. Then the real activity begins.

'What does this activity teach us about change?' I ask. The answers come quickly, and usually include:

- 'We all have different capacity for change. Some people have lots they can change about themselves, while others have very little.'
- 'Some changes are obvious to everyone, while others are harder to notice.'
- 'Some people enjoy change, while other people find it uncomfortable.'
- 'When we try to make changes we can look and feel quite foolish.'
- 'We need to be "aware" of what can change. I could think of things my partner could change, but they couldn't.'

These are all great answers, and are generally true for most people. By this time everyone feels they have a pretty good handle on the ins and outs of change. The conversation has gone on for several minutes.

Then I ask, 'Who has changed their appearance back to how it was at the start of the activity?'

In almost every case, the entire audience has undone all of the changes they made to their appearance during the activity. Their shoes and socks are back on. Ties are done back up. Hair is tidy and jewellery is back in place. Shirts and blouses are tucked back in. Glasses are perched where they were most comfortable. Belts are re-threaded.

'Why?' I ask. 'At no point did I tell everyone to change back. You've all just done it. Automatically. Out of habit.'

At this point, the answers become even more insightful because my audience realises that those changes occurred without them even thinking about it. Everyone changes back to the state that feels normal out of habit.

What does this have to do with making my family happier?

Let's say that I was in the habit of matching my child's volume when dealing with challenging behaviour but that I vowed to change – to speak softly and kindly. If I want to change that habit, I need to respond to my daughter yelling in a way that is different to my normal response until my *new* response becomes automatic. While I'm concentrating, I'll probably do okay most of the time. But when I am hungry, angry, lonely or tired (or stressed or sick), or when I'm not being mindful, my best attempts will often fail. My new kind response is not automatic yet. The new neural pathways are not formed strongly enough. I'm still in that old groove. If I'm not paying attention, I'll change back. It's my least practised habit.

It is only as I continue to incrementally strengthen the association between the stimulus (my daughter yelling) and my chosen response (answering her softly) that I create a new habit. When I am responding to that stimulus efficiently with a lack of attention because I don't need to concentrate and control myself so much, then I am making that new behaviour my habit.

Habits are powerful. In family life, habits can disrupt and damage our relationships, forcing parents and children (and spouses) into impossible situations where criticism and condemnation infuse every interaction, and where the smallest provocations (or perceptions of provocation) stimulate angry outbursts. Yet when they work for us, habits can do incredible things to foster and promote warmth, love, availability, communication and happiness.

Does it really take 21 days to make a habit and 21 days to break one?

This adage has existed for decades in spite of there being almost no empirical basis for the claim that it takes 21 days to make a habit and 21 days to break one.[6] Such a generalisation fails to take into account the type of habit being made, the temperament of the person attempting to make the habit, the context related to the habit, the complexity of the habit, the strength of the habit needing to be broken, and so on.

I don't buy the claim that doing 'x' for 21 days results in a new habit. If you've ever moved house but stayed near your old neighbourhood, chances are you have accidentally driven to your old address (or at least part of the way there) at least once or twice. But it probably didn't take you a full three weeks to feel as though the journey to your new home was automatic.

Comparatively, if you have ever tried to stop nail-biting, nose-picking, teeth-grinding, swearing, saying 'um' or 'like' or other verbal crutches, interrupting when other people speak, or obsessively checking your devices for email or social media messages, there's every chance it took longer than three weeks of concerted effort. Perhaps you're still working on it today after several years!

So why 21 days?

Changing the way you parent can be a complex thing. There will be days where you get it wrong, or miss out on opportunities to practise the habits you want to create. You're trying to undo something that has been a neural superhighway for the entire time you've been a parent, and potentially the entire time you've been a human!

I suggest that you read each chapter of this book carefully. There are 21 different things you can do to make your family happier. Choose to do *one or two relatively simple things*. Work on making them automatic and as you feel them becoming your natural way of doing things, slowly build on that with other ideas. You can and will change how happy your family is almost every time you use one of these methods successfully – and it will only take 21 seconds in most cases, and not 21 days! But it does take a while for that new idea to become a habit. So be consistent. Do it over and over, every chance you get, and you will see a real and measurable difference in your family's happiness.

Now, a note of caution. If you were to do all 21 things recommended in this book, you might be adding a degree of complexity to your life that dooms you to failure. Some of the ideas I describe are really simple – like asking your children what they are grateful for while you have dinner or while you put them to bed. Other ideas require ongoing focus and effort, like being mindful or accepting life and all it throws at you. These concepts may take much longer to incorporate as an automatic way of being a parent.

Are you willing to consider how you might change your parenting habits? The only way that things can change is if we change. I'm sad to report that in the story of Sonya, Michael and Abbey, Michael chose not to change. His pride and resentment combined to work against him, and against his family. Rather than working on new habits, he clung to his belief that it was up to his daughter to change – and thus nothing changed.

Comparatively, a couple called Frances and Laurie who believed their family was doomed flew me interstate for some one-on-one parenting coaching. Laurie was angry. Frances was trying to change him. Their relationship was antagonistic, and their children bore the brunt of their psychological inflexibility – the inability to change the way they thought about things. We spent some time together and looked at the habits they had developed as a family. They committed, together, to make changes. My last correspondence with Frances, nearly six months after my visit, showed that habits can shift quickly, and for the long-term. While still not entirely automatic, the changes they made altered the climate of their family.

'After a rocky start our family is so much more united,' Frances told me. 'As soon as I stepped back and allowed Laurie to work on improving his relationship with [our son], things started to improve for them. [It created a] much calmer environment for everyone.'

This book is not a prescription. Instead it is a description of a range of scientifically based strategies, habits and practices that parents can implement to improve the wellbeing of family members, and the quality of our family's functioning. The book is full of ideas to make your family happier. You may find that every single idea is of worth to you and your family. If so, great! But if not, you might find it useful to skip ahead to the next chapter and focus on the ideas that work for you.

I believe that if you work on developing the ideas in this book into habits, you will find greater joy, meaning and happiness in your family – fast. Those I've coached have found the ideas I share here have led to new habits and happier families in just a few days. In Michelle's case, it was just a few minutes. Their new habits and ways of thinking have made an enormous difference in the climate of their family. We can make a *decision* to change in less than 21 seconds. Change starts now. A happy family starts now. It's as simple as a decision, made now, and then repeated every time you feel like going back to your old habits.

Are you ready? Do you want to change? Do you believe you can change? The pathways to a happier family are in the following pages. With a clear goal, helpful pathways and a willingness to have a go, your relationships can be better now.

CHAPTER 1

Step one to a happy family: setting your course

When you do not know which harbour you are
making for, no wind is the right wind.

Seneca

It was a Friday morning and I had a presentation to deliver. I arrived at the venue feeling calm with time to spare – until I realised I had forgotten my notes! I was being paid to deliver an all-day training session, and I didn't know what I was going to say beyond the first hour or so. I called my wife, Kylie, in a panic.

Fortunately the training venue was only an hour from home. I apologised to Kylie for destroying her morning, gave her the address, and made what preparations I could. We took a slightly early morning tea and I rang Kylie.

'I thought you'd be here by now,' I said. 'Where are you?'

'I could ask you the same thing,' Kylie responded.

I was perplexed. 'I gave you the address.' I then proceeded to name the street and suburb again.

'I'm on that street,' replied Kylie, 'but I can't see any building with that name. What number is it? I've driven all the way to the end of the street where the building should be but I'm stuck next to a paddock!'

I had no idea of the number, but found out quickly and gave Kylie the information. Within moments we realised the road had two ends divided by a paddock and the technology we were using didn't seem to recognise the obstruction. Kylie eventually found her way around the paddock and gave me my course notes.

In family life we need to know where we are going. The clearer our direction, the more likely it is that we can get there. Kylie knew the suburb and street, so she got close to my location, but without precise detail, she couldn't get to me.

Mission statements, manifestos and guiding principles

You've probably heard of the idea of a mission statement or a manifesto. If you have, please don't roll your eyes and sigh, thinking this is all too hard. Remember that stuff in the Introduction about habits being hard to break? Well, this is step one. We need to know what habits we want to make, and a mission statement or some similar statement of intent may be a remarkably useful tool to work that out. You must imagine a new future before you can create it.

Initially popularised in organisations by management guru Peter Drucker[7] in the 1970s and then given a worldwide popularity boost in the late 1980s in Stephen R. Covey's bestselling *The 7 Habits of Highly Effective People*,[8] a mission statement is a creed or a statement of our values or philosophy. It outlines what we want to do – our *goals*. It also emphasises what we want to be – our self-definition – when we are at our best. The idea is that it metaphorically points us towards the harbour we seek.

> You must imagine your new future before you can create it.

Because of the way mission statements have been used, a lot of people are sceptical about trying to run their business or their family according to a mission statement. They don't work so well when they're written by a couple of people at the 'top of the tree', when the mission statement sits on a wall or shelf with occasional lip service being paid in its direction. Additionally, writing a mission statement, creed or manifesto requires *thought* and *introspection*. It can be hard work, and you can be forgiven for feeling like it is just one more thing you have to do. But the worst thing is that once it's written, it serves as a constant reminder of everything we're not doing! Every time we fall short of our ideals, it can make us feel guilty.

At least, that's how I used to feel about mission statements. But when we look at them with an alternative view, we can begin the process of changing the culture of our family to fit the new philosophy – a mission statement gives us a chance to develop new routines and habits.

Research really does confirm that well-done mission statements work. But we need to get a handful of things right for a mission statement to make our family successful, such as the points that follow.

1. Everyone should buy into the mission statement
2. Everyone needs to have some say in how it is created
3. The mission statement has to make sense for everyone
4. Everyone must be committed to follow it.[9]

The impact of creating a mission statement varies based on how well those principles are followed, but it seems the direction the statement provides helps steer companies in the direction of their goals. They are also useful for individuals who create them for their own lives. But do mission statements work in families?

There are plenty of people who say, emphatically, 'YES!' And even though empirical research is lacking, people are using them regularly to support and strengthen families with quantifiable results. Jodie Benveniste, an Australian psychologist and author, provided dozens of case studies in her book *The Parent Manifesto*[10] where families created a vision for how they wanted their family to be, feel and act, with gushing reports from those involved in the process. Similarly, Stephen R. Covey wrote an entire book suggesting his 7 *Habits* were as valuable at home as they were at work – if not more so – with the mission statement acting as the keystone to family harmony.[11] Russell Grieger, a US behavioural therapist, has commented on using a mission statement in couple relationships:

> I have found that assisting couples in writing their 'Marital Mission Statement' ... is a powerful tool in helping them choose to act in ways that mutually benefit each other and the relationship. The mission statement and values serve as a beacon for correct action much like a lighthouse guides ships to shore. When two people participate fully and genuinely in creating these and then responsibly, without anger, use them to direct how they act with each other, their relationship often soars.[12]

Think of it like this: there are times in your life when things are great. So what is happening in your family relationships at those times? (And, no, I'm not asking you to suggest family life is happiest when the children are asleep or at their grandparents' house.) Creating a happier family relies on tapping into the values and ideals that make things work best – but we really need to take the time to identify those values and ideals and then practise them as much as we can.

Where is your family heading?

In my youth I used to do a lot of surfing. Often, strong currents would push me away from where I wanted to be, and I had to consistently look towards the beach to get my bearings. I would choose a landmark and try to stay in line with it as I paddled and caught waves. Whenever I stopped focusing on the landmark in the distance and instead looked directly in front of my surfboard, I would often find myself drifting away from the place I needed to be to catch the best waves. Sure, there were usually still waves to be caught, but they were never as good as the ones in the prime spot. The landmark kept me focused and in position so I could enjoy the best the ocean was serving up.

Because of the short-term focus and reactivity of being 'in the moment' in family life, it is easy to lose sight of those landmarks on the shore that keep us on course and in the right spot. A mission statement helps us to regularly take stock of what matters to us as a family unit, and steer ourselves consistently in that direction (even if we're drifting away from our ideal place a lot of the time). The more often we check in with that distant landmark rather than focusing on the issues, challenges and distractions immediately in front of us, the more we are able to continue heading towards that safe harbour we seek.

So, what is it that you most want for your family? And what is it that everyone else in your family wants?

Take a minute before you read any further and think about those questions a little more deeply. Be really specific about them. Don't just say 'I want my family to be happy'. Instead, really ask yourself (and your family, if you can) what your ultimate goals are for your family. What does 'a happy family' mean? How does it look? What are you doing (or not doing) to get to that goal? You might consider answering the following questions:

- When has our family been happiest?
- When has our family been most focused and together – united?
- When I was a child, what did I want most from my family?
- What has happened to cause problems? Will doing something different change that?

- If we just picked one or two things to shift our family
  focus to a better place, what would they be?

If your children are old enough, get their perspective and involve
them in your thinking. Remember that buy-in is key, and is most
likely to be achieved when everyone works together.

Ultimately, you know your family best – and certainly better
than I do. Listen to what that something inside you, that no one
else has access to, is telling you. Focus on the direction it suggests,
the goals it makes you aspire to, and the plans you know you need
to get there.

You can't steer a parked car. To get to your destination you
have to start moving forward. However, we don't get into a car
and start driving without knowing where we are going. We make
a plan. We have a reasonable idea of the route. While we might
change our course once we are on the road, we always do so
knowing the ultimate destination we are working towards.

To reach a goal requires a vision of where we want to go, and a
commitment to move in that direction. The greater our clarity, the
more likely it is we will get there (or closer to it than we are now).

Head in the right direction

There is no perfect way to work out what your mission statement,
creed or manifesto should be. What does seem to be clear, though,
is that we need to know what we are aiming at *as a family* in order
to go in that direction. The more explicit we can be in declaring
our intended direction, the more likely it is that we will move our
family towards that.

Just as Kylie needed precision in order to get my workshop
notes to me, we need the same level of clarity for our family to
reach the harbour we seek. Australian psychologist Steve Biddulph,
who has sold more parenting books than anyone in the history of

the world, suggested the thing that will be of most use is to have a map of where we are going – to keep us on track when we are stuck in the significant struggles of family life.

> We don't get into a car and start driving without knowing where we are going…

My family mission statement is not really a mission statement at all. Instead, it is a simple mantra that we repeat as a reminder to keep our family on course. Help others; Have fun; Be grateful. That's all. Just a list of three key concepts that our family has identified as critical in creating the environment we value. We don't even think about it as a mission statement – it's just a shortlist of our 'family principles', or our 'family mantra'. We have found this is easier, more practical, and more memorable than a lengthy manifesto that uses jargon to describe our family's values.

The interesting thing about our experience with this concept and what has become our 'mission statement' is that when we don't talk about these values regularly, emphasising how we are living them each day, we find ourselves losing sight of them. We drift. We forget the 'address', we fail to find the harbour we are seeking, and we notice that we are a little less focused, a little less kind and fun, and a little more challenged in living the way we identified as ideal. When this happens, family life doesn't serve up the best it could, just like the waves when we are swept away from the ideal break. As such, we make time each day to talk through the way we are living these values, emphasising each of them at our evening meal, or our morning meeting.

It doesn't matter what form your mission statement, creed, mantra or manifesto takes. What matters is that you have one. I've seen examples that are a page long in small print. (Interestingly, no one in that particular family could ever remember what their mission statement was really about.) I recall reading one that was just three words: 'No empty seats.' This family valued inclusiveness, unity and participation. They wanted everyone to always feel sufficiently loved, understood and valued that they would always want to be with the family. They never wanted to look around the room and see a seat empty because someone felt excluded, misunderstood or offended. What a simple but powerful statement for that family, whose every word and action can so easily be guided by a three-word mantra. Other mantras that have resonated with me include: We're all in this together; kindness begins with me; we can do hard things; and you've got a friend in me.

When we know what we are aiming to accomplish and we work towards it consistently, we achieve far more than when we react to things on a moment-to-moment basis without a vision of 'the big picture'.[13] Whatever you create, do it together and have fun with it. Don't expect that you'll get it right the first time you discuss it, or even the second or third time. Developing your family's mission statement can, and should, take a while. The process is at least as important as the actual outcome. The main thing is that you start thinking about, and chatting about, what matters most to your family right now. It is only as you identify what matters most that you can create a clear road map to get there.

Still don't like mission statements?

Perhaps you feel resistant to goals and a mission or mantra for your family. If so, maybe you feel more role-oriented than goal-oriented. In other words, you are more focused on the *kind of parent you want to be* than the things you must do. If this is you, then the following question may be helpful in determining the overarching objective for your family.

What is your highest priority? Is it peace, happiness, independence, closeness, discovery, cleanliness, fun or something else? It may be enough to choose one word that describes *who* you want to be, or *how* you want to be – or how you want your family to be – and work towards that. In other words, keep it short and simple. Because complexity can become the enemy of happiness.

It is only as you identify what matters most that you can create a clear road map to get there.

Take-home message

Once you've worked out – precisely – what your family is really working toward (in whatever format you decide is best), the most important thing you can do is to keep your eyes on the long-term goal described in your mission statement or manifesto. Keeping in touch with your mission statement will keep you aligned with where you aim to go, regardless of the metaphorical tides and currents that distract you and pull you off course.

This includes the whole family. Mission statements, creeds, family philosophies, mantras, or guiding principles give us something to aim for as a family. If we take the time to write ours carefully and in unity, and spend a few minutes each day focused on a different aspect of the statement, it will offer us hope for what we can become, and give direction for our daily decisions.

Happy family focus:
Simple steps to set your course

Have a conversation with your spouse or partner and children about what it is to be a happy family. Talk about how you each most want the family to feel. What kinds of activities do you want to do? How would you all like the family members to speak, think and act towards each other? Play around with ideas and be creative. You might use a vision board, a poem, a phrase, an anagram, or a few short sentences that identify your ultimate values for how you want your family to act, what you want your family to do, and the kind of family life you'd like to have.

Be creative in the way you represent your mission statement, values or guiding principles. It does not have to be an official document. In fact, you can start writing your immediate thoughts in the space below and add the ideas of the other family members too.

That's it!

You're now a family on a mission – and if you work at it consistently, and follow the ideas in this book, your family will be happier in 21 days.

CHAPTER 2

Step up your parenting style: going autonomy-supportive

Rewards and punishments are the lowest form of education.

Unknown

Bree and Jacob felt their three children were out of control. They had come to me for help and we were discussing their parenting styles. What I mean by parenting style is the consistent decisions parents make in their interactions with their children. It's how we parent. To help them establish what their parenting style was, I drew a table with limit setting ratings across the top, and love and warmth ratings on the side (see below),[14] and worked through it with them.

	Low limits and boundaries	High limits and boundaries
High love and warmth		
Low love and warmth		

'Some people are really low on love and warmth towards their children, and they're also low on limits and boundaries. In other words, they don't care what their children do, and they don't really care about their children,' I explained. 'How would you describe those kinds of parents?'

Jacob responded immediately. 'They're neglecting them, pure and simple.'

'Spot on,' I replied. 'That's precisely the psychological term we use, too. We call it neglectful parenting.' As I wrote the word 'neglectful' in the bottom left box of the table I added, 'As I talk with you two, I get a strong sense that you don't fit in this box. Children raised in this kind of environment don't typically fare too well in life unless there is *someone* outside the family who they can rely on to be a stable support. They're likely to battle against boundaries, struggle to socialise and under-achieve academically. You guys value your children too much to be considered neglectful.'

Pointing to the box at the top left, I went on. 'There are some parents who are ultra-loving and super-warm, but they're so concerned with kindness they actually choose to forego limits and boundaries.'

Bree interrupted. 'That's me,' she said, laughing. Jacob nodded his head almost accusingly. Bree may have been proud that she loved her children, but it was clear that they had a parenting style mismatch. Jacob looked upset at Bree's admission and almost said something, but then held back.

'What would you call this parenting style?' I asked.

This time Jacob didn't wait. 'It's permissive. Totally permissive. And indulgent.' Jacob was speaking directly at his wife. I agreed, and wrote the two words in the top left corner of the table. 'It can also be called laissez-faire,' I added. 'There are differences in permissiveness, indulgence and laissez-faire approaches, but for the last 30 years they've all been put into that box. What outcomes might you expect in children who are raised in these environments?'

The two parents sat quietly as they pondered the question. Jacob spoke first. 'I suppose they'll feel entitled. Spoiled.'

26

'Yes!' I exclaimed. 'Some research indicates that permissiveness and indulgence can create that response in children. What else?'

Neither Jacob nor Bree was sure what else to add, so I filled in the silence by adding, 'Research also tells us that these children may struggle with boundaries. There is also some evidence that children raised in a laissez-faire, permissive environment might feel helpless, lack resilience and not want to work too hard for anything, which can impact on their schooling, too.'

We worked our way to the bottom right corner of the table and I asked, 'What about when we get low levels of love and warmth and high demands for boundaries and limits?'

'Yeah, that's me – 100 per cent.' Jacob was willing to acknowledge his parenting style immediately. 'I'm pretty hardcore. I'll say it once. I expect them to do it. And if they don't, I crack down hard on them. I'm not talking for the fun of it.'

Then Bree jumped back in: 'Actually that's me too. I give and give and give. I'm kind and permissive, and I let the children keep getting away with more and more and more until I can't take it anymore. Then I lose it. I blow up and things get totally out of control.'

'That's a common response from a lot of parents,' I replied. 'In fact, your patterns of responding are consistent with many mums and dads I talk to. Mum is permissive until she can't handle it anymore and then she goes hard-core authoritarian – that's what we call it when we get stuck in that box. We swing like pendulums in a grandfather clock. The children test us and we are permissive, permissive, permissive … and then finally – SNAP! And Dad is generally strict and straight down the line.' I scrawled the word 'authoritarian' into the box.

Both of them nodded, and then Jacob asked a question that immediately illuminated his motives and heart. 'So that's not ideal, either. And you're leaving the other box for last for a reason. What do I have to do to be in that box? That's the one I want.'

27

'Don't get too excited yet,' I replied. 'That is authoritative parenting, which is built on a combination of warmth and boundaries. And in psychological scholarship, many see it as the gold standard of parenting styles.'

I went on to explain that even though it is considered the 'gold standard', I believe there's something even better. Bree and Jacob seemed puzzled.

Beyond the gold standard

In her original concept of authoritative parenting, Diana Baumrind – the researcher credited with developing the parenting styles model – suggested that authoritative parents ought to rely heavily on their power to coerce their children to comply with limits. And that they should just do it *warmly*, where possible. Baumrind strongly advocates for using 'extrinsic contingencies', such as removal of privileges, to achieve control. (Extrinsic contingencies occur when we manipulate the external environment to change our children's behaviour. This suggests that we motivate them externally, rather than helping them be intrinsically motivated.) Baumrind's early writings demonstrated a clear approval and endorsement of extrinsic contingencies, even with the gold standard of authoritative parenting. She advocated smacking children and showed an unapologetically strong leaning towards punishment as a means of ensuring boundaries are kept.[15] In his book *The Myth of the Spoiled Child*,[16] author Alfie Kohn points to a 1972 article where Baumrind stated, 'The parent who expresses love unconditionally is encouraging the child to be selfish and demanding.'[17]

Let me emphasise that quote, because it matters enormously. Baumrind was clearly against unconditional love in parenting. Such an approach would lead to unhappiness in families, she argued, and so we should show what psychologists call 'conditional positive regard' instead. This is the equivalent of saying to a child, 'I'll only love you and treat you well when you behave the way I want you to.' And, unfortunately, this is the crux of the parenting style that is still held up by many 'experts' as the gold standard. Think about time out. It is one of the world's most popular 'discipline' techniques, yet it is all about conditional acceptance of our children. (I'll speak more about this idea when we look at discipline more closely.)

'I'll only love you and treat you well when you behave the way I want you to' is still held up as the gold standard of parenting by far too many people.

In his critically insightful treatment of Baumrind's research, Kohn points out that as early as 1981 researchers were beginning to poke holes in it. They discovered that the *controlling* aspects of authoritative parenting appeared to be unhelpful, and the *warmth* aspects of authoritativeness were what mattered. Similarly (and I know this is getting a bit technical, but stay with me for a brief moment), Baumrind lumped permissive parents in with indulgent parents. You can see how if a person is low on limits but high on warmth, they could potentially still be good parents by being loving, and by gently giving children choices and guidance. Some might call this permissive, and in some circumstances it might be so. But some parents might be highly democratic and willing to defer decisions to their children because they believe it helps them to become more responsible.[18] Research indicates that we experience better outcomes with our children in both the short and long term when we adopt this style compared to a controlling style.

The last technical note, is that where other studies have shown authoritative parenting to be superior to other styles, they've often redefined what authoritative parenting is, shifting it away from Baumrind's original control-based concept. Their definitions have incorporated a much greater emphasis on democratic processes in the family, with lower levels of control. That is why so many 'experts' still promote authoritative parenting – because the style appears to have changed from what it was originally. More recent research (that is largely ignored by too many parenting researchers and most parenting writers) suggests that *autonomy-supportive parenting* may be the real ideal.

I explained all of this to Bree and Jacob.

'Why did you walk us through the model if it's wrong?' asked Jacob, a high achiever who wanted answers about the ultimate parenting aspiration.

'We need to look at where we are and identify what we are doing so that we can work towards change,' I replied. 'If we don't know where we are on the map and what the alternative directions are, it can be hard to work out the correct route. Now we know what your parenting styles are, we can look at what the ideal is and figure out how to move in that direction.'

Autonomy-supportive parenting

Like most parents, Bree and Jacob were big on punishment and reward. Praising and rewarding behaviour they liked and ignoring or punishing challenging behaviour was their *modus operandi*. This approach is entirely conditional, and flies in the face of what we know about autonomy-supportive parenting practice. So what does it look like if we don't punish and reward?

Autonomy-supportive parents prefer to avoid 'manipulating' their children with bribes or threats, rewards or punishments. They also lean away from being controlling. Instead they prefer, where possible, to actively allow and encourage their children to make their own decisions. When a wise decision is made, the parent steps back. When a poor decision is made the parent steps in – but not to control. Instead, the parent invites the child to think through the choice, and consider potential alternative choices. Autonomy-supportive parents focus on teaching their children, asking them questions and problem-solving challenges together. The following points summarise the approach of autonomy-supportive parents.

1. They give their children a clear reason (or rationale) for behavioural requests
2. They recognise the feelings and perspective of the child
3. They offer choices and encourage initiative and problem-solving
4. They minimise the use of controlling techniques.[19]

In other words, there is clearly involvement on the part of parents (so no neglect), and there are certainly expectations about what behaviour is and isn't appropriate (so not permissive). And the research shows that it is remarkably effective.

In a study of mothers and infants, one-year-old children were taught to play with some toys by their mum. Then the children were observed as they played on their own. When mothers were controlling in the way they taught their children to play, the children were less persistent and motivated to play with their toys than those children whose mothers had been more autonomy-oriented in the way they taught. Children with autonomy-supportive mothers were delighted to have some free play, and enjoyed playing with the toys even when their mum was gone.

What was the difference? The controlling mothers were the ones who were hovering over their children, giving lots of direction, and quite literally controlling the play process. They might say things like, 'No, not like that. Like this.' They were highly directive, and allowed little space for the child to discover what to do alone. It was almost as though mistakes were not allowed. These mums loved their children and had good motivations. They were controlling, however, because they felt like their child should play with those toys the 'right' way.

The autonomy-oriented mothers allowed their children to explore the toys a little more. They asked questions more than they gave directions. 'Oh, is that what it does? What else can it do?' 'Does it feel good to hold it like that?' They encouraged exploration and broader thinking in their children. They presented choices and options to their children, whereas controlling mothers wanted their children to do it the way they felt it should be done.

A follow-up study eight months later showed those children with autonomy-supportive mums (at the original play session) were still more willing to persist in their play, and were actually more competent in the way that they played.[20]

> Autonomy-supportive mothers encouraged exploration and broader thinking in their children. They presented choices and options to their children, whereas controlling mothers wanted their children to do it the way they felt it should be done.

Support autonomy at every age

A similar study involving six- and seven-year-olds with their mothers showed the same pattern of results. Children played with 'construction toys' with their mum. The way mums spoke to their children was coded as controlling, autonomy-supportive or neutral. When the play session was over, children were left alone for five minutes for a free-play session. Results showed that mums who were controlling in their talk had children who showed less intrinsic motivation to play.[21]

That is, mums who said things like, 'Okay, now put this one over there,' or 'I think you should ...' impacted their children's sense of control, and made the child feel like 'mum's in charge here'. A 'do this, do that' approach to playing with children reduced the child's motivation and led to poorer motivational outcomes. Children whose mums encouraged them to explore and create by saying things like, 'Wow. What's next?' Or 'Gee, what do you think is the best thing to do now?' promoted a sense of curiosity and discovery, and a stronger motivation to continue the activity even when the experiment was 'over'.

Other research adds to the story – and not just for infants, toddlers or young school children. The idea of autonomy-support matters for adolescents as well. Researchers have discovered that the more controlling parents are, the less positively adjusted their children are at school. Conversely, the more autonomy-supportive parents are, the greater their children's school adjustment. And teens whose parents are autonomy-supportive have much higher psychological and social functioning than teens whose parents are firm and controlling.[22]

Picture this: your child is old enough to make decisions about which friends she will spend time with after school or on weekends. You feel uncomfortable about the friends she wants to be with. You know they behave in ways that are inconsistent with the values you have taught your child. When your daughter is with them, she seems to change – for the worse. Her attitude is difficult. Her school achievements drop off. You are convinced she is smoking, drinking and using drugs. She may be doing other things you'd rather not know about too. What do you do?

The old-school model suggests a combination of demanding improvement and being warm (authoritative parenting). According to the authoritative model, we are supposed to make it clear that we don't like what is happening, request change, and provide a clear overview of consequences (read: punishments) if things don't change the way we'd like them to. In short, we are supposed to be controlling, but in the nicest, most sugar-coated way possible.

Such an approach leads to conflict, power-struggles, and unhappy outcomes.

My experience shows that in such a situation, most parents will either sigh and say, 'Children will be children,' (indulgent/permissive/laissez-faire) or get mad and come down hard on them (authoritarian). Once again, we know that the outcomes with these parenting patterns are negative too.

When it comes to setting boundaries around drug use, friends, school expectations and treating people kindly, the autonomy-supportive results come up trumps against anything considered either passive or controlling. Passivity only creates a culture of acceptance and a sense that parents endorse their children's challenging behaviour. Control pushes the child away, builds resentment and leads to children becoming sneakier so they don't get caught. Here's an example:

In a longitudinal study involving 335 adolescents, teens that experienced the best outcomes in each of four areas (avoiding drugs, avoiding deviant peer associations, school engagement and behaving prosocially) had parents who scored lower on controlling parenting styles and higher on autonomy-supportive parenting.[23] These parents did not tell their children what to do. They did not make demands, prescribe 'consequences', or shrug their shoulders and turn away. Instead, they let their children know of their expectations, listened to understand their child's perspectives, problem-solved together, and worked hard to minimise the use of any controlling techniques (extrinsic contingencies) that might have created division and disharmony in their relationship with their child.

Control the controlling

Controlling parents can be found making important decisions for their children, solving their problems and intervening in their children's conflicts – all with the very best of intentions. A 2015 study involving 438 undergraduate students found that control undermines the likelihood of positive outcomes in our children's lives.[24] The students in the study responded to questionnaires about their parents' controlling behaviour and warmth, as well as their own self-esteem, risk behaviours and academic achievements. Controlling parents were perceived by their children as lacking warmth, and that perception increased risky behaviours and decreased feelings of self-worth in children. But the lower the control (and the more autonomy) combined with increased warmth the person experienced, the more the student felt engaged with school, and the less risks they took behaviourally. This change did not eliminate risks and negative outcomes, but the negative effects were greatly reduced. In summary, too much control is too much, no matter the parents' affection and support. And these findings apply at all ages, from infancy to early adulthood.

How to support your child's autonomy

From the time that our children are young we should aim to be warm, kind and loving to our children. That is a simple principle of positive relationships regardless. We should also be clear on what our values are, and the boundaries and limits we want to encourage in our children. The groundwork we established in Chapter 1 is helpful here, with the family's vision, guiding principles or road map agreed upon and firmly in place.

Rather than 'enforcing' limits, autonomy-supportive parents talk to their children about things, even when they are little. They *work with them* on problem-solving and finding solutions in a collaborative, understanding manner – even when they are little. They recognise that children are people too, and that they have feelings and desires. In short, as much as it is possible, and in accordance with their child's development, they support their children's autonomy by giving them opportunities to be autonomous – which leads to superior outcomes. Autonomy-support for a three year-old might be 'who do you want to put you to bed?' They may not be old enough to choose their bed time (although most young children can and do regulate their sleep quite well if we allow it), but we give choice where we can. Our four year-old might be given choice as to which of three shirts he'll wear, but he may not choose whether he goes to playgroup today. We do have to control some things. But where choice is viable, we offer it in an autonomously supportive way, clearly presenting our preferences and listening to our child's, before problem-solving together.

Autonomy-supportive parenting changes as our children mature. When they are young, we are more likely to cocoon our children from things we are concerned about. We establish a limit clearly, discuss why, and resolve any concerns our child has. This is pretty simple at the age of three or six, or even 10. But as they mature, the process changes, becoming one that involves greater levels of reasoning together, until they are finally old enough for us to simply defer to them and offer our guidance where needed.

Our parenting style matters enormously. The way we parent casts a long shadow into our children's lives. Our choices as parents can impact on the way our children feel about themselves, the kinds of relationships they develop throughout life, the quality of their academic outcomes, the way they regulate their behaviours and emotions, the likelihood of them developing mental illness, alcohol and other drug habits, and even their sexual decisions. Parenting style is even related (quite powerfully) to the likelihood of our child being physically healthy, or battling obesity[25] or anorexia,[26] so it pays to consider what the research says and follow it as best we can.

In summary, the more controlling we are of our children, the poorer their outcomes. That even includes authoritative parenting as it was originally defined (and as it generally remains defined). Autonomy-supportive parenting, more than any other parenting style, consistently corresponds (and leads) to our children enjoying optimal outcomes. If they feel good about themselves and feel they have autonomy and our support because we work with them and defer to them, it seems that generally they flourish, make wise choices, and experience high levels of wellbeing.

> The way we parent casts a long shadow into our children's lives.

If our children experience our parenting as controlling or lacking in warmth, they tend to struggle to develop the self-regulation that will help them be resilient in the face of challenges and setbacks. They may struggle with a range of concerns related to self-worth and feelings of inadequacy, a desire to act in a delinquent fashion, or perhaps they'll experiment with alcohol and other drugs, or sex.[27]

If our children receive neither warmth nor boundaries from a significant and stable adult in their lives, research consistently emphasises that these children will typically struggle and languish. The effects of this parenting style will leave children feeling worthless, helpless and despondent, or aggressive, resistant and defensive.

What is your parenting style?

Let's look at a basic scenario: imagine that your four-year-old keeps snatching a toy from your six-year-old. What do you do?

If you fall into the 'neglectful' box (which is unlikely given that you're reading a book about being a better parent) your response would likely be aggressive or annoyed, or you might ignore them.

Either way, your primary goal would be to make sure the children don't bother you. No warmth. No boundaries.

If you're permissive, there is a range of potential responses you might show. The first might be indulgent, meaning you will probably go and get another toy for one of the children to keep them both happy. You will be focused on meeting your child's needs, but will probably not focus too much on guidance. Or you'll just leave the children be, surmising they can sort things out themselves.

If you're authoritarian the obvious response is to get very serious, demand they sort it out, or take the toy from them! An authoritarian parent will automatically disapprove of the argument over whose toy it is, saying things like, 'Cut that out!' or 'Stop that fighting at once!' Or, ironically, exclaim 'I have had enough of you children and the way you treat each other! Give me the toy right now and go to your rooms right away! Don't come out until you can be nice to everyone in the family!'

An authoritative parent will be clear, but warm. There will be a discussion of consequences and expectations. The parent will tell the children what is expected: that they find ways to cooperate and play nicely. The children will understand that their parents will punish or reward according to their behaviour. The decisions the children make are not really their own. Should they choose contrary to their parents' will, they can expect 'consequences'.

Autonomy-supportive parents will focus on meeting their child's needs and providing guidance. They will see the challenging behaviour as an opportunity to empathise, teach and problem-solve instead of claiming it as a violation of the rules with a demand that the child be reprimanded, punished and 'learn a lesson'. Importantly, because they accept their child unconditionally and seek opportunities to express love for whom their children are (rather than making that love contingent on their children's behaviour) they will try to see the world through their child's eyes to better understand the behaviour and his reasons for it. Then they will talk with their child and provide that child with opportunities to make decisions about what is best in these situations. Questions they might ask include, 'What is the best way to deal with this now?' Or, 'What do you think we should do to make things better?' If the child gives poor answers, the parents will ask for alternatives, or offer their own suggestions. These parents will also recognise that such an approach takes time and will not work when a child is stressed, or when the child has an audience. As such, many of these conversations will take place well after challenging behaviour occurs. Sometimes they will decide that a new toy for another sibling is the perfect answer. Other times they will determine that sharing will work best. Alternatively, they may decide together that distraction, or a nap, or some special time with a parent is ideal. It is the process that matters.

Work with your children

Okay, reality-check time. I have six children, and I know that in the real world it is not always possible to be quite so calm and controlled or to spend this amount of time working through issues with our children. Being warm and loving is great, but sometimes we have to make things happen NOW! Sometimes that means autonomy takes a back seat. On such occasions children have no choice. They must wear a seatbelt. They must keep devices out of their rooms. They must not drink alcohol if they are underage.

Please note, however, that autonomy-supportive parenting is not about pretending everything is loving and soft and gentle. Autonomy-supportive parents are absolutely clear and direct in how they manage challenging behaviour. The difference is that they manage it by *working with* their children. They turn towards their children and their emotions, seeing the world through their child's eyes. They acknowledge difficulties and help their children repair problems and relationships.

39

Take-home message

Our parenting style has a clear effect on the wellbeing of our children in pretty much all aspects of their lives. Research confirms in myriad ways that the optimal parenting style is one where we are autonomy-supportive, having a clear rationale for our requests, and a willingness to work with our children on suitable outcomes with minimal (but occasionally necessary) control.

Happy family focus:
Think about your parenting style

Are you controlling, dictatorial and authoritarian? Or are you a permissive and laissez-faire pushover?

How could you move towards a more engaged style of interaction with your children where you set clear limits on behaviour in a way that respects your children's perspective and minimises the use of control? In other words, how can you work with them more to find good solutions, rather than doing things to them because your solution is the one they must adhere to?

Next time your child behaves in a challenging way, calm things down, and then sit and chat. Ask them, 'Do you know what I expect in this situation?' And listen carefully to their response. See things from their perspective, and then ask, 'Well, what do you think is the best thing to do now?' Problem-solve together, and then ask, 'What will you do if it happens again?' Then hug them and reassure them that you love them.

CHAPTER 3

Getting your parent-child relationship right

> Where did we ever get the crazy idea that in order to
> make children do better, first we have to make them feel
> worse? Think of the last time you felt humiliated or treated
> unfairly. Did you feel like cooperating or doing better?
>
> **Jane Nelsen[28]**

The diagram below shows an empty bucket. Take a moment to read the two labels that describe what is in the bucket.

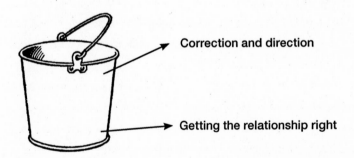

Correction and direction

Getting the relationship right

At the top of the bucket is correction and direction – what we give our children to help them act in good, kind ways (see Chapter 11 for more about that) – and at the bottom, 'Getting the relationship right'.

Imagine you were asked to place water into the bucket in direct proportion to the amount of time you spend in your relationship with your children that's focused on correction and direction versus time spent on getting your relationship with them right. For example, if you think about 50 per cent of your interactions with your children are focused on correction and direction, place a line at the halfway point in the bucket. If you feel you spend nearly ALL your time on correction and direction, perhaps you would place the line 80–90 per cent of the way towards the bottom.

In my work with parents, most of them immediately draw a 'relationship' line that symbolises a splash in the bucket – it feels like the majority of their time is spent telling the children what to do, how to do it, when to do it, and that they'd better hurry up and do it! And there is a problem with this approach.

Correction and direction are all about control. As we saw in the previous chapter, higher levels of control lead to poorer outcomes in our children, and in our family. The reality is that none of us likes taking correction and direction all the time. It undermines our sense of autonomy. It can also be bad for our relationships. When someone is always correcting and directing us, we feel that they do not trust us. This creates a sense of resistance. If our children feel we don't trust them because we are always telling them what to do, correcting them, or checking up on them, they will resist us. Our influence will wane. So where does the trust come from? We need to build it by trusting our children – from a young age. And we will struggle to build something that can withstand storms, winds and tempest unless we deepen and strengthen the foundations. Our family foundation is no different to a building foundation in this regard – stronger foundations make for stronger outcomes. If we trust them to do something and they fail, our response to that failure matters. A willingness to understand and work with them to develop a mutually satisfying solution will build trust more quickly and deeply than a heavy mix of correction and direction with little regard for their feelings or for the relationship.

Building trust and earning influence

Consider your relationship with a significant person in your life – perhaps your spouse or partner, or a parent or very close friend. Imagine them being highly controlling, telling you how to do everything from the way you dress to the way you drive. Think how you might respond to them if rather than patiently listening to and trying to understand your constant complaints and challenges, they just told you how to fix things. Visualise them picking at you for what you eat, how little you exercise, or your lack of discipline when it comes to housekeeping or yard maintenance.

It doesn't feel good and it doesn't work because too much focus on correction and direction undermines trust and diminishes influence – it leaves little room for getting a relationship right.

> Too much focus on correction and direction leaves little room to get a relationship right. It undermines trust and diminishes influence.

It is interesting that correction and direction is often served up with the very best of intentions. A husband might lovingly say to his wife, 'Honey, when are you going to start exercising again?' But if she perceives the question as controlling, she will likely become resentful and retaliatory. A mother might suggest to her daughter, 'Sweetheart, what you're wearing is not very modest.' Most teen girls are unlikely to consider the suggestion and respond with, 'Good point Mum. I think I'll go change, and then I'll drop these clothes off at a charity bin while I'm out tonight.' A father might reprimand his four-year-old son: 'Stop crying. Man up, son.' Maybe a wife tells her husband, 'If you would just look at our daughter instead of the TV when she talks to you, I'm sure she would open up more.' Consider the standard morning in so many homes: 'Where is your lunchbox? How many times have I told you to put your lunchbox on the bench when you come home in the afternoon? Now I can't clean it ... Oh, great, you didn't eat what I packed yesterday ... You have to eat or you'll get sick ... I should make you eat yesterday's lunch today ... Okay, what do you want today? While I'm making your lunch, go and get dressed ... What do you mean you can't find your shoes? We go through this every second day ... You need to put your shoes away!' Sound familiar?

These controlling interactions that are built on correction and direction do not increase trust and build influence. Our intentions in saying such things might be good – we are trying to help – but approaches that focus on fixing faults in others all too often undermine the very thing we want more of – trust and influence. They are the basis of getting relationships wrong, not right.

Trust and influence in action

Some years ago I came across the following true story in a newspaper article about cyber-bullying. After her husband passed away unexpectedly, Nicole decided the best way she could support her young family was to return to school and finish her degree. While she completed her qualifications, Nicole was fortunate enough to get part-time work in a university professor's lab studying the impact of cyber-bullying. One morning as she worked in the lab she received a phone call from her daughter's school. Nicole was informed that her daughter was to be suspended because, ironically, she was bullying another girl online. Nicole drove to the school in shock. 'How could she?' she thought.

As Nicole sat with the principal, she asked her daughter why she would do such a thing. Her daughter responded indifferently and unapologetically.

'This is another human being!' Nicole exclaimed, and recalled that her words were met with a shrug of the shoulders as her daughter admitted, 'Yeah, it's true, and so what?'

44

Nicole was at a loss. Her daughter needed to learn a lesson. So Nicole removed privileges – she grounded her, and took her phone and computer. Far from working to fix the situation, these actions led to even more animosity between mother and daughter. They barely talked for several weeks, and what communication did exist was primarily screaming, defensiveness and slammed doors.

As time went by, Nicole and her daughter began taking long walks together, talking about nothing and everything. They rebuilt their relationship, carefully avoiding discussions of the 'incident'. Her daughter began to become the girl Nicole remembered her being before the incident. Their relationship slowly improved. As they discussed life, Nicole began to see that her daughter was grieving the loss of her father. So consumed with her own pain, coupled with the enormity of the task of raising her family alone while also studying and working, Nicole recognised for the first time that she had never really taken the time to understand what was going on in her daughter's emotional world. All of that pain, fighting and tears – this was a revelation.

Nicole had assumed her daughter was a problem, and that was the problem. Had she stepped back a little, Nicole may have realised that rather than her daughter being a problem, she was experiencing one. That approach may have helped get the relationship right, and should have led to far better outcomes. It was not the correction and direction, but the building (or re-building) of her relationship with her daughter that made the difference in her girl's behaviour.

After this remarkable insight, Judy bought a puppy – Milo – to help her daughter learn more responsibility. Her daughter adored her puppy. One day Nicole asked, 'Would you want anyone to be mean to your dog? Throw rocks at Milo?' A predictable 'No!' was the response, to which Nicole replied, 'Bullying other people's children is just like that. How do you imagine those parents feel when they see you figuratively throwing rocks at their children?'

Her daughter broke down and cried as she saw, perhaps for the first time, the impact that her actions had on others' lives.

Let the heat go out of the moment

As we dissect this story, we see a couple of important principles that relate to getting relationships right and creating a happy family. The first is entirely obvious, but often ignored and forgotten by over-zealous, or at least frustrated, parents. Correction and direction is ineffective in the heat of the moment. Screaming 'No!' and banning our children from the things they want ultimately undermines what we are trying to achieve. We diminish influence because our children stop trusting us. They do not believe we will act in their best interest (the very essence of trust) when we get them in trouble and tell them what to do.

My children have regularly attended the parenting presentations I deliver. After a particularly frustrating exchange between one of my children and I, I demanded she give me her iPad. Her response was classic. 'Do you think giving up my iPad will change my behaviour Dad?' My influence and our relationship was undermined because of my emphasis on correction and direction (and consequences/punishments).

This doesn't mean we should give up on limits, but what it does mean is that we don't communicate particularly effectively with our children when we are upset, especially about limits. It emphasises that there is a difference between limits and punishments. And it is a pertinent reminder that while ever our children are caught up in the moment, they are not receptive to our efforts to help them be better people.

> While ever our children are caught up in the moment, they are not receptive to our efforts to help them be better people.

Relationships before discipline, understanding before instruction

The second central message from Nicole's story is this: before we can discipline effectively, we need to get our relationship right with our children. Typically a parent goes straight in for correction and direction. We say 'No'. We begin the process of making claims and demands, and ramping up our expectations of our children. We start punishing, even though punishments undermine the relationship. But without a strong, trusting foundation, children will throw out blame, excuses, and either denial or defensiveness, usually accompanied by dramatic outbursts. Alternatively they will pay us lip service, telling us what we want to hear with no internalisation of the behaviours and principles that matter most.

This highlights how important it is to really understand what is happening in our children's lives. We must avoid giving direction and correction until our children feel safe – emotionally as well as physically – and understood. They need to really trust us. And that means our children have to deeply believe that we are here to act in their best interest. At the risk of being repetitive, we must invest in getting relationships right before we start telling children what to do.

To put it another way, statements of understanding should always precede statements of instruction. Nicole's daughter clearly did NOT feel safe or that those with authority over her were acting with her best interests in mind. She did not feel understood. The adults in her life may have believed that they were trustworthy. They may have believed they were trying to help her. But it is her perception that matters. It is her perception that determines whether she trusts them, and whether she will be influenced by them. And the only way that will occur is if she feels they understand how things are for her – what is going on in her life, what her unmet needs are, how she sees the world.

Trust means believing that another person will act in our best interest. This is the foundation of influence.

Feeling good goes with doing better

Take a look at the quote that begins this chapter. If our entire relationship is built on bossiness and criticism, with us directing and correcting all the day long, do you suspect that our children will trust us? How would you respond to a boss who spent 80–90 per cent of her time micromanaging you at work, checking up on your systems and processes and adherence to her instructions? Would you like to work for someone who peered over your shoulder every time you were on the computer to make sure you were working and not looking at your favourite website or app? Or who double-checked every decision you made? But don't we do that to our children?

When we spend all of our time on correction and direction, we disempower our children. We reduce their feelings of security and trust in us, and our relationship. We leave them feeling lousy, and that leaves them unmotivated to do much at all, except avoid us.

Statements of understanding should always precede statements of instruction.

Explore before exploding

The loss of her father doesn't excuse Nicole's daughter's poor behaviour, but it helps us to recognise that her state of wellbeing was far from ideal. It doesn't just take significant life changes like death to promote challenging behaviour in our children, either. A parent I once coached decided to take my advice and try to cuddle her toddler whenever she was behaving in a challenging way. She described that her little girl was having a tantrum, hurting her sisters and being terribly troublesome. She wanted to be mad at her little girl, but paused and picked her up to hug her instead. Then she realised her daughter had a temperature and was sick.

Our children's behaviour may seem entirely irrational and even inexcusable to us, but they will almost always have a reason for what they do, even when they cannot explain it. Remember the acronym HALTSS to understand what is driving difficult behaviour. Whether they are hungry, angry, lonely, tired, stressed or sick, your children will rarely behave in challenging ways just for the joy of it. Children don't get out of bed in the morning thinking, 'Hmmm, how can I destroy my parents' day today?'

Our responses matter. We need to get our relationships right, even when the situation is challenging. Simply recognising that challenging behaviour is a result of an unmet need (remember HALTSS) can be all it takes to shift our focus from correction and direction to getting our relationship right. It seems to turn us towards our child, and promotes perspective and empathy, kindness and compassion.

Giving time and attention

So how do we go about getting our relationships right? How do we build that trust?

In my first book, *What Your Child Needs from You: Creating a Connected Family*, I wrote that just as dollars are the currency of our economy, attention is the currency of our relationship.

What that means is that we get a relationship right when we focus on it and build it in positive and constructive ways. Think of any relationship you might form with another adult – someone you hope to work with productively in the future. Chances are that you find opportunities to spend time together. You explore common interests. You send relevant emails or text messages. You make sure you maintain the relationship by investing in it consistently in positive ways (you likely avoid giving too much correction and direction in that relationship), and with your time. Time is that precious resource that our children need so much, yet we give so sparingly. If your new friend or colleague is having a difficult time, you take time to be with them. You offer understanding and empathy, or perhaps you share some gentle encouragement. You might even ask if it's okay to share your experience, or if they mind if you take over and show them how it's done because you're quite experienced.

> Just as dollars are the currency of our economy, attention is the currency of our relationships.

Does that seem different at all to the way we respond to our children when they are challenged or having a difficult time (which means they are screaming, having a tantrum, or being defiant)? Are we proactively looking for opportunities to build our relationship in those challenging instances, or even when things are calm? If our children are online do we shoot them a quick text message or email to tell them we are thinking about them? Do we give them attention when things are good as well as when things are bad? Do we pack a special love note in their lunchbox to let them know we care? Are we empathic, compassionate and understanding when they struggle with challenges – from potty training through to being self-disciplined when it's time to study for exams?

Parenting with passion

In addition to making ourselves as available as possible for our children and seeking opportunities to connect with them and understand them, there are two other ways to get our relationships right. The first is related to our 'orientation' towards our children.

Research that I conducted at the University of Wollongong with over 1000 parents looked at the feelings parents had about being a parent. In essence, I asked mums and dads whether they felt that being a parent was just a 'job' they had to do, or whether it was something more than that – a 'calling' or 'vocation'. My research identified that when our heart is really in this parenting role – when we see it as a part of who we are – we invest more in it, and we work harder at it.

The most interesting aspect of this research was the correlation between our approach to the parenting relationship and the wellbeing of our children. As parents' sense of vocation increased, so too did their children's wellbeing (as well as their own wellbeing). In other words, when we put a great deal into our parenting we are happier and so are our children.[29]

Humility helps

The second way that we can get our relationships right is perhaps a little bit counterintuitive. I suggest that humility may strengthen relationships and encourage kind, positive and respectful bonds. When we are humble we consider the feelings and preferences of others – we acknowledge that we don't always know what is best, or what they feel or need. We express our vulnerability. We tell our children we are sorry, that we are learning, and that we want to be more open to their ideas. We engage more with our children to learn from them and to work with them.

> Time is that precious resource that our children need so much, yet we give so sparingly.

Making time for our children, putting in the effort to really understand them, having a real desire to be a great parent and modelling humility are valuable steps in getting our relationships with our children (and other family members) right. Supporting autonomy is another powerful way we can improve our relationships. In fact, you will find that most of the chapters in this book will load you up with many more ways we can get our relationships right. Practising them will boost your relationship satisfaction, your life satisfaction and your children's wellbeing.

Putting the relationship first

The next time you are inclined to go for correction and direction, consider the relationship. Is it built on a strong enough foundation for you to start telling that person what to do? I confess that correction often spills out of my mouth before it should, and I have to back up, spend time understanding, and then work with my children on appropriate solutions rather than acting as the dictatorial know-all.

Take-home message

It is our natural reaction to go for the jugular when our children act in challenging ways. Direction and correction are typically our default responses, and all too often that direction and correction comes in unkind ways that betray a lack of humility, understanding, perspective or compassion. However, by strengthening the foundations of our relationship we build trust with our children. With a strong foundation of trust, developed through availability, humility and understanding our children, our correction and direction is more likely to be well received, and we'll probably need to do a whole lot less of it.

Happy family focus:
Exercise relationship-building every time

Make opportunities to interact with your child in ways that build your relationship. Each time you want to offer correction or direction, pause and ask whether it is really necessary, and consider what you can do instead that will be better for the relationship. If correction and direction is needed, think about how you can offer it in a way that builds, rather than tears down, your relationship.

CHAPTER 4

Being where your feet are

Few of us ever live in the present. We are forever anticipating
what is to come or remembering what has gone.

Louis L'Amour

My family recently purchased several large self-assembly furniture
items. Miraculously all the pieces were there and I was able to
follow the instructions closely enough to assemble the furniture
without any major mishaps. We were left with several large
cardboard boxes. It was early autumn and the sun was shining
bright and warm across a perfectly blue sky so I suggested to
the children that we might carry the boxes the short walk to the
nearby school and slide down the *very* steep embankment beside
the playground on them. We opened the boxes out so they were
flat, and I hefted them above my head. Together five girls and I
raced to the schoolyard and spent the next hour sliding down
the slope.

At some point in the activity and excitement I recall feeling, for
just a moment, that I was wholly engrossed in the moment. There
were no thoughts of deadlines or demands. I wasn't thinking
about the fact that we needed to get moving so we could get dinner
organised, or run baths and get ready for bed. I was absorbed.
And so were the children. Nothing mattered in that moment other
than *the moment.*

I stood, watching my children in awestruck wonder as they
scrambled up the hillside and slid down the grass on their boxes,

enormous grins dividing the top of their faces from the bottom. For just a moment I wished that the entire world would stop so we could enjoy the experience forever. It was perfect.

Breathtaking moments

Perhaps you have had a similar experience. Maybe it was as you stared at your baby and she smiled at you for the first time – and it was a real smile, not gas. It could be that perfect moment where you watched your children smiling, laughing and talking like friends. You may have felt it at the dinner table as you watched your spouse and children eat, talk, and engage with each other. Or maybe it was while one of your children played a musical instrument for you, or ran around on a sports field. Sometimes it sneaks up and hits us in the middle of a precious hug. Other times it stuns us as we take note of our teenager grabbing the car keys because he can now drive. We watch as he smiles and drives away, and we are so entirely absorbed in the moment we cannot even move our feet or think of what we were supposed to do next.

There is an old saying that life is not in the number of breaths you take, but in the moments that take your breath away. Being mindful allows us more of those breathtaking moments.

The power of the present

Mindfulness has been the buzzword in Western psychology for a couple of years. Research on the topic has exploded. The word is out – mindfulness can change our lives.

A common misconception is that mindfulness means emptying our minds and getting rid of thoughts and emotions. Most of us would find that impossible and few would be interested in it.

To the contrary, mindfulness means that we are fully attentive to what is happening right now. Our thoughts are in the present.

We feel our emotions based completely on what is happening here and now. And we are open to the moment. We are even curious about it, noticing how we feel, think and act. We are flexible, too, able to respond to everything as it happens because of our open acceptance and presence.[30]

If that sounds a bit too airy-fairy, perhaps it is easiest to simply remember that mindfulness is being fully in the moment – right here, right now. End of story.

> Life is not in the number of breaths you take, but it is in the moments that take your breath away.

Being mentally elsewhere makes us unhappy

I have a strong scientific background, and initially I found the whole mindfulness fuss a little bit New Age and fuzzy. But as I paid attention to the science, I started to come around. Mindfulness (being focused on the here and now) has been shown as an effective strategy in reducing severe mental illness, improving management processes, decision-making[31] and emotion regulation,[32] enhancing athletic performance, as well as preventing relapse in depression[33] and substance abuse.[34] While mindfulness is not a stand-alone solution, it appears to be a critical part of the foundation for wellbeing. With ancient roots and newfound scientific credibility, perhaps mindfulness can play a part in boosting the happiness, positivity and wellbeing we experience in our families.

Being mindful is *not* the natural way we respond to life. Our minds are wired to wander (and wonder). Rather than being mindful, we spend time imagining our futures, reliving our past (and wishing we'd said or done something different), and thinking about all the things we're not doing. Being mindful is pretty hard work. Researchers at Harvard University suggest we're mentally somewhere else about 50 per cent of the time – particularly when we're driving, working or staring at a screen (hopefully not doing all three at once, though!).[35] To examine our mindlessness and mindfulness, these researchers constructed a website (www.trackyourhappiness.org) and invited people to download an app that connected them to the site. Their database (at the time of this study) contained information from over 5000 participants in 83 countries and across a large number of occupations.

Each day during the study, participants would receive random alerts from their app and respond quickly to the following simple questions.

- How are you feeling right now? (Responses were on a scale from 0 –100, with 0 being very bad)
- What are you doing right now? (22 possible activities were displayed, based on previous research. They were broad enough to provide sufficient clarity for the purposes of the study)
- Are you thinking about something other than what you are currently doing? (Responses were either a) no, b) yes, something pleasant, c) yes, something neutral, or d) yes, something unpleasant)

With the exception of sex, people recognised that their mind was not on what they were doing 47 per cent of the time. (With sex, they were thinking of other things about 10 per cent of the time!) What people were doing (with that one exception) seemed to have no bearing at all on whether their minds were on the activity in front of them or not.

Importantly, people's wellbeing was *lower* when their minds were wandering, regardless of what they were doing. It seems that there is nothing we can do that can't be made worse by wondering what else we could be doing instead!

Dazed and distracted

There is actually research that shows people will hurt themselves in order to be distracted from the reality of mindfulness. A 2014 study published in *Science* involving over 700 participants across 11 different experiments showed that most people feel uncomfortable when asked to simply sit with their thoughts 'in the moment'.[36] We prefer to be distracted and will go to odd lengths to not simply sit, be still, and take in our surroundings. In one experiment, 64 per cent of men and 15 per cent of women gave themselves electric shocks when left alone to think. Ironically, prior to the experiment these same people had said they would *pay money* to avoid being shocked. Yet self-administration was a welcome distraction from being present, alone with their thoughts.[37]

> The opposite of being mindful is being mindless.

Distraction may be the curse of our modern culture, and it is impacting on our children's wellbeing and our family's happiness. The sense of busy-ness and distraction is exacerbated with the always turned-on allurements of technology. Our distractions pull us away from the things that matter most. Perhaps you have had the experience of opening up your phone, tablet or computer to 'just check this one thing', and found yourself completely absorbed 15, 20 or even 30 minutes later. Maybe you have been at the park or beach with your children and responded to a text message (or pulled out your phone to take a photo of the children playing) only to realise you had a few of those little red flags in the top right corner of your apps ... and soon you failed to notice your children's presence at all.

Research published in mid-2015 showed that when parents are in the park they are easily distracted from their children, with unwelcome results. Scientists from the University of Washington found that when a child attempted to interrupt a parent on a mobile telephone, the caregiver completely failed to respond, to speak or even to look away from the phone in 56 per cent of cases. Those children were entirely and completely ignored! When parents were doing other things (such as helping another child, chatting to a friend, or staring into space), they failed to respond in just 11 per cent of cases.

> Distraction may be the curse of our modern culture, and it is impacting on our children's wellbeing and our family's happiness.

The researchers interviewed people after observing their phone habits in the park and discovered that parents feel guilty for using their phones! They are aware of it. They know they are ignoring their children. They sense the distraction and do not like it. They know they are not being mindful at all. Wellbeing drops, children get poorer quality attention, their memories of the moments in the park are lower … no one benefits. Yet we remain transfixed by these devices and their capacity to draw us in.[38] We don't mean it. But we keep on doing it.

How being mindful works

If you are aware of your emotions, your actions and the way you are thinking or feeling about things, then you are moving into mindful territory. A mindful person observes what is occurring (rather than judging it) and turns toward whatever it is that has caught her attention.[39]

There is an old quote that says, 'To a child, LOVE is spelled T-I-M-E.' If that is the case, I can't help but wonder what 'Hurry up' might mean to a child. In spite of the fact we usually know we are allowing ourselves to be distracted, we still struggle to be present, in the moment, where our feet are. Let's be honest, hearing about your six-year-old's day at school is not always entirely engaging. Watching your child do the same trick on the trampoline or swing for the hundredth time can fail to satisfy. I have heard parents mutter, 'Kill me now!' under their breath as they rolled their eyes while their child sought their attention for one more piggy-back, one more 'round and round the garden', or one more, 'Mummy watch this!'

Our agenda easily takes over. We are busy. It is easy to be distracted by the messy kitchen bench, the unprepared dinner, the looming extracurricular deadlines, that phone call you were supposed to make, and the drama your best friend is sharing all over social media. It becomes even harder, again, when you're driving your six-year-old home from school while your toddler screams because he woke up later than normal and he doesn't want to be in his seatbelt – and it's raining, and there is traffic everywhere and ... so it goes.

Other children, our own exhaustion and issues, media and *life* get in the way of being mindful of our child's stories about what Mrs Smith told him in class today about the bugs living in the front garden. It is not all about social media and technology.

In spite of this, a mindful parent is able to be in the moment and appreciate it for what it is, and even be curious about it and respond to it constructively and actively.

One of the best ways to know if we are being mindful is to ask those who can be impacted by our *mindlessness*. Occasionally, my wife and I invite our children to let us know how we are doing. While I play with the other children, Kylie takes one child at a time into a quiet room and interviews them. She individually asks each child questions like, 'Do we show you we care about you?', 'Do we remember things that are important to you?' and 'Do we make you feel wanted?' We try to understand whether the children feel we are truly mindful and attuned to them. We take notes based on their responses, so the children know we are taking it seriously – and they take it *very* seriously.

These interviews are always insightful. They are often satisfying and uplifting. Occasionally, they leave us feeling humbled, with a powerful drive to do more. In one recent interview one of our daughters said: 'When you are busy you don't listen to me properly. Like when Dad's on the computer or you [Mum] are doing craft, you're not available to me. It feels like they're more important than me.'

Then she added, 'You say you're listening, but you're not because you keep doing what you're doing.'

Our little girl's honest and heartfelt insight was a marker in the road for me, signifying a turning point. She reminded me more clearly than all the studies on mindfulness and being present that she needs me to show her that she is important – that she matters. Saying I am listening is not enough; she knows when I'm not.

How mindfulness can build resilience

Andrew Fuller, well-known Australian child and adolescent psychologist, has been conducting a long-running study about resilience with approximately 16,000 Aussie youths. The children who were most resilient almost universally agreed with two statements that children with the lowest resilience disagreed with. They were:

- I have a parent who cares about me
- I have a parent who listens to me.

Take a moment and ask yourself whether your children would say 'Yes' to those two statements. Perhaps you might even ask your child these two questions: 'Do you feel like I care about you?' and 'Do you feel like I listen to you?'

Now, think about what made you feel cared about as a child. When did you feel listened to? And most importantly, how did feeling cared about and being heard make you feel?

If you are like me, it is not the big holidays or major events that built your sense of worth and your resilience. Instead, it was the consistent, small interactions that added layer upon layer upon layer to your feelings that you were valued for who you were. Those small interactions will typically have come through one of your parents taking the time to acknowledge you, to be with you, and to really connect with you. These moments do not usually occur when mum or dad is distracted with phones and tech, other children, or home and work responsibilities. Instead, they occur when time is stopped, agendas are dropped, and parents are right in that moment with you.

Mindfulness may be a simple strategy for helping us build stronger relationships with our family. Extending from the previous chapter, mindfulness is part of the process of getting our relationships right. It means we pay attention to those around us and respond to them openly, with curiosity, and with acceptance. In spite of the intrinsic propensity we have for allowing our minds to wander, or to think that we are the centre of the universe, getting ourselves into a mindful state is as simple as reminding ourselves to be present.

A simple mindfulness check

Next time you are with your child, focus fully on being in the moment. Yes, you might be doing some tasks or working to an agenda. That's fine. But just be there. Don't think about the past or the future. Simply work on being present. Ask yourself, 'What am I hearing right now? What am I seeing? What am I feeling? What do I sense?'

Keep observing what your senses are telling you, and how your mind and body are responding. Whenever you notice that you are 'not where your feet are', especially when your children or partner are trying to communicate with you, tune right into them and see what a difference it makes.

Keep in mind that this is not something that we like. In spite of all of the personal wellbeing benefits that come from being mindful, a surprisingly large number of us would prefer to give ourselves painful electric shocks than be mindful. It doesn't come naturally. It can be hard work. It is often inconvenient to drop the agenda and really be there. But just try it. Put down the book, don't glance at your phone, and notice what is going on around you. It is fine to interact with people and your environment, but as you do it, ensure that you are intentional and focused. Pay attention to how it feels. Could you live more mindfully? Can you see it impacting your family life in the positive ways some research suggests it might?

Take-home message

Philosopher and poet of Ancient China Lao Tzu instructed, 'In family life, be completely present.' Being mindful tells our children that they matter – their feelings matter, their voice matters, their story matters, their life matters. *There may be no message more important for our family's happiness and resilience than that* – and it extends beyond our relationships with our children to ALL of our relationships, and especially with our spouse or partner.

Happy family focus:
Exercises in daily mindfulness for parents

1. Make time to be present. An old quote says that, 'To a child, LOVE is spelled T-I-M-E.' If that is the case, I can't help but wonder what 'Hurry up' might mean to a child. Or 'I'm too busy right now.' Saying hurry up, especially when a child is trying to tell us something, does not show a willingness to be in the moment. The message it sends to a child may be harmful, too. When we are too busy for our children, or when we are rushing them, they suffer. They withdraw. They miss out on opportunities to connect with us. And our relationship with them may suffer when they are older.

2. Switch off and tune in. There may be no greater sign that you care, and that you will listen, than to power down your phone – or at least go to flight mode – when your children want your attention. Studies show definitively that the mere presence of a phone detracts from the quality of our conversations. Put the phone away when you are talking, and listen with interest and attention. Respond actively and in a way that builds the conversation. Psychologists call this 'active and constructive' responding, which requires mindfulness and presence, and builds relationships. The opposite of active and constructive responding is passive and destructive responding. If you were to experience one or the other, which would you choose?

3. Build screen-free time into your schedule. You might find it is easier to be mindful if you make certain parts of the day screen-free – no TV, no tablets, no phones – and just focus on the people in front of you. That means

no texting, reading, swiping or playing games. It means no beeps, pings, whistles or reminders. It's just you, your children and conversation. Perhaps it might be at a mealtime, or maybe while you travel. When you decide to do it is less important than making the decision to do it.

4. Engage with eye contact. Mindfulness can be increased when we pause what we are doing and look the person we are speaking with in the eyes. Physically turn towards them and pay attention to them in a way that makes it clear you really are right there.

5. Be all ears. When your children come to you with problems, put down your tools and listen! When they tell you about a friendship drama, a challenge on the netball team, a teacher making them feel rotten, or another difficulty, ask them to tell you all about it. Listen carefully. When they are finished, ask, 'What do you think you should do?' and listen again. Usually that's enough. You don't have to solve their problems. The answers are inside them and they merely need your presence and a listening ear. Be mindful.

6. Reach out and touch somebody. In our home, we have a habit of always touching each other as we move past one another. It might be a squeeze on the arm, a stroke of the hair, a caress on the cheek, or an arm across the shoulder. The touch is an acknowledgement that you are passing a real person. It is recognition that you have seen and noticed your child (or spouse). It is a way of being mindful of others. It feels nice to be noticed. Plus, research shows it can boost wellbeing. I also find that if a child is struggling, one of the best things we can do is hug them. In fact, the times our children deserve our hugs the least, are the times they need them most.

CHAPTER 5

Being loving, being there

Happiness is love. Full stop.

George Vaillant

If there is only one thing you do as a parent, be emotionally available.

When our children are upset and everyone is running late for school, it is not unusual for a parent to become frustrated and begin making threats and demands that a child shape up, get their act together, and do as they're told. One morning this happened in the home of Melissa and Simon. Their six-year-old, Corey, was upset because his big sister had a note to take to school for the teacher. He was insistent that he had to have a note too. Simon explained to Corey that he didn't need a note but that his sister did. And then he angrily dismissed Corey, telling him to hurry up and get ready because they were late. Corey's outburst grew. Melissa rushed into the family room to see what was going on. Amid Simon's hurried explanation (and justification) and Corey's wailing, Melissa walked over to Corey and hugged him.

'You want a note because your sister has one?'

Corey sobbed and nodded 'Yes'.

'Come with me and I'll help you.' Melissa took his hand and walked to the kitchen bench where she grabbed a pen and paper and wrote him a note, explaining that he could give it to the teacher when he arrived at school. Corey was satisfied and the morning proceeded calmly.

When Corey arrived at school, he gave the teacher his note. She read:

'Dear Mrs Rowe, Corey was upset this morning because his sister had a note and he didn't. This is his note. Now he is happy.'

A measure of warmth in relationships

The Grant study[40] is arguably one of the most important studies into human development ever undertaken. It is the longest study ever conducted (and probably one of the most exhaustive, too). The study commenced in 1938 and followed 268 privileged men who entered Harvard University as undergraduates, through until these men were in their nineties. The aim of the study? To track those men for the remainder of their lives, measuring their progress, following their development, and analysing their responses to life's challenges. The researchers behind the Grant study wanted to know everything possible about the young men they had selected to participate, believing that they could unlock the door to understanding what attributes and characteristics of our lives lead to ultimate success and happiness.

Grant study participants were subjected to 75 years of in-depth (and invasive) interviews ranging across topics as diverse as when they stopped bedwetting through to discussions of their family pedigree. They spent long hours with psychiatrists, and took questionnaires year after year. They interpreted Rorschach inkblots. They were poked and prodded. They submitted themselves to physical tests measuring everything from the amount of lactic acid they produced after five minutes on a treadmill to the length of their scrotum, as well as every other body measurement the researchers could think of. (At the time it was thought that success in life might be a function of body measurements.)

The researchers observed the full range of human possibility and achievement in the men selected for the study. Some participants took their own lives, some experienced alcohol and drug addictions, depression and multiple divorces. Others led full and flourishing lives into their nineties, enjoying the blessings of wealth, marriage, leadership and contribution. Some participants struggled to find and keep meaningful employment, and others led significant and successful enterprises. In 2009 it was revealed that one of the participants in the study made it all the way to the Oval Office as President of the United States.[41]

The Grant study is full of fascinating facts providing glimpses into what makes a good life. It turns out that our body measurements and anatomical proportions are not important to living happily. But there are a few findings that are particularly relevant to how families can be happy.

Perhaps the most relevant result (and certainly one of the central findings) of the multi-decade study is this: the warmth of the relationship the men experienced with their parents mattered in terms of their mental health, financial success and life satisfaction. The study's director for over three decades, George Vaillant, described relationship warmth as the greatest predictor of life satisfaction of all the variables in the study. His conclusion: 'Happiness is love. Full stop.'[42]

This result has been replicated in similar longitudinal studies – although none quite as ambitious and remarkable as the Grant study – throughout the world.[43] Researchers consistently highlight the remarkable power of parents who warmly and compassionately recognise that their children want nothing more than to be welcome in their world, and who make space in their lives for their children. Our children's wellbeing is improved when they feel our warmth, care and availability.

The warmth of the relationship the men experienced with their parents mattered in terms of their mental health, financial success and life satisfaction.

Just how warm and available are we?

If happiness is a response to the loving and warm quality of our relationships, how are we demonstrating our love and warmth to our children?

Data from the Early Childhood Longitudinal Study (ECLS), a nationally representative US study of 14,000 children born in 2001, showed that as a society, parents are not doing too well at demonstrating it at all. Warmth and availability typically lead to children being 'securely attached' to their parents and caregivers. Attachment describes the quality of the relationship shared between a child and his or her primary 'attachment figure' – usually the mother. Children who experience secure attachment have far more positive outcomes in their lives – and experience more happiness and wellbeing – than children whose attachments are insecure. In their analysis of data from the ECLS, researchers found the following.

> While the majority of children are securely attached, 40 per cent are *insecurely* attached. This is split into the 25 per cent of children who learn to avoid their parent when they are distressed, because the parent regularly ignores their emotional needs (avoidant attachment), and the highest risk 15 per cent of children, rising to 25 per cent in disadvantaged cohorts, who learn to resist the parent because the parent often amplifies their distress or responds unpredictably (disorganised or resistant attachment). The bond that children develop with their parents, particularly as babies and toddlers, is fundamental to their flourishing.[44]

How being emotionally available works

One of the clearest ways of showing our children we love them is to be emotionally available to them – and that means when you are busy doing a task of some kind (from sending an email to talking with a friend to hanging out the washing) and your child starts calling out to you, the simple act of stopping what you are doing to pay attention to your child means you are being emotionally available. It means you are helping your child feel secure around you, to trust you, and to believe that you are a predictable and safe person. You are creating a secure attachment.

> Researchers consistently highlight the remarkable power of parents who warmly and compassionately recognise that their children want nothing more than to be welcome in their world, and who make space in their lives for their children.

In my experience with a broad range of parents, it seems that the data from the ECLS are relatively accurate in the Australian context: in too many cases we are not particularly good at being emotionally available. And I wonder if this is because our parents were not emotionally available to us. David Brooks made the following insightful observation writing for the *New York Times*.

> If you go back and read a bunch of biographies of people born 100 to 150 years ago, you notice … things that were more common then than now … Many more children grew up in cold and emotionally distant homes, where fathers, in particular, barely knew their children and found it impossible to express their love for them.[45]

But I don't think we need to go back 100 years to experience this. In many families I visit with today, there are children experiencing that distance from their parents. There are solid emotional walls that interfere with too many parents' ability to be emotionally available to their children. In addition to the barriers described by Brooks, many of us have created a host of new impediments to being emotionally available by running overflowing schedules for our families, by being incessantly connected to devices (for work and pleasure – Candy Crush anyone?), and by being absorbed (often understandably) in our own 'stuff'. (I mentioned a lot about this in the previous chapter so I won't labour this point.)

Making a bid for connection

When our children reach out for us, they are doing what leading relationship researcher Dr John Gottman calls *'making a bid for connection'*.[46] He suggests that our relationships are strong or weak – and our families happy or unhappy – based on the way we respond to these bids to connect. Every time our children try to interact, whether it is through a look, a touch, sharing something or speaking to us, they are making a *bid* for connection. The way we respond to those bids indicates the extent to which we are emotionally available. Gottman further explains that we typically respond to these bids in one of three ways: we turn against our children, we turn away from our children, or we turn towards our children.

Turning against our children

We turn against our children's bids for connection when we show frustration and anger with statements such as: 'I've had enough of you', 'Would you just cut it out and leave me alone?' and 'I don't like it when you do that'. Threatening them is also turning against our children: 'I tell you what, you keep that up and I'm going to lock you in your room until you can behave the way I expect you to.' I have watched a mother at the beach turn against her seven-year-old daughter by screaming in her face for not complying with a basic request. Perhaps you have seen something similar. Parents with children in shopping centres, parks and other public places provide regular examples of disapproval associated with 'turning against', often in aggressive ways. A further example of turning against our children is the situation described in the introduction of this book, where a father refused to respond in any positive way to his teenage daughter's bids for connection until she apologised to him for the way she had behaved.

If you live in a relatively functional home such scenes would ideally be entirely foreign to you, but the fact is whenever we are disapproving of our children we are seeing them as an impediment, an obstacle or an object in our way. We voice our disapproval as a way of short-circuiting their bid for connection and demand that they leave us alone or solve their problems without our intervention. We show negative regard for them, invalidating their behaviour and emotion, and leaving them questioning their worth. It is rare that a response like this will lead to a happier family. To the contrary, turning against your children is a sure-fire way to achieve an unhappier family.

Turning away from our children

Ignoring our children when they want to connect with us or trivialising their feelings is equivalent to turning away from them. We may say things like, 'I'm not going to listen to you if you're going to speak to me like that.' Or we may ridicule them with a response like, 'Hmmm. Someone put his cranky pants on this morning.'

Turning away can also be as simple as the inattention we display by saying, 'Not now,' as we focus on someone or something else. It gives a clear message: your bid for connection is not important. Or, sometimes, we might dismiss (or turn away from) our children in seemingly well-meaning ways, such as sighing and kindly saying, 'Oh no! That's no good. Oh well, you'll be okay.' Maybe you recall your grandmother responding when you told her you had just broken up with your first love: 'Oh, never mind, love. There's plenty more fish in the sea.' How did that feel?

Regardless of whether the turning away is meant kindly or as a way of shoving off a child, it is a dismissive approach, it harms our relationships with our children and will ultimately lead to an unhappier family.

Benign parental neglect

Professor Neal Halfon, the director of the UCLA Center for Healthier Children, Families and Communities, has described this turning away as 'benign parental neglect', and argues that too little availability when our children need us can promote what he calls 'parental attention deprivation disorder'.[47] He suggests that when we are diverted from healthy interactions with our children and they fail to get our attention despite their best attempts, the compounding effect could be the genesis of the various developmental disabilities and childhood mental health problems we see escalating in prevalence each year. And Professor Halfon advocates what John Gottman and other child and parenting experts also suggest – that we turn towards our children.

Turning towards our children

The reality is that often our children are seeking to connect because they are biologically wired to be close to us – emotionally and physically. They need us to be responsive to them! Alternatively, they might be experiencing a challenge and they see us as a way to have a need met, or to be understood. This was mentioned in a previous chapter, but it is worth noting again: usually our children will seek us out and make a bid for connection when they are hungry, angry, lonely, tired, stressed or sick (HALTSS). When we turn towards our children and actively and constructively respond to them, we are acknowledging their bid for connection. If they are infants, we coo and laugh and tickle, if they are older we speak more to them. We invite them closer. We see their bid for connection (or their challenging behaviour, which is really just an uncivilised bid for connection) as an opportunity to be intimate and near them. Then we do the ordinary and the simple. Rather than leaving our children to feel that they are unimportant, we treat our children like the human beings they are and respond to them with our full focus and attention.

At the conclusion of one of my speaking events, one mother, Lisa (a psychologist) described a lengthy challenge she had experienced with her daughter, Mia. At around age 12, her little 'angel' began to exhibit some challenging behaviours. Eventually their relationship became deeply troubled. With each infraction of family guidelines Lisa would *turn against* Mia, voicing her disapproval, and demanding that things change. The relationship was all correction and direction. Rather than getting the relationship right, mother and daughter bickered regularly. Often conversations descended into name-calling, and angry disputes arose from innocuous comments. Foot-stomping, door-slamming and yelling were the currency of their interactions. Lisa recognised that she had conditioned herself to become 'pre-agitated' with Mia. As soon as her 12-year-old entered the room, Lisa would bristle with annoyance. It was as though she were preparing for the battle. The slightest provocation was all it took. Many times she found herself being accusatory only to be wrong, but this did not change the way she felt.

As their relationship deteriorated, it became clear to Lisa that something needed to change. But Lisa recognised that she was the adult in the relationship and after one particularly bitter dispute, realised that it was up to her to act like one. She made a commitment to do the unexpected – maybe even the impossible. Every time she saw Mia, Lisa decided she would offer her a hug. Then she would bite her tongue and simply be with (or near) Mia. The change only took two or three weeks to happen. Soon Lisa was excited to be with Mia because it meant hugs. Their relationship took a turn for the better. It was kind, courteous and loving.

> It became clear to this mother than something needed to change. She recognised that she was the adult in the relationship and it was going to have to be up to her to act like one.

It is this kind of response that forms the secure bonds our children so desperately need for wellbeing and happiness. It is also this response that is missing for almost half of all children (across all social classes) by the age of three.[48] Such a kind response seems antithetical to what so many people think their children need. But coming down hard on the children with correction and direction does not make families happy. Loving them does. Lisa still needed to discuss and maintain limits with Mia, yet those limits were so much easier to work through when the relationship was happy. This one change – a response that entailed turning towards, rather than against or away – led to greater emotional availability, and a happier family. And it happened in less than 21 days.

> Coming down hard on the children does not make families happy. Loving them does.

The need to belong

Feeling like we do not matter to someone, or being ostracised, may be one of the most painful human experiences we know of – for children and adults.[49] Research has provided an easy-to-understand experiment to demonstrate.

Imagine walking into a psychology lab and being told you will join in a game of catch with two other 'participants', but you are not aware that the two others who are playing are actually confederates of the experimenter. After playing catch for a few minutes the two confederates exclude you from the game, and only throw the ball to each other. Being excluded would likely leave you questioning whether there was something wrong with yourself, how you could have offended these people, and maybe even whether you are a 'good enough' person. This is a classic set-up for ostracism experiments, and whether the game is played on a field with a real ball and real people, or on a computer with a program designed to ostracise someone, the results are the same. The ostracised person experiences feelings of embarrassment, self-consciousness, and decreased self-esteem, self-efficacy and wellbeing.[50]

The ostracism research highlights the powerful intrinsic need people, whether children or adults, have to belong – that is, to matter to someone. We want to be significant in the lives of those with whom we interact, even if that interaction will only be for a few brief moments while we throw a ball to each other in a seemingly meaningless psychology experiment.

The opposite of being ostracised is belonging. A Japanese term, *amae*,[51] describes the feeling we each have to depend on another person, to connect and be attuned to those close to us, and to share emotional intimacy and kindness with others, but there is no clear English-language equivalent. Perhaps it is best described as the desire to receive love, or the desire to matter and to belong. There may be no better way to fulfil our children's *amae* than by being emotionally available, and turning towards them when they need us.

When mattering matters

During the first 12 years of life, our children seek *amae*, or belonging, consistently. They want to be near us; they love to talk to us; they want to connect with us, and they actively make bids to form connections by having us turn towards them. As we do, they feel safety, security, predictability and fulfilment. While very little research has been done on *amae*, research on a related term, *mattering*,[52] provides important lessons for us in the way we make ourselves available to our children, and in the way we boost their feelings of belonging. The studies show that people feel good when they perceive that other people value them. That means our children need to really feel that they matter to us. The best way to demonstrate that is through being emotionally available.

Secondly, feeling that we matter and belong are based on comparisons. We (and our children) evaluate the degree to which we matter by comparing the attention we receive from someone versus the attention they give to other activities, friends and things.

Thirdly, when we know we matter, we feel good.

There may be no better way to fulfil our children's *amae* than by being emotionally available, and turning towards them when they need us.

Creating belonging through being emotionally available

The lesson from this chapter is simple. We make our families happy when we down tools and focus on them, showing our children that they matter to us, and that they belong to a close-knit, loving family. We all have challenges in being available. Some parents are doing it solo, and have limited time and other resources. Other families are juggling two parents working long hours, and a host of other responsibilities. In some families, one child demands more than anyone else. The challenges are complex and the answers are not always easy. But, ultimately, it is finding a way to regularly give precious quality time to each child in a meaningful way that builds happier families and more resilient children.

To make your family happier in 21 days, you might try to find time today (or as soon as you can) to spend with your children.

It may be in a park, at the beach or on a bushwalk. It could be in those quiet 10 minutes before bed. It could be at the local café with an iced chocolate or while you walk the dog or drive to a sport or a music lesson. Just be there, focused and without distractions. Your children will love being in your space and will feel special. Note, also, that some children may respond more slowly to your efforts than others. It may take more than one date – especially for older children – but if you put your attention into your relationships, they'll become enriching sources of happiness and meaning for you.

Take-home message

Mums and dads who make themselves emotionally available for their children have happier families, and their children will benefit in their relationships, their schooling, their resilience and their overall wellbeing.

Happy family focus:
Commit to a totally available moment

Take a minute to think of a time when you were entirely available for your children. How did it feel for you, and for your family? How was it received?

Take time, at least once today, to really be there. Compare how that feels to the way things feel when you are not so available.

CHAPTER 6

Developing an attitude of gratitude

Gratitude involves wanting what one has rather than having what one wants ... gratitude may help people appreciate the gifts of the moment.

Jeffrey Froh[53]

Imagine that we were together in your lounge room. I hand you a life-saver or mentos or some other small sugary treat and tell you to pop it into your mouth. I also hand you a stone and ask you to put it into your shoe. Then I instruct you to go for a short walk, perhaps 15 seconds or so. After your walk around the room and down the hall and back I ask you to describe your experience. What do you think you might say?

If you're like 99 per cent of people I do this activity with on stage during my presentations, you'll say, 'It was uncomfortable', or 'hmmm, it wasn't that bad ... but I'd rather not walk around with a rock in my shoe.'

In most cases, people describe their experience in terms of the level of discomfort they experienced because they had a rock in their shoe. It is extremely rare for anyone to comment favourably because they were chewing on a tasty treat.

Each of us, individually and as families, is walking around with metaphorical mentos in our mouths and rocks in our shoes. Some people have more rocks than others. Some have more mentos than others. Some have bigger or smaller rocks. But we all have things we can complain about, and things that we can be grateful for. Gratitude is an attitude that is not dependent on our possessions, comfort levels, or wealth. It is an attitude that is entirely dependent on the choices we make about what we will focus on.

We have a saying in our home: 'You can be grateful or you can grumble.' It's a gentle, but tough-love reminder of the impact that a grateful attitude has on how we feel about life.

The essence and impact of gratitude

Gratitude is a recognition and acknowledgement of people, events and things in our lives that we appreciate. We can feel grateful for *anything* at all – from waking up and seeing a sunny blue sky to appreciating the way our children cleaned up after themselves at breakfast, or even for the trials of a challenging relationship because of the growth and learning we received from it.

The impact that gratitude can have on our happiness and wellbeing cannot be overstated. Dozens of studies have demonstrated that an attitude of gratitude makes us happy – and that when we're happy we are more likely to be grateful.[54] Some people feel that they should be more naturally grateful, but the knowledge that you can work at being grateful (and develop more happiness as a by-product) is amazing.

As a brief example, Professor Robert Emmons, one of the world's leading gratitude researchers, conducted a 10-week study[55] involving participants who were randomly assigned to one of three groups. The first group was asked to make a note of five things they were grateful for each week. Group two was requested to list five hassles or negative events from their preceding week. The third group was invited to write down five general events from the past week, but there was no instruction regarding whether they should emphasise the positive or the negative. Additionally, each day participants completed a questionnaire where they provided detailed ratings of their moods (things like distress, sadness and stress, as well as happiness and excitement), physical health (such as any aches, pains or sickness they felt) and their feelings of wellbeing.

> The impact that gratitude can have on our happiness and wellbeing cannot be overstated. Dozens of studies have demonstrated that an attitude of gratitude makes us happy.

The results? Gratitude makes a *big* difference. After 10 weeks, those who had listed five things they were grateful for each week felt better about their lives and were more optimistic about the future than those who wrote about general events or those who wrote about hassles. Those who were grateful reported fewer headaches and less illness, and exercised more than those in the other two groups. And for the gratitude group, happiness was up! Way up.

Later research has shown that a variety of gratitude 'boosters' can not only improve our health and wellbeing, but also make our relationships stronger. In my Introduction to this book I described how important relationships are for our happiness. And it seems that gratitude is a key to having good relationships, as well as greater wellbeing. Further, gratitude was shown to increase the amount we help others, decrease loneliness and depression, and even improve our sleep![56] Gratitude builds trust,[57] and it makes people more pleasant to be around. And gratitude benefits can go both ways, too. It's good for us to give thanks, but it is also a wellbeing boost to receive thanks.

The ingratitude of entitlement

The opposite of gratitude is entitlement – when we say 'No thanks', as in literally 'I'm not saying thanks, because I deserve this.'

Our children's way of voicing their feelings of entitlement, depending on their age, is through statements such as, 'That's not fair! If she gets to do that, then I should get to do it too!'

They will often add a 'You're mean!' and 'Oh, far out! Why do you always want me to do everything!?' And as they get older, this sentiment will be conveyed by a simple eye-roll followed by a dismissive 'Whatever!'

Often these phrases are really just our children venting a little and showing a need for some emotional support and validation, but when their use escalates, the message they are sending is: 'I *shouldn't* have to do anything I don't like, and good things *should* simply come to me.' Notice the prevalence of the word *should*? Entitlement is focused on 'should', and a sense of deservingness and pride, while gratitude is built on a foundation of recognition, humility and appreciation. And it is gratitude, not entitlement, that makes us happy.

Building gratitude in families

The rest of this chapter is packed with ideas for strategies that make people more grateful and, by default, more happy. Many can be easily and effectively applied in you family, and are so simple you could start doing them tomorrow!

Some of the ideas below have been experimentally validated, while others are simply fun things to do, but all of them can increase our gratitude and make our family happier. As you read through this chapter, think about how you could start 'doing more gratitude' at home, and how your family might respond. If you try and you are met with resistance, explain what you are doing and try again in a softer way, perhaps just focusing on what *you* are grateful for. (You might even be grateful for the resistance that comes your way, because that can give you a chance to turn towards your family and continue working at get your relationships right.)

Entitlement is focused on 'should', and a sense of deservingness and pride. Gratitude is built on a foundation of recognition, humility and appreciation. And it is gratitude, not entitlement, that makes us happy.

Grateful chatter

Our family has a tradition of talking about grateful things around the dinner table each night. Each person gets to share a couple of things they're grateful for. 'Dinner' is one of the more common answers we receive, although responses usually also include interesting things that have occurred during the day for our children. But the conversations serve other purposes too. Firstly, they focus the family on gratitude. Secondly, we gain insight into our children's lives – the ups and downs of their days. Thirdly, our discussions show the children they matter – that they belong. It is a chance for us to really listen and be mindful. We are also filling our minds with all of the good things life offers. And finally, our conversations about what we are grateful for offer some great teaching opportunities.

We get to share things that we are grateful for that seem unusual, such as, 'I'm grateful that I was caught in the thunderstorm today and got wet. It reminded me of how fortunate we are to have a home that keeps us dry and warm.' Or, 'I'm grateful that things are challenging at work right now. I'm learning about patience, and how to work with people who see the world differently to me.'

Our grateful things are usually simple, but sometimes they're profound. And when Kylie or I fail to talk about our grateful things immediately, the children take over! If I have been too distracted to ask the question within a minute of sitting down, one of the girls will take on the grateful things leadership mantle and begin asking her siblings what they were grateful for. They love it – and it makes our family happy.

This may be the simplest gratitude exercise to implement in your family. It requires nothing more than a conversation about what you are each grateful for. It's simple, usually fun, and it is almost certain to increase feelings of wellbeing. Recently we have expanded our grateful chatter to incorporate sunshine (what we're grateful for), storms (what has challenged us), and rainbows (what was good that came from the storm). It can be a useful conversation that points us to the way we can find benefits and things to be grateful for during tough times as well as in good times.

> 'I'm grateful that I was caught in the thunderstorm today and got wet. It reminded me of how fortunate we are to have a home that keeps us dry and warm.'

A gratitude tree

In a previous home we had a beautiful tree just outside our front door that we named 'the gratitude tree'. One evening as we discussed our grateful things we made tags describing all of the things we were grateful for. Then we attached the tags to the tree, and over the subsequent days we continued to add tags to the branches. The tree served as a symbol of all that we had to be grateful for.

I'm not aware of any research on the effects of gratitude trees, but it's a fun family spin on the idea of making lists of what we are thankful for. One of the best things about our gratitude tree was that every time we walked past the tree, we had a powerful visual reminder of the enormous quantity of goodness and blessings in our lives.

Secret thank you

It may be one thing to say 'Thanks!' to someone who has done something you appreciate, but a secret thank you goes the extra mile. To develop an attitude of gratitude and to strengthen relationships, consider encouraging your children to take a few minutes each week to give a secret thank you to someone in the family for something that has happened during the week. They might go for a quiet walk to say thanks, or offer a special hug. Perhaps they will write a short note and hide it in a shoe, or drop a treat into a pocket. A secret thank you can start a spiral of positive reciprocity in your family that builds unity and love, and strengthens relationships.

You can start it off by sneaking a note of appreciation into your children's lunch boxes. In my talks around the country, employees are inspired to do something similar in their staff rooms. A gratitude box is placed in a public place and staff place small gratitude notes into the box, highlighting things (or people) in the workplace that they appreciate. In staff meetings a few of these notes are shared with the team, and someone types up the remainder into an email to share all of the things staff were grateful for during the previous week. Regardless of how you do it, saying thank you seems to improve relationships and increase happiness.

> To develop an attitude of gratitude, encourage your children to think of a way they can give a secret thank you to someone in the family for something that has happened during the week.

Gratitude letters

Writing a gratitude letter is a well-documented, empirically-validated way of building relationships through expressions of appreciation. Think of someone who has done something for you that is significant, but who you may never have truly thanked. They may or may not be a family member. Write them a letter detailing everything you can about what they have done and how it has impacted you. When the letter is written, take it to the person, read it to them and leave it with them.

For younger children who can't do this on their own, mum could easily pen a letter to dad, or someone else, on their behalf. She simply has to interview their child about all the great things that person does, ask the child how that person makes him or her feel, and write it down. Similarly, encouraging our children who are old enough to write their own letters of gratitude to grandparents, teachers, coaches and neighbours can also promote a strong feeling of gratitude within our family.

The gratitude letter is not for everyone, and practitioners have suggested that some people don't receive great benefits from the process, perhaps due to the way the recipient might react or because of personal anxieties. But for most people, this is a strategy that gives long-term happiness boosts and brings joy to relationships.

Model it

Say thanks. Talk about what you're grateful for. Chat with your children about how much you appreciate different people and things. Leave little thank you notes under pillows or in pockets. The best way to grow grateful people is to be grateful people ourselves.

Tell stories that promote gratitude

Some time ago we went through several weeks of listening to a couple of our daughters whining about going to school. We listened carefully but found nothing was wrong – they simply didn't want to go. Their whining was contagious, and soon no one wanted to go to school. So we shared the remarkable story of Malala Yousafzai. Malala is a girl from Pakistan who, at the age of 11, wrote a blog for the BBC about life in a place where the Taliban ordered girls out of schools. She continued to attend school, and gained prominence for her strong views on why girls should be allowed an education. At the age of 15, Malala was shot in the head in an assassination attempt, ostensibly because of her outspokenness. Malala survived and has become an amazing example of courage and strength to people around the world.

After sharing that story with our children, we asked our daughters what they thought, and how they felt – both about Malala and about education more generally. We took time to describe the society we are fortunate to live in, and compared it with the village in which Malala was raised. Our motive was not to guilt our children into a sense of indebtedness. Rather, we gently opened their eyes to what they are blessed to have that so many others don't have. And the result was instantaneous. Their gratitude for freedom, education and safety changed their approach to school, and to helping out at home, in an instant. Amazing stories that promote gratitude are everywhere, and they can change the way our homes and relationships function.

Look for the good

Sometimes bad things happen. We experience trials and difficulties. Next time your children struggle with something, wait for the appropriate time and ask them what good has come out of that struggle, or what good will come out of it. Benefit-finding[58] is a remarkable way of reconstructing challenges and viewing them as blessings, and is also a strategy for increasing wellbeing. After particularly difficult experiences, gratitude can foster post-traumatic growth (rather than its negative corollary, post-traumatic stress).

> After particularly difficult experiences, gratitude can foster post-traumatic growth.

One of my daughters was struggling after an altercation with her friend. Feelings were raw and life had become uncomfortable. On a quiet afternoon I asked her if she could think of anything to be grateful for about the ongoing relationship challenges she had experienced with this particular individual. Her response: 'I'm grateful for what I'm learning about friends and friendship. I think this is teaching me how to choose better friends, and how to be a better friend.'

Take-home message

Gratitude is, according to the ancient Roman philosopher Cicero, the greatest of all the virtues. It builds our relationships, our character, and our wellbeing. And it does so, simply by us taking the time to recognise the good (and not so good) things in our life, and acknowledge them for the blessing that they are.

Happy family focus:
Exercises in gratitude

1. Find at least three opportunities to say thank you to people in your family today. Say it sincerely and describe to them *why* you are thankful. Go beyond 'Thanks,' and say 'I really appreciate you doing _____ because _____.' (You fill in the blanks.)
2. Try doing grateful chatter at dinnertime.
3. Do some gratitude craft – perhaps making a gratitude tree or wall.
4. Write thank you letters to people who deserve a heartfelt and meaningful thanks.
5. Bake some treats, attach anonymous thank you cards, and do secret drop-offs to people you think deserve thanks. Maybe they have helped you personally, or perhaps they are people you know who help others in the community and may not get thanked very often.

CHAPTER 7

Using hope to make your family happy

Even the darkest night will end and the sun will rise.
Victor Hugo[59]

One of my favourite stories describes Christmas morning in the home of two young brothers, aged five and eight. The older brother, who was somewhat pessimistic, was told that he had been very, very good throughout the year, so he should expect something nice from Santa. On Christmas morning he opened his stocking after some coaxing from his parents. Inside he found a beautiful gold watch. He held it carefully, told his parents he appreciated it, and then described all the ways he was worried it might break. There was no excitement; only concern for what might happen to the watch in the future.

His younger brother was a vibrant, wide-eyed optimist who was forever getting into trouble. He had been warned that Santa might not visit him because he had not been quite so good as his well-behaved, cautious brother. In spite of the warnings, as soon as he was allowed to, he raced to his stocking and hefted it. There was something in there. He yelped in excited anticipation. He tipped the stocking upside down and jumped backwards as horse droppings fell from the stocking and landed at his feet. In an instant he was racing for the back door. His father called him back and asked him where he thought he was going. The boy responded with excitement, 'Santa brought me a pony but it looks like he's gotten away. I've got to run and find him!'

At the risk of being provocative, there's a good chance that, like the youngest brother in the story above, you are deluded. Yes, you. The person reading this book. Deluded – not in touch with reality. And to be fair, I am just like you in that regard.

The three essential delusions for wellbeing

It seems that most of us experience positive illusions about ourselves and our future as part of our normal, healthy function – illusions that in actual fact make us deluded. The people who don't experience those delusions are typically depressed or struggling with other mental illness. This is the counterintuitive, and compelling, argument made by psychological researchers since the late 1980s. We have to be deluded by these illusions about ourselves in order to be healthy. If we are seeing things the way they really are (and are therefore not deluded), we are typically not psychologically healthy. Go figure. Social psychologists have indicated that we generally 'suffer' from three specific illusions about ourselves, and it is these illusions that make us normal and help us cope with life in a healthy way.[60]

The first illusion is that we think we are better than we actually are. For example, ask most people whether they're better-than-average, average or below-average drivers, and chances are that you'll get a strong bias toward being better than average. That is mathematically impossible, of course. If the average is around the midpoint but everyone believes they are above that point, then the average has to move! We can't all be above average. By definition, we must have a group of low-ability people to counter-balance the high-ability people.

Continuing this positive illusion (or delusion), we tend to judge positive character traits as more representative of who we are than negative traits, and we feel that we possess those positive attributes in greater degree than the average person. Finally, people typically feel that when success is achieved it is primarily due to their contribution, while when failure occurs, the blame lies in factors (or people) outside their own control.

It seems that most of us experience positive illusions about ourselves and our futures as part of our normal, healthy function – illusions that make us deluded.

The second illusion that psychologically healthy (and therefore deluded) people experience is an unrealistic belief in our ability to control things. A simple example of this can be seen in a game where dice are thrown. Many people believe that they have some kind of control over the dice, and insist on throwing them rather than allowing someone else to roll the dice on their behalf. They even go through special routines, shaking the dice in a predetermined way in an attempt to exert some kind of control, or blowing on the dice in their hands as though their breath has magical controlling properties. Some people *kiss* the dice, believing that expressions of love matter to the six-sided cube they are about to throw on the table. Other researchers have shown that when people expect a certain outcome, even when it occurs entirely by chance, they overestimate the extent to which they can claim responsibility for that outcome. In short, we do not attribute fortunate experiences to luck. We believe we control things over which we have no control. And this belief boosts our optimism and hopefulness.

The third illusion is based on an unrealistic optimism that mentally healthy people enjoy. Research shows that most of us think that we are quite likely to experience pleasant future events at rates well above the likelihood of those events actually occurring. We think we will get good jobs, promotions and pay rises. We

91

expect our children will be healthy and happy. We anticipate that our relationships will be successful. These optimistic expectations keep us happy and positive. We similarly expect that our futures will *not* contain unpleasant events that statistics indicate are far more likely to occur than we suppose, such as becoming a victim of crime, divorcing, being involved in a car accident or getting cancer.[61] By believing that such things will not happen to us, we maintain a higher level of wellbeing than we might if we spent our days dreading the time when it will all come crashing down.

While these illusions are fun to talk about, and fascinating to consider, they really do appear to be linked to our good health and help us to be happy. And it is the third of these illusions that I will focus on throughout the remainder of this chapter.

Understanding optimism and hope

Optimism means we feel good about the future. We are hopeful about it and we expect good things will come, even during – and sometimes because of – the difficulties we face. The optimist is the 'glass half-full' kind of person. Poets and novelists have written countless odes to optimism, promising rising suns, bright futures and endless possibilities to those with courage, optimism and vision. Optimism is positively related to our psychological wellbeing[62] and physical health.[63]

To better understand optimism, it can be helpful to take a look at its opposite. Pessimism is associated with depression, stress and anxiety. People who are strongly pessimistic expect lousy things to happen in the future, and in some cases develop what we know of as *helplessness*, believing that when something difficult occurs, nothing they do can make things better, so it's not worth trying anyway.

So how does hope fit in? In scientific literature there are some technicalities that distinguish optimism from hope, and they are important. While most of us have a natural tendency towards being optimistic, it is something of a personality characteristic. Hope, however, is different. Hope can be learned. And while optimism builds wellbeing, hope can be even more powerful.

To have hope, we (and our children) need three things: a vision or goal, pathways towards that goal, and something psychologists call agency, or efficacy, which is a belief that by taking action we can achieve our goal. In a sense, this entire book is an exercise in building hope. You have read the early chapters and spent time thinking about what your vision or goal is for the future of your family. You are reading the subsequent chapters to understand the various pathways you might take in order to achieve that goal. And if you have the belief, you will be able to take active steps to accomplish what you set out to achieve.

The research on hope is compelling. Hopeful people enjoy more success in life than those without hope. They make more effort. They work towards achieving great things. And whether they actually get to where they hoped to get or not, they often come closer to it than they would have if they had not hoped at all.

> To have hope, we need three things: a goal, pathways towards that goal and a belief that by taking action we can achieve our goal.

How to enhance optimism and create hope

Creating a hopeful family offers us tremendous promise in terms of wellbeing – and achievement. Hopefulness demands that we create a plan or vision, develop strategies, and work towards achieving our goals. If we do it well, it can enhance our opportunities to be increasingly emotionally available and mindful, and to get our relationships right, making our families happier. But how do we do it? By creating a pattern or habit of looking forward to things that are meaningful, and identifying ways to make those things happen.

In *The Optimistic Child*,[64] Professor Martin Seligman describes a simple conversation that he asks parents to enjoy with their children to encourage a positive future-orientation – or optimism. He suggests tucking our children into bed at night, sitting with them, and asking them to describe something that they're looking forward to. Our children will share their hopes and dreams with us. We will learn what is meaningful to them. Trust in our relationships will deepen, and security will be strengthened. This optimistic view of the future is the beginning of true hopefulness.

To generate a more powerful sense of hope as a family, we can work towards meaningful goals. Take a moment now to reflect on what the last meaningful goal your entire family worked towards together with a shared enthusiasm and sense of purpose. What was the goal? How did you plan on getting there? How did you create the belief you could achieve it? How did it feel for you to progress in the right direction? What are you, as a family, working towards now? If something has immediately popped into your head, that's great! Does the whole family know about it and do you have specific plans and motivation to work together to achieve it?

Making hope happen

A few years ago our family decided to create a sense of shared purpose around a hopeful theme: 'I can do hard things.' We spoke about a bunch of challenging things we might do as individuals and set some personal goals. Then we picked a single, hard thing we could aim for as a family. The challenge was decided. We would hike to the top of Australia's highest peak, Mount Kosciuszko. While no Everest, Kosciuszko's peak sits 2228 metres above sea level. It is at altitude, which makes everything – including breathing, walking and carrying children – harder. And while

94

there is no actual climbing involved, it is a long uphill hike: the path is around 8 kilometres, which is a good walk for an adult, and a huge effort for a child, particularly at altitude.

Everyone looked forward to the hike for about nine months. That was the optimism part taken care of. Kosciuszko is a six-hour drive from home, which meant we had to go away on a mini-holiday to achieve our goal. This increased the enthusiasm and optimism everyone felt. We invited cousins and grandparents to join us, which made it even more exciting. And then we started training. This was the 'pathways' and 'agency' part of building hope. The children (including our young ones) had to get used to walking for long periods while going uphill. Our youngest had to get used to sitting in a toddler carrier on my back for those same long periods. When times got tough, we talked about doing hard things, and described the hike we would be doing. These conversations kept us focused on our goal when agency (efficacy/ self-belief) was low. If self-belief faltered, even a bit, we zeroed in on the goal, and how we were going to achieve it. We looked forward to the holiday, time with family, and the feeling we anticipated we would feel being at the highest point in Australia.

Finally the day arrived and we packed the car for the six-hour drive. Even though it was summer, the temperature in the mountains was only a couple of degrees above freezing. But in spite of the long drive and the cold weather, the family was excited.

The walk was memorable. We ate lunch at Australia's highest point, took photos and shared a joyful experience. Then I carried *two* children back down the mountain because they were so exhausted!

Your family goal does not need to be so taxing. It could be as simple as going for a weekly walk to the library for new books, or going camping twice a year somewhere new and beautiful. What matters is that you set the goal, work out how you might achieve it and take action to make the goal a reality.

Where hope dies

Think back to previous chapters about discipline, getting relation-ships right, and being both mindful and emotionally available. You will recall that the heart of each of those chapters was really about building strong relationships with our children because that is what creates resilience. Sadly, when our relationships with our children are poor, they tend to have lower levels of hope, and the whole family suffers.

I had the opportunity to travel to a relatively remote community to work with schools, community workers and families on building happiness habits that might improve the wellbeing of children and parents in their community. We discussed hope and a Department of Child Services (DOCS) worker shared some stories that left the audience feeling hopeless. In an interview with a challenged teen from a highly dysfunctional and aggressive family, she had asked him, 'What do you hope for in your future?' He had responded that he hoped to be like his father. The worker hung her head in sadness. The boy's father was in gaol. As we discussed his plight we recognised that he had the goal, he had the pathway mapped out and he had the belief he could get there. It was highly likely he would get what he was hoping for.

Chloe was a 13-year-old girl. I worked with her grandparents as they sought to improve her circumstances and the choices she was making. She had high hopes of becoming a childcare worker or a hairdresser. Chloe lived with her mother and stepfather. Her father had washed his hands of his daughter. While only in Year 8, Chloe was no longer in school. She was on the contraceptive pill, and was drinking, smoking and using drugs including ecstasy and ice. Chloe seemed to be a great kid who was terribly confused, felt unloved, and was making some poor choices. As we focused on her goals, a sense of hope infused our conversation. With Chloe's agreement, her grandparents used some relationships they had with someone who owned a hair salon, and Chloe was offered a trial with a hairdresser. If the trial went well, a traineeship and eventually an apprenticeship were possibilities.

Chloe began day one full of optimism and enthusiasm. She had a goal, and a pathway. But did she have the agency, or self-belief, that she could actually make a go of things? By about day three, Chloe's attitude was changing. Working was hard! After making some small mistakes and being spoken to by the boss, Chloe crumpled. Her self-belief disappeared. Without resilience, she gave up and chose not to return.

Hope requires more than a blind and cheerful optimism. While that certainly helps, hope demands a pathway to a goal, and a belief that we can walk along that pathway – or try other paths if the one we are on fails. It seems that hopeful children – the ones who have a vision plus the pathways plus the belief – are most often found in families where parents are there for them, stand beside them and believe in them.

An activity that creates hopeful children

Shane Lopez is a senior scientist with the Gallup organisation and one of the world's leading researchers on hope. In an article describing the process of building hope in children he indicated that those children who are actively engaged in hopeful activities enjoy high wellbeing. He described how this meant they were working on goals that mattered to them, and that kept them future-focused.[65]

He described an evening he attended at a local school. A teacher asked fifth and sixth grade students to spend a week taking photos that documented hope in their lives. If they saw something that made them hopeful, they were to snap it and store it. At the end of the week, in consultation with their teacher, the students chose the one photo that best represented hope. They were asked to write brief stories describing why they had made their choice. The photos and stories were matted and framed in preparation for an art show for parents and teachers. As Shane and his wife took in the displays and spoke to the students, they learned about many of the challenges and fears the children had, and how looking at things that inspired hope helped the children see specific pathways – actions – they could use to make their futures better. The project focused them on things that made them hopeful. It pointed them to pathways that led to the positive outcomes they wanted. It enhanced their sense of self-belief, and encouraged them to keep on trying to get where they wanted to go.

Ode to can

When Henry Ford said, 'Whether you think you can, or you think you can't, you're probably right,' he appears to have been advocating for hopefulness, resilience and a 'can-do' attitude.

Some years ago a major Australian bank created a campaign based around the word 'can'. Our family memorised a poem that was written as part of the campaign.

There's a four-lettered word as offensive as any
It holds back the few, puts a stop to the many.
You can't climb that mountain, you can't cross the sea
You can't become anything you want to be.
He can't hit a century, they can't find a cure.
She can't think about leaving or searching for more.
Because can't is a word with a habit of stopping the ebb and
*   the flow of ideas*
It keeps dropping itself where we know in our hearts it's not
*   needed*
And saying 'don't go' when we could have succeeded.
But those four little letters that end with a T

They can change in an instant when shortened to three.
We can take off the T, we can do it today
We can move forward not back, we can find our own way.
We can build we can run, we can follow the sun
We can push we can pull, we can say I'm someone
Who refuses to believe that life can't be better
With the removal of one insignificant letter.

Can't or don't want to?

Many years ago my mother told me, 'Justin, "can't" means "don't want to".' I hated that. Every time I heard it I felt that my feelings were invalidated. Mum didn't understand. And I honestly believed that I couldn't do whatever it was I was whining about. But mum would patiently explain, 'You *can* do it, but you just don't want to. If you really wanted to, you would find a way.'

That quote has stayed with me for decades, and reminded me of hope. Anytime we find ourselves or our children crying out, 'I can't! I can't do it. I can't make my family happier. I can't be kind. I can't be patient. I can't make this relationship work!' we are really saying we don't want to. If we really wanted to, in most – if not all – cases, we would find a way. We would set up a vision or goal, figure out the pathways, and then take action with the self-belief that it could really make a difference. And who knows. It just might.

Take-home message

Being hopeful and optimistic about the future should lead us to be motivated, make plans and work towards meaningful goals. The process, when worked through as a family, can strengthen our relationships, build a sense of shared purpose, and increase our happiness as we anticipate a positive and exciting future.

Happy family focus:
Try these ideas for making your family more hopeful (and happier)

1. Ask your children, often, what they are looking forward to
2. Create a vision board, as individuals, and as a family
3. Set a big, challenging, audacious goal to work towards as a family
4. Talk about the different pathways to achieving your goals
5. Have quiet conversations with your children where you can confide in them that you believe in them
6. When your child is struggling, be patient, compassionate and understanding, then ask, 'What options do you have?' and work with them on creating pathways.

CHAPTER 8

Creating strong family traditions

Family traditions counter alienation and confusion. They help us define who we are; they provide something steady, reliable and safe in a confusing world.

Susan Lieberman

My maternal grandparents lived around a 90-minute drive from our house. As a child we would make regular trips to visit Nan and Pop, usually on a Sunday afternoon. Nan would invariably have a roast dinner waiting for us. While the grown-ups would talk about boring stuff, we would play at the park and ride our bikes along the path near the poorly named Duck Creek (there never being any ducks, and I don't recall there ever being enough water to consider the watercourse a creek). We occasionally played cricket in the backyard and regularly had to crawl under the house (which sat about half a metre atop stubby brick posts) to collect the ball someone had hit, hoping to avoid the bugs, spiders and imaginary monsters we were sure existed under there.

I'm not really sure how it started, but as we drove away from Nan and Pop's house and they waved farewell from the end of the driveway, our entire family would stick our heads out of the car windows and scream at the top of our lungs, 'Bye!' We would extend the farewell as long as we could, continuing to cry out until our breath was spent and we were well out of earshot. 'Byyyyyyyyye!'

It became a family tradition.

My Nan has passed away, but we still visit my grandfather and he gets the same treatment. And now, when Kylie and I take our children to visit their grandparents (on either side of the family), the neighbours all know when we're leaving because all of our children have their heads out the window as they shout their goodbyes in a single 30-second ear-splittingly fun syllable that lasts to the bottom of the hill or the corner where we are well out of earshot. I confess that Kylie and I are as enthusiastic as the children in our goodbye too.

Making life make sense through traditions

Our family traditions form part of our family culture. At the heart of every family tradition is a meaningful experience that has the potential to increase our wellbeing. Traditions have the potential to bind us to one another through shared experiences, and the shared meaning attached to those experiences. We use traditions to transmit (often unconsciously) our values to our children, or to remind us of the warmth that exists in our relationships. They also help us feel happier as we look back and reflect on the tradition. (Psychologists call this process *savouring* and it is strongly linked to happiness.)[66]

A definition of tradition

When I used to think about family traditions I would roll my eyes and think, 'It's all too hard.' I pictured enormous family reunions with hundreds of strangers trying to hug me and tell me how we were related. I don't think I really understood what a tradition was – and how simple it was to create one. In fact, we create them all the time.

A tradition is a behaviour that we repeat in a certain way at the same time each week, month, or year, or with the same people, or in the same place. Often the tradition will include the same people at the same time in the same place!

Traditions differ from our routines or habits because we carry out these traditions with a specific purpose and degree of intentionality – we are trying to achieve something very specific to create bonds, impart values, promote shared experience and build memories. Whereas routines are designed to become automatic and to make life simpler, traditions and rituals are about being mindful of the moment, and are designed to demand attention and imbue life with meaning.

Why traditions matter

In *The Book of New Family Traditions*,[67] author and journalist Meg Cox suggests traditions matter in significant ways, and identifies 10 good things they do for our family (as long as the tradition is healthy and helpful).

1. Traditions impart a sense of identity
2. They provide comfort and security
3. They help to navigate change
4. They teach values
5. They pass on ethnic or religious heritage
6. They teach practical skills
7. They solve problems
8. They keep alive a sense of departed family members
9. They help heal from loss or trauma
10. Traditions generate wonderful memories.

I'm sure that our family is known as the 'loud goodbye family' by the neighbours of our parents and grandparents. And even if they don't think of us like that, we do. It's part of our identity.

Our traditions and rituals create a sense of who we are and how we are different to other families. In the instances where we extend traditions from one generation to the next, those traditions can strengthen ties between our children and their grandparents. This enhances our sense of family identity even more, and research again shows that traditions boost wellbeing[68] through stronger relationships, meaning and a sense of 'This is who we are'.

Traditions and rituals help life make sense to our children. They increase predictability so our children feel secure, because knowing what to expect increases feelings of comfort and safety. In a 2015 study involving approximately 250 teens (aged 15-20), researchers discovered that the practice of family rituals and traditions had a significant and important protective role in increasing social connectedness for teens, and for reducing their experiences of anxiety.[69] Those who participated in family rituals also experienced less depression. It seems that the sense of family connectedness tradition and ritual provides deep roots in which our children's self-esteem and wellbeing can develop and grow, and protects them from the stresses that so many teens experience.

> Traditions and rituals help life make sense to our children.
> They increase predictability so our children feel secure.

Traditions mean shared experience

Traditions don't have to be huge, wildly creative or over the top. My paternal grandparents had a tradition of following their favourite football team to every match they played each winter. Because all of the games were held in the local Sydney league (at the time there was no national league organised), they were able to take my dad and his sister to cheer on their team every weekend. From around the age of five, my dad cheered on the Magpies, rarely missing a game. This continued until he met my mum, who hates football, and the tradition changed from going to the games to watching the game on TV every weekend with me, my brother and our sisters.

I asked my dad what that tradition meant to his family. You won't be surprised to find that several of the themes in this book were strongly echoed in his response. He said, 'We were always excited about what was going to happen during the coming weekend. When summer was ending, we'd get excited that autumn and winter were coming because the football would be back.'

The tradition promoted hope, optimism and a positive future-orientation. He also said, 'It gave us things to bond over. We were always talking about the last game, or the next game.'

The tradition promoted a sense of shared experience and emotional closeness.

Simple is good

Kylie and I have our own simple traditions or rituals that we practise regularly – not as an automatic routine, but as an intentional standard designed to bring our family closer together, strengthen our sense of family identity and teach specific values. As you will see from the examples I have shared below, traditions don't have to be big, once-a-year celebrations centred on religious or holiday festivals.

- Every morning I play a song on the piano to wake everyone up. When they hear that song they know it is time to come to our lounge room where we talk about our day and share a story, a quote, or something inspirational and uplifting – perhaps something related to our family principles – to start our day off positively.
- We set aside one evening a week for uninterrupted family time. There are no activities scheduled, no electronic devices (unless they're an intentional part of our night)

and no interruptions. It's just us, the children, and a night to be together, talk, play and teach.

- I cook pancakes for lunch every Sunday, and every Sunday night we have a roast dinner.
- Every night before bed we read stories to our children.
- Each year at Christmas we visit my parents' house. Their home has a short private jetty, and our Christmas tradition (aside from eating far too much seafood) is doing backflips and somersaults off it into the water.
- Kylie and I are establishing a tradition of having an annual break – just the two of us – for a few days to rejuvenate and strengthen our relationship. We also have created a regular date night tradition to make sure we reconnect on a weekly basis – without the children.
- When each of our children turn 16, we have determined that we will take them to a holiday destination of their choice (within reason!) to spend time just with us. We'll use that holiday to talk about the big issues and the small ones, to strengthen our relationship with them and to prepare them for the increasingly close arrival of adulthood.

Dip into the tradition trove

There are endless opportunities in life to develop traditions that are unique to your family, and here are more ideas to get you thinking about them.

Positive daily rituals to try

I've already described my family's wake-up music and morning time together as a family. Other families I have quizzed, or use as models of excellence, have traditions like saying a morning or evening prayer together, saying goodbye in a special way when they leave for school or work, or having special and specific conversations at bedtime, such as those that promote gratitude or hope as I have talked about in previous chapters.

Developing weekly traditions

A regular Sunday roast, or a weekend tradition of playing or watching sport, are examples of easy-to-do weekly traditions. Perhaps dad might take the children to get a Saturday-morning milkshake or hot chocolate while mum sleeps in. Or you could make Friday night a family movie and pizza night, or Sunday afternoon could become special one-on-one time between parents and a child.

Embracing seasonal traditions

Many families take advantage of long weekends and holidays to take their family away for a camping trip or a break at the same place each year, and build up a reservoir of memories and treasured experiences at those special spots.

There may be religious or cultural traditions that bring meaning to your family, and a sense of identity and wellbeing. Christmas, Easter, Ramadan, Hanukkah, Baptism, Bat Mitzvah or Bar Mitzvah and the Boxing Day cricket match (or the Boxing Day sales at the shops) all offer opportunities to build traditions.

Establish simple traditions around your children's birthdays and meaningful milestones in your children's lives. A tradition might be created for the first day of summer with a trip to the beach, or lighting the first fire of winter, or going on a hike each year on the Queen's Birthday long weekend.

One mum described to me an annual tradition around a favourite TV show – *Dr Who*. Every year Katie and her daughter watch the previous series again to remind themselves where the series is up to. There's the sighting of the first episode trailer on TV; the countdown to the starting day, and then the First Episode. No appointments, lessons or activities are planned for that night. It is just Katie, her daughter and a big bowl of popcorn.

> Traditions give the promise of wonderful memories, but they also give our children, and us, something to look forward to. They build optimism and hope.

As you reflect on this list of potential activities, you can probably see that traditions give the promise of wonderful memories, as well as making our family happier by impacting positively on our future-orientation. Traditions give our children, and us, something to look forward to. They build optimism and hope.

The all-important bedtime traditions

Bedtime can become a wonderfully special time for families. One of my favourite traditions occurs at bedtime each night in our home – or at least the nights when I'm home and it hasn't been too chaotic. We try to make bedtime, including for our bigger children, a time of quiet connection and relationship strengthening. During the dramas of the day we can easily overlook our children's emotional needs and struggles because we aren't always available or can't always be mindful. Often there is just too much else to do for us to be focusing on getting our relationships right. As often as we are able, we enjoy our favourite bedtime things – our bedtime tradition.

We read stories, exposing the children to classics, humour, adventure, wisdom, biography, fantasy and more. Once we have read to them, we tuck them into bed and do something that's difficult – we intentionally forget about the dishes, and we leave the email and social media accounts alone. Instead, we sit softly on the end of our children's beds and talk with them. We ask if there is anything they want to talk to us about, and we find out what was great about their day, or maybe what they're looking forward to doing tomorrow.

One of the most commonly shared pieces of marriage wisdom

is that we should never go to bed angry with our spouse. The advice applies to our children as well. If, during the course of the day, we have not been our best selves, these final few minutes of the day are a valuable time to make much needed relationship repairs. Letting our children know we are sorry for not being our best teaches leadership, humility and humanity, and it shows a willingness to put a relationship ahead of frustrations and grudges.

As our five or so minutes draws to a close, we tell our children that they are loved, wanted and important to us. Such statements – heartfelt and meaningful – matter so much. Honest, caring listening may be the most important thing we can do to show our children we care about them, and to help them really feel it.

I believe that this tradition, during those final minutes each night, provides a precious time – almost sacred – for listening, repair and love.

Take-home message

Traditions tend to grow organically through us as parents being mindful of what we do with our families. When we become aware of and appreciate wonderful and meaningful events as potential traditions, we can consciously shepherd our family towards repeating them. Traditions have the potential to unite our families, impart values, create a climate of anticipation, build delightful memories, and provide a strong sense of identity and belonging for our family. They can promote a sense of safety, certainty and security. Traditions can be big or small. They can be elaborate or simple. What matters is that we have them and that we celebrate them.

Happy family focus:
Start building on your family traditions

Traditions are not created in a day – it takes time for them to build meaning and momentum. But perhaps you can take a minute to think about some of the meaningful (or perhaps unintentional) traditions and rituals that exist in your family.

How can you build meaning around those traditions? Think about how you can emphasise them, and make them unique to your family, so you can say, 'This is what we do! This is who we are!'

CHAPTER 9

Routine matters

*The only possible way to have it ALL is with structure
and the discipline to keep to it, to make it a routine.*
Margot Hattingh

What is it that makes your life meaningful? What gives you purpose? Have you found something that drives you and gives you a reason for living? Perhaps it is your family? Your work? Your particular 'cause'. We are much more likely to be happy if we have a sense that our life is meaningful. More meaning usually means more happiness. That may be why family life makes us happy (when it's not driving us crazy). It is not necessarily because we feel good being parents. It can be hard, exhausting, dirty, frustrating, and inconvenient work and it often fails to make us even a little bit happy *in the moment*. But it provides great meaning – and it is that meaning that has a dramatic impact on our happiness. There is something about being an invested, intentional parent that makes everything feel meaningful and important. We know we are doing even the most mundane and banal duties for a reason. It is for our children. And when we see them progress, make good decisions, and grow up to be better than we are, we glimpse what it is all about.

In a surprising piece of research, participants were divided into two groups and invited to complete five maze puzzles. One group completed five mazes that had similar solutions, thus creating a kind of habit for how to get through the mazes, whereas the second group's five maze solutions were entirely random. When invited to complete a subsequent questionnaire about meaning in life, participants in the first group reported significantly higher levels of meaning than those in the second group. Other research shows that people who say they do 'pretty much the same things every day', according to a survey of daily routines, find life more meaningful, even after the researchers control for mindfulness, positivity and religiousness.

> The coherence of a routine and well-ordered life provides a foundation for the pursuit of larger goals, which promotes greater meaning in life, and happiness.

In other words, there appears to be something meaningful about routine. Life makes more sense. We are happier with mundane routine than ongoing spontaneity, surprise and chaos. The coherence of a routine and well-ordered life provides a foundation for the pursuit of larger goals, which promotes greater meaning in life, and happiness. This probably seems counterintuitive. If you were asked about the most meaningful experiences of your life, you're more likely to agree that marriage, the birth of a child, graduating, or other significant life events are what makes your life meaningful. This research is suggesting that it is the simple, basic routine of getting up each day and doing the same things – a la Will Ferrell in *Stranger than Fiction* – that actually gives life meaning.

How's the meaning of your life going?

What is your home like on a typical morning? A smoothly running well-oiled machine? Do the adults in the house wake up at the same time each day, and move seamlessly and effortlessly from one activity to another in preparation for the day ahead?

Do the children get out of bed at the right time and automatically commence their routine of getting dressed, eating, packing a bag and getting organised? Or is your family more toward the other end of the spectrum, with harried parents stressing because they've overslept, and children sitting on the floor in a screaming heap because they can't find their shoe, lunch box, hair brush or some other necessity? Is it a well-ordered system that moves each person to the exits on time? Or a chaotic shemozzle of barked commands from stressed-out adults who don't quite have their own routine worked out, let alone that of their children?

Which sounds more like you? And perhaps, more to the point, which of the two alternatives would you prefer?

Most of us sit somewhere between those two extremes and the situation can change dramatically from one day to the next. Strict routine is not for everyone, and a lack of flexibility can be unhealthy. However, as I work with parents, I find that one of the most powerful ways for families to improve the level of wellbeing they enjoy is to create a routine that can work for everyone in the family. Routine matters, particularly in the mornings and evenings. A good routine reduces the negative impacts of 'arsenic hour' or 'witching hour'. Of course, no matter how good your routine is and regardless of how well you stick to it, children will still have challenges, tantrums and difficult moments. However, on balance, a carefully constructed routine will make families happier. It reduces tension. It improves children's (and parents') behaviour. It even helps us sleep better, and our children do better at school, and with friends.

A good routine make families happier. It reduces tension. It improves children's (and parents') behaviour. It even helps us sleep better, and our children do better at school, and with friends.

Routine reduces cognitive stress

One of the main purposes of creating new routines and habits is that, in time, they become automatic and happen without thinking. This is important because using our brains to work things out creates stress and fatigue for our brain, and it saps our willpower – that important intangible that helps us stick with a commitment when the emotion of making the commitment has passed. If you can keep the white bears away ...

Whatever you do, don't think of white bears

The white bear phenomenon[70] describes how thinking about things – or trying not to think about things – actually depletes our cognitive resources and reduces our ability to keep focused on the things that matter. In a series of studies conducted by Harvard psychologist Daniel Wegner, participants were randomly assigned to one of two groups. Each group was given a five-minute task to complete. Wegner asked participants in both groups to verbalise their stream of consciousness for five minutes – meaning they were to talk into a recording device about everything that popped into their minds. One group was told they could think about (and speak of) whatever they wanted – including white bears. The other group was told they could think about (and speak of) whatever they wanted – except for white bears. He then instructed this second group that should a white bear come to mind, they should ring a bell on the table.

Wegner found that in spite of the clear and direct instruction to avoid thinking about white bears, those participants who were told to avoid the thought of a white bear still had one pop into their consciousness five to six times on average during that five-minute timeframe. This was not markedly different to those who were allowed to think of white bears.

The study becomes interesting during the next phase, when

participants were then asked to carry out the exercise again, talking to the recorder for five minutes about all of their thoughts. Nothing changed for the group that had been allowed to think about white bears, but this time Wegner told the second group it was now perfectly fine to think of white bears. When the exercise was repeated, these participants thought of those white bears significantly more than those who had been allowed to think of whatever they wanted. The psychological term for the phenomenon these participants experienced was 'post-suppressional rebound'. It reflected how the mental effort required to suppress the thoughts of white bears weakened the capacity of the brain to the point that when it no longer had to follow those rules, the white bears went wild!

Releasing my own white bears

After I learned about this study, I tried it out in a workshop. I wrote out the instructions and rather than talking, the participants simply sat quietly and thought. Some were told to think of white bears and note it down when they thought of one. Others were told not to think of white bears, and to note it down when they thought of one. We did the exercise a second time, allowing all participants to think of white bears, then calculated the results. Sure enough, those who weren't to think of white bears during the first phase did so anyway – at a significantly higher rate than the group for whom it was allowed. And in the second run through, they thought of them many more times than those who were allowed to think about them the whole time.

To make it even more interesting, I had placed bowls of lollies on the participants' tables. We calculated the results and discussed what the results meant, and then I asked the participants to count the number of lollies that were left in their bowls. They didn't know it, but I had carefully counted them before I handed them out and the results were amazing. Participants who had been suppressing their thoughts ate almost all of the lollies they'd been given. Participants on the other side of the room had barely touched theirs.

When participants were placing their brain under strain (by not thinking about something), their cognitive resources became depleted. Their willpower waned. They seemed less able to resist something that was tempting to them, and so they ate most of their lollies. The group that had not been under any strain at all seemed to have greater capacity to resist the sweets. There was less internal pressure, and they made better choices.

Parenting with brain strain

Anything that requires our brain to work hard seems to deplete it of capacity to withstand subsequent stress. As parents, the more we have on our mind, the less capable we are of exercising willpower. This means that if we are making our brains work hard, we are decreasing our cognitive bandwidth for other tasks – which may make us less patient, more likely to raise our voices and at greater risk of parenting in ways that do not fit with our ideal. The more we have going on, the less capacity we have to be mindful, the faster we forget our goal of what type of family we are striving to have, and the quicker we become reactive, with the potential that we may struggle to get our relationships right.

In a parenting context we may not be suppressing thoughts, but we are experiencing multiple demands, which can tire our cognitive and emotional resources and affect our ability to parent in harmony with our values and vision. That's where routine can help.

> Experiencing multiple demands can tire our cognitive and emotional resources, and affect our ability to parent in harmony with our values and vision. That's where routine can help.

The pros of having a good routine

Without a routine our brains have to constantly work hard to think through what is supposed to happen next and what we need to do later. This means that we will likely have less bandwidth to deal with unexpected challenges that come our way, like a child who refuses to get out of bed, squabbling siblings, an upturned bowl of cereal or a missing sock. It also means we can more easily forget things and mess up our morning or evening. Routines reduce the cognitive stress and fatigue we might otherwise experience by creating habits that are implemented automatically, freeing up our cognitive reserves for more important things.

Routines promote security and stability

Importantly, children thrive when they feel safe and secure, and when life is predictable. If our children know what is coming and when, they feel comfortable. This means they can explore, be curious and always come back to 'routine' if they feel uncomfortable. If life is unpredictable, feelings of security and safety are generally lower, and children will generally have higher levels of the stress hormones cortisol and adrenaline in their systems.

Routines can also be helpful for making family life happier because of another aspect of predictability – our children can look forward in anticipation to story time, play time, park time, or whatever it is that falls naturally in their routine, when it is well established and predictable.

Routines help improve social-emotional health

Our children's relationships with others are happier and they are more emotionally healthy in those relationships when we have positive family routines. Data gathered in the 2014 Early Childhood Longitudinal Study[71] came from examining the family routines that 8500 preschoolers engaged in with their families. The routines the researchers considered were eating dinner as a family five times per week, and singing, storytelling, reading and playing at least a few times a week. They found that in families where none of these routines were practised, just one in 10 children experienced high social-emotional health and were judged emotionally and socially competent and ready to attend school the next year. Comparatively, when families did all five of those routines, one in four children had high social-emotional health.

> Children's relationships with others are happier and our children are more emotionally healthy in those relationships when we have positive family routines.

The numbers are not huge, and there are certainly other things that can impact on our children's social-emotional health, but this is still a significant difference between the two groups. Children with routines were more than twice as likely to thrive socially and emotionally when compared with children without a routine. It is also important that for each additional routine the children participated in, the social-emotional health of the children increased – oddly, with the exception of reading. (But reading has sufficient benefits to suggest we should keep doing it anyway!)

Routines improve sleep, schooling and learning

Data suggest that, on average, school-aged children tend to have inconsistent sleep routines, going to bed at a different time every night. Some nights, dinner may be late, other nights there might be extra-curricular activities that end well into the evening. And other nights they may not be tired enough to go to bed. Just as limited hours of sleep are associated with behavioural and learning difficulties, so too is 'bedtime latency', or inconsistent bedtimes.

The greater the degree of variability in the evening bedtime sleep routine, the stronger the chance of significant behavioural challenges in children. Research indicates that when our children have a good sleep routine they sleep better, learn better and regulate their behaviour more effectively.[72]

Routine doesn't mean total rigidity

Some people criticise routines due to the need for a level of rigidity that they are uncomfortable with, and while I agree that being too rigid is most likely to be unhelpful and create stress, a good routine can be invaluable. A routine should be a framework that supports us, rather than dictating our every move to the minute. In fact, an added bonus of routines is that they give you the power to be flexible if needed, because you can always come back to the structure of the routine at a later time.

Take-home message

Routines create predictability, and establish times for specific key activities to anchor our mornings and evenings. An effective, positive routine can help to provide a useful framework to guide us through the busiest times without overloading us with decision-making fatigue, stress and demands. Instead, our routines can make a range of things automatic, leaving us and our family empowered with the capacity to focus on the things that really matter. They lay the groundwork for us to have the flexibility to move towards the big-picture goals and vision for our family's happiness.

Happy family focus:
Do a routine overhaul

Chat with your family about your current routine (or lack of it). Take a close look at what is working, and what else needs to be done to make things work better. You might draw up a schedule, create some artwork to design your routine creatively on paper or cardboard, or develop another strategy for illustrating your routine and encouraging your children's buy-in. The new routine will take some time to bed down, but it *should* make family life easier, smoother and happier.

CHAPTER 10

How parents become their children's enemy

The natural parent is an enemy to children.

Dr H. Wallace Goddard

Having an afternoon nap with two young children unsupervised in the house is never a good idea. But it happened, quite by accident, to Anne. She had lain down beside her 18-month-old son, Aaron, to help him get to sleep. Fatigue led to her drifting off, while Aaron climbed off the bed and went to the lounge room where his four-year-old brother, Daniel, was watching a movie.

Anne awoke a little over an hour later startled by the fact she had drifted off. Realising what had happened, she walked downstairs to make sure both the boys were okay. Entering the lounge room, Anne's impulse was to let out an angry growl at what she saw, but she hesitated. Daniel was throwing washing around the lounge room as Aaron laughed; four loads of freshly washed, folded and ironed washing that Anne had intended to put away once Aaron was asleep. Each time Daniel threw another piece of clothing into the air, Aaron would squeal with delight. He loved this game.

Anne's initial reaction was to let Daniel have it, but by pausing and taking the time to consider how screaming at him might impact the entire family, she drew on her patience and – somehow – changed tack.

Calmly she asked Daniel, 'Son, what are you doing?'

He noticed her for the first time, and smiled. 'Hi Mum. You were sleeping upstairs, and Aaron was getting cranky and crying, and he was going to wake you up, but this made him happy.'

Anne's immediate response when she saw the undoing of all her hard work had been anger – Daniel had to be punished, no questions asked. But had Anne followed that entirely understandable and natural response, she would have hurt her little boy for doing what he thought was helpful and kind. He would have been confused. His mum would have seemed like a dragon – an enemy – and he would have felt like a victim.

What are our typical reactions when we see our toddler refusing to share with friends or siblings? What is our standard response when our teenage son ignores repeated requests to get off his devices and make a contribution to the household? Our typical responses make us enemies of our children.

Curbing the classic response

What are our typical reactions when we see our toddler refusing to share with friends or siblings? What is our standard response when our teenage son ignores repeated requests to get off his devices and make a contribution to the household? Can you recall how you last responded to a child who couldn't find her shoe when it was time to leave the house, or who spilt milk, sugar or cereal over the table and floor at breakfast time, or who refused to go to sleep even though she had been asked several times, or ... you get my point I'm sure.

The following example illustrates how frustrating our children can be when we are already under pressure, and how our typical responses can lead to unhappiness in our home. The mum in question was 'over it' after an exchange between her seven-year-old son and his four-year-old sister. The little girl had bounded into the house after preschool and began excitedly telling her father about her day: 'Dad, Dad, guess what? At preschool today a fireman came to visit and he showed us his truck and his hat and ...'

The story was interrupted by her brother, who said, 'No he didn't.'

The little girl immediately responded with, 'Yes he did.' Then the back and forth began, 'Na-aah.' 'Ye-eah.' 'Na-aah.' And so on.

As the argument became even more heated the mother flipped out, told her son to butt out with an angry, 'What would you know?' and sent him to his room.

Talking with the mother about the incident later, she asked me, 'Why would he do that? He wasn't there. He didn't see anything. He wouldn't know whether or not she saw the fire truck. Where does this opposition come from? Why does he antagonise her like that?'

For many parents, our typical immediate reactions include giving warnings of consequences, threatening removal of privileges, yelling, using time-out, bribing or even hitting. At the very least, we become short and curt with our children, often ironically demanding respect in a manner that fails to display respect for them in any form.

Our demeanour changes so quickly in this kind of situation, from calm and reasonable to frustrated and critical in no time – made worse by existing fatigue and emotional stress. And we are especially quick to switch into punish mode when our children are showing anger or frustration, or what we judge to be rudeness or disrespect.

We often stop seeing our children as people, and begin to see them as a problem.

See your children as people, not problems

Take a look at those typical responses to challenging situations. Whether we make demands, threaten, take a toy from squabbling children, yell, punish in some other way, or bribe, there is a common denominator underlying each response. We see our children's behaviour as problematic and we use our power to stop the problem as quickly as possible. In so doing, we often stop seeing our children as people, and begin to see them as a problem – just as I had viewed my toddler during my initial epiphany many years ago.

When we respond to our children in this way, we objectify them. We see them as *things* that we stumble over or as *problems* that disrupt our otherwise well-ordered life. And so we react to them by using our power and *doing things to them*, riding roughshod over their feelings, turning against them in anger and disapproval, or turning away from them with dismissive annoyance. In short, we make ourselves into their enemies – people who they see as not caring and who are unwilling to listen or help.

Our typical response to challenging behaviour from our children involves approaching them entirely from our perspective, without pausing to consider what is driving their behaviour or how they are feeling. We then label a child's behaviour as problematic (and in many cases, we label the child too), and use our power to 'discipline' (read 'punish') them.

You might also notice this typical approach of using our power to coerce our children does not require any real thought, only reaction. Our spontaneous response is automatic, unthinking, habitual and all too easy. And it goes precisely against the explicit purposes of this book.

Rather than being intentional and mindful about our responses, developing the relationship with our child and getting it right, creating new positive patterns of behaviour and practising them until they become our new habit, we simply react. This reaction requires no skill, perspective or compassion; it is simply a case of wielding power.

Dr Sean Brotherson, a family science specialist at North Dakota State University, calls this kind of reliance on being big and threatening, 'puffer-fish parenting',[73] because when a puffer fish feels threatened or afraid, it blows itself up to be as big as possible, attempting to eliminate the threat or challenge.

Effects of puffer-fish parenting

It is this type of automatic puffer-fish reaction that makes us our children's enemy, for fairly obvious reasons. If someone reacted to you like that consistently, you might well decide the relationship was unhealthy and leave it. At the very least, you would be defensive and try to make changes. But our children don't have that option and they're stuck with us – their enemies.

Living like that can make it tough to have a happy family. So let's look at why these responses don't work, and begin to explore what we can do to change the situation.

Bullying is not effective parenting

These natural reactions are bad for relationships. Yelling, threatening, removing privileges, forcing isolation and hitting all have the potential to create resentment, fear, sadness and anger. They can even promote helplessness, or a sense in a child that she or he can't do anything right so why even bother trying. Receiving this kind of response promotes a sense of unworthiness in a child and reduces their resilience.

Responding to our children in angry and disapproving ways, or by ignoring them or being dismissive, also teaches our children that when they want something, wielding their power is the way to get it. After all, that's what we are doing. Some research suggests that children who are bullied at home (and that's what much of this highly reactive, coercive puffer-fish parenting is), are much more likely to bully other children.[74]

> It eventually stops working. Our threats or physicality lose their impact. Our children stop being afraid or, alternatively, their unwanted behaviours are driven underground.

One of the paradoxical outcomes of this typically reactive approach is that it eventually stops working. Our threats or physicality lose their impact. Our children stop being afraid or, alternatively, their unwanted behaviours are driven underground. We may feel that we have stamped out this kind of behaviour, but all we have really done is made our children increasingly subversive and clandestine.

Perhaps most concerning of all is that if we go for these automatic, low-skill, low-thought, low-perspective approaches, our children may not learn *why* their behaviours are not okay. Sure, being dominating can get a result. If that's all we want, the 'natural' ways of responding will get the outcome. There are costs to the relationship and to our children's self-esteem, but the outcome will be achieved. Compliance.

The bigger issue is the why behind our requests. Children who are coerced are unlikely to learn why it matters that they are kind, or that they share, or that they go to bed at a reasonable time. What do we want our children's reasons to be for complying with us? Do we want them to comply out of fear? Or out of an understanding of how their behaviour affects other people? Do we want them to always need to have an external supervisor to monitor and control their behaviour for them using rewards and punishments, threats and bribes? Or do we prefer that they develop a personal, deeper understanding of why something matters so that they can regulate their behaviour without us constantly acting as a punitive overlord?

Do what doesn't come naturally

I was once asked by a frustrated parent during a radio program what I thought was the best way to deal with a screaming pre-schooler who was refusing to sit with his seatbelt on in the car. I asked what this person's typical response to this difficult behaviour was and predictably he told me that he made demands, counted to three, yelled and finally escalated the situation to physical punishment. I suggested that he do precisely the opposite of what seemed natural – I let him know I wasn't sure this was the 'best' thing, but I felt the most unnatural thing he could do in the circumstances was to let go of his agenda and pull over and stop the car. He might then walk to his child's door, open it, and let his child out of the seat (carefully … we're on the roadside here!), before hugging his little boy and letting him know he understood how upset he was. By focusing on getting the relationship right, his son might be more open to receiving correction and direction. It is always best to give a statement of understanding before a statement of instruction.

Getting to the bottom of the problem

When our third daughter, Ella, was eight-years-old, we encountered a serious school refusal challenge one morning. My attempts at calmly helping her were futile. I was in a rush to catch a flight (ironically I had to go and help make other people's families happy!), so I handed things over to Kylie and left for the airport. Kylie patiently sat with Ella and tried to understand by carefully empathising with her and seeking to understand her: 'You don't want to go to school? Want to talk about it?'

It took a while, but Ella finally revealed she didn't want to go to school because she needed a new school bag. Sure enough, there was something that had once been an item of food in the bag that smelt really, really bad. Kylie couldn't identify exactly what it once had been, but removed it, cleaned and deodorised the bag, and finally got Ella ready for school. But Ella still wouldn't move. So Kylie remained patient and waited, asked more questions, showed she understood, and did all she could to help Ella feel safe enough to talk more.

Over the next 10 minutes, Kylie discovered the smelly food in Ella's bag had nothing to do with her not wanting to go to school until she had a new bag. Instead it came down to this: Ella told Kylie she felt unliked, unwanted and unpopular at school. She didn't want to go to school unless she had a new school bag. Ella felt as though having a new bag might increase the other students' interest in her and make her a bit more popular.

To be clear, Ella was not being bullied. She was just feeling like she had no friends. She felt a new bag could bring her some attention and interest, because all the kids would see her new, really cool bag and want to talk to her. In her eight year-old mind, this was the solution to her popularity worries. Our little girl didn't need a new bag. She needed some love, friendship and compassion.

Ella did not get a new bag, but because she felt genuinely understood, she no longer felt a need for one.

Controlling the pendulum

As you reflect on Ella's story, think about what your natural reactions might have been if your child was refusing to get ready for school and wouldn't tell you why, and then started demanding a new bag. If you are anything like many parents I deal with daily, you may have started out calm, but as Ella resisted your attempts to encourage her to get ready for school, that calmness might be like the pendulum in the grandfather clock I alluded to in Chapter 2 – calm, calm, calm, calm … kaboom! Many parents expect compliance from their children, and when it's not forthcoming, they will resort to anger, frustration, threats, yelling and demands.

If we believe that children are supposed to comply with our every request, and that it's our job to make them obedient, we will typically react to their noncompliance by doing things to make them so uncomfortable they see no other option but to acquiesce. The trouble is, we'll end up being seen by them as angry, manipulative, coercive and lacking in compassion, empathy and understanding. They will lose trust in us and believe we are acting only in our own best interest – not theirs. And we will make ourselves into our children's enemies.

Explore the reasons behind the behaviours

An emphasis on compliance and consequences means we essentially *ignore* the reasons for our children's behaviours. Often those reasons are deep, painful and important, but while we threaten and bribe we will remain oblivious to them. On the other hand, an emphasis on developing character in our children through problem-solving and collaboration leads to an autonomy-supportive parenting approach.

If we believe that our children's sometimes less-than-civil behaviour, back-chatting, attitude and temper is something for us to *work with* and *understand*, our approach will allow us to work together to find solutions. The problem behaviours may not even require consequences once *we understand why* they are happening. Ella didn't need reprimanding, but understanding. Aim to be open to seeing your children's perspective, and about explaining yours. Work together to solve problems with a minimal emphasis on control, punishment and reward.

The problem behaviours may not even require consequences once we understand why they are happening.

Creating a solution versus becoming the enemy

I shared the story about Ella on social media shortly after it occurred. One parent responded, 'If that was my daughter I would have smacked her bum, told her to stop being silly, and sent her off to school.' Such a response is all too typical, and had we done that, we would have instantly become an enemy in her eyes. She would have gone to school feeling that she had no friends in the playground or classroom, and no friends at home, either. But the remarkable thing about the situation is that once Kylie understood clearly why Ella did not want to go to school, it became immediately clear that consequences were never going to be an appropriate solution to the problem. (They rarely, if ever, are.) The conversation led to discussions with her teachers and, ultimately, a new school with a new peer group and good friends. Our daughter became happier because of a mum who listened and understood – and didn't turn herself into her daughter's enemy.

Take-home message

Our typical reactions to our children's challenging behaviours make us their enemies, because those reactions are generally based on a foundation of judgement and a view of the world from our perspective only. When we see our children as *things* that we need to *do things to*, we act with frustration, impatience, anger and disrespect – all of which undermine our relationships and turn our children against us. Avoid power, control, manipulation, and coercion. Punishments and rewards ignore the root of the problem and focus only on short-term results. Instead, seek collaboration, perspective, understanding, and problem-solving. Rather than being your child's enemy, you will become his or her support and advocate. It will change your relationship for the better.

Happy family focus:
Plan ahead for a positive relationship

The secret to avoid becoming our children's enemies is simple to say, but difficult to implement:

- Plan ahead of time how you want to react to your children's more difficult moments.
- When the time comes, down tools and focus.
- Respond to them as people who need our assistance and encouragement. When you have a 'how can I help you get what you want in a way I can feel good about?' approach, you're on your way.
- Be open to suggestions as you problem-solve together.
- Take the time to understand them and work with them to achieve a positive, happy outcome.
- Offer choice wherever possible, but make sure the choice is within limits you're satisfied with. 'You can wear these pj's or those ones. Which do you prefer?' 'I can pick you up at 9.30pm or your dad can pick you up at 9.30pm. Who would you rather?' Or 'I'm happy for you to spend as much time with your friends on Saturday as you want. Who do you want to spend time with?'
- Minimise the use of control.

CHAPTER 11

Getting discipline right

'If a child doesn't know how to read, we teach.
If a child doesn't know how to swim, we teach.
If a child doesn't know how to multiply, we teach.
If a child doesn't know how to drive, we teach.
If a child doesn't know how to behave, we...
Why can't we finish the last sentence as
automatically as we do the others?'

Tom Herner

When it comes to raising children, discipline is *the* hot button issue. Every time I run a seminar or workshop, parents inundate me with questions along the lines of:

How do I get my children to _____?

What do I do with my children when they _____?

I've tried _____ with my son and it doesn't work. What am I supposed to do?

How can I discipline my daughter?

Overdosing on vitamin 'N' isn't the answer

Some experts advocate dishing up more vitamin 'N' – vitamin 'No'. They argue that if parents would grow a spine and be parents, rather than friends, to their children, then those children would not be so challenging. It is absolutely correct that children need to be told 'No' from time to time for their own safety and wellbeing.

Limits show we care. But when 'No' is required, the way we say it matters as much as the fact that we say it at all. When we place compliance with our (often arbitrary) rules ahead of understanding and perspective, we run the risk of rupturing our relationships.

Consider how regularly you say 'No' to your children compared to how often you say 'Yes'. Studies indicate that young children are prevented from doing something they want to do *every few minutes*. While this is understandable for safety reasons, the most common reasons we say 'No' relate to what is convenient for us as parents rather than our children's protection.

Researchers have found that a pervasive 'No' culture leaves children feeling they are neither cared for nor understood. Such a 'No' is painful, dismissive and often signals disapproval. When repeated too often, 'No' undermines self-worth, disempowers children, and promotes a sense of despair and helplessness. 'No' may be needed from time to time, but when it is pervasive, it undermines trust in our relationships, meaning we have less influence with our children. It can be hard to get your relationship right with a pervasive 'No' approach.

> Young children are prevented from doing something they want to do *every few minutes*. While this is understandable for safety reasons, the most common reasons we say 'No' relate to what is convenient for us as parents rather than our children's protection.

Besides, vitamins should promote good health. 'No' often fails this test – at least psychologically.

There's another vitamin 'N' that's good for our children, however, and that's 'Nurture'. It is nurture, rather than 'No' that leads to resilient, happy children who make a contribution to our communities. It is nurture that helps us get relationships right, and leads to much more effective discipline.

There's another vitamin 'N' that's good for our children, however, and that's 'Nurture'. It is nurture, rather than 'No' that leads to resilient, happy children who make a contribution to our communities.

The question of discipline

There may be no question I hear from parents more than, 'How can I discipline my child?' The answer to this question depends on what we mean by discipline. The Merriam-Webster dictionary[75] contains an interesting insight into what is meant by *discipline*. The first definition is a single word: punishment.

If all we are interested in is punishing our children, we need look no further than those typical, punitive reactions described in the previous chapter. And we hardly need parenting experts to guide us in the various ways we might discipline in that manner.

The second definition that Merriam Webster provides is the one that intrigues me. It reads, '*OBSOLETE:* instruction.'

It appears that the meaning of discipline has shifted over time. Until recently, discipline has always meant teaching, instructing and offering guidance. This is the definition that I prefer, and the one that is most consistent with the origins of the word. Merriam-Webster describes the roots of discipline as being Latin – *disciplina* – which means 'teaching', and the root of that word – *discipulus* – meaning pupil. I find it interesting that the Latin for discipline also means pupil. In other words, when we discipline our children, we guide, teach and instruct them to be our pupils, students or followers. Our aim is not to punish. It is to teach them good ways to act.

With that definition in mind, we might ask how effectively we teach our children good ways to act when we use our power to punish. What does it do to our relationship? And when our power is gone and there is therefore no deterrent (because our children are not afraid, or because we are not present) how will our children think and behave?

Disobedience, deception and the device dilemma

During a school break our family took a beach holiday. Before we headed off on the long drive to get there, we agreed that family time would be our priority and so we should leave all devices behind. That meant no phones, tablets, laptops, electronic games – and not even TV or DVDs when we were there.

We found the eight-hour drive challenging. Five children in the car for that length of time can be tough. But we reached our destination without too much fuss, and immediately started to settle in.

The following morning everyone bounded out of bed at sun-up, ready to swim at the beach. Everyone, that is, except one of the children. The rest of us waited patiently ... and ate ... and played ... and waited some more. By 8am I was convinced something was going wrong. At 8.30 there was still no sign of her. At 9am I was struggling to stay calm. This was selfish! This was a family holiday, not a sleep-fest.

> When we discipline our children, we guide, teach, and instruct them to be our pupils, students, or followers. Our aim is not to punish. It is to teach them good ways to act.

One of the other children said something she probably wasn't meant to, but let enough slip that I started wondering whether perhaps my sleepy-head daughter had broken the no-phones agreement.

I woke her up and asked in my best non-accusatory voice whether the phone had come on holidays with her. Denials flowed fast. I was accused of being rude for interrupting much-needed sleep. Further questions were met with frustration and more denials.

I checked suitcases, drawers and shelves but I couldn't find a phone. Still feeling that something wasn't quite right, I told my daughter that I expected honesty and I felt like I was being duped. My manner was still calm, but I could sense I was not far from tipping into 'Captain Cranky Pants' territory. Strident denials followed so I checked under the pillow and began searching the beds. Before I got beyond the first doona my daughter produced her contraband phone from under her mattress.

My first, natural reaction? Anger. I was supremely angry. I wanted to smash that phone against the wall and I felt entirely justified. I had been disobeyed. I had been lied to over and over again. I was beyond furious.

As a parenting expert, of course I knew couldn't smash the phone. That would not help me make my relationship right with my daughter. I would become her enemy. (It would also make for a terrible story if it ever got out!)

My next reaction was that I should share out loud every thought that was racing through my mind – nasty names for my daughter, my feelings about liars and the very good reasons I had for wanting to lock her in the hotel room for the rest of the holiday. But again I recalled that our typical reactions to our children's challenging behaviours make us their enemies, and I bit my tongue.

I looked angrily at my daughter and then issued a clear time-out – for myself. I stormed out of the room and told Kylie something along the lines of, 'I'm going for a long drive. I'll be back when I've calmed down.'

I began to drive north, deciding to use my time-out as productively as I could by filling up the car with petrol. When I got to the petrol station I found myself responding angrily to the attendant because there was no diesel, and I realised I was still irrationally upset. So I decided to keep driving. The next petrol station was nearly 100 kilometres away. I drove for an hour and filled the car. On the way back to the hotel I realised I had not worked out a clear solution because I was still so mad. Every solution that popped into my head was punitive. So I stalled. I called in for groceries at the supermarket and finally returned to our hotel nearly four hours after I had left. I sat in the car and contemplated, still seething.

> How effectively do we teach our children good ways to act when we use our power to punish? What does it do to our relationship? And when our power is gone and there is therefore no deterrent how will our children think and behave?

My central thought through all of this was, 'How can I use this challenge as a teaching experience?' How can I discipline my daughter by teaching her good ways to act?

All I wanted to do was hurt her. The list of potential punishments was growing exponentially, but I was not getting closer to a satisfactory solution that would teach her. It was all about causing pain, not learning.

I was dealing with two issues, both significant: disobedience and deception. Recognising that I couldn't stay in the car all day (or the ice-cream I had just purchased with the groceries would melt) I took a deep breath and walked into the hotel room.

'We're going to the beach for a swim,' I called out. 'Race you to the water!' The whole family was changed and running for the sand in moments, and we dived into the waves. After we had body-surfed for 15 minutes, having a terrific time, I called out to my daughter. She swam to me and I asked her a question: 'How did what happened this morning affect how much I can trust you?'

As she answered we began a conversation that lasted the duration of our swim. I asked questions about trust and about why we had the rules that we had.

Our discussion continued beyond the swim. But the point was this – it was a discussion. It occurred when we were both calm enough to talk without the conversation becoming emotionally overwhelmed, and without injuring one another, emotionally or otherwise. The purpose of the conversation was not to punish. Instead, it was to teach. And the conversation was principally built around me asking questions to encourage my daughter to think, internalise and improve.

A second purpose of the conversation was to understand. I had arbitrarily set a rule about devices. She had protested but I did not consider her protests or perspective. I made a unilateral decision that ignored her valid reasons for wanting to be able to use her phone to stay in touch with friends, take photos, and so on.

There were some bigger issues around technology use that were unresolved, so my daughter handed her phone over and we agreed that while some of her reasons for keeping the phone were valid, she would have it back when she could identify the reasons for our rules, and demonstrate that she clearly understood them. Our subsequent conversations centred on what appropriate guidelines are for technology use in our home and, most importantly, *why we have those guidelines*. A short time later, her phone was returned.

As an aside – and in the interests of full disclosure – while I was writing this book I asked my daughter to read that story to confirm its accuracy. She agreed with all of it, except for one point (which I might still dispute). Her version suggests I may have raised my voice and called her a liar. Okay, so I'm not perfect. But we both agree on the rest of the story.

I asked her to describe how she felt about my approach, and her response was informative: 'Dad, if you'd done what you wanted to do, I would never have talked to you again. And there's no way that you could really ever stop me doing what I wanted to. I'd just have gotten sneakier so I didn't get caught.'

I did not like what I heard, but it was an honest and clear message: punishments drive wedges into relationships and push our children further from us, usually at the time that they need our wisdom, presence and love the most. Punishment also promotes more sneaky, underground behaviour and self-centred behaviours.

Our relationships with our children are primary

A central element to effective discipline – that is, effective teaching and instruction – is that it cannot happen when emotions are high. It also cannot happen if the foundation of trust, emotional availability, and a willingness to be truly in the moment and mindful with our children is absent. We *have* to get our relationship right before we can discipline – or teach.

Even though my relationship with my daughter is mostly right most of the time, in that moment it was not right. My immediate reactions were making the relationship wrong, and making me my daughter's enemy. I had to get myself back to a place where I could put our relationship right, and then focus on discipline, correction and instruction. The proportions have to be in order or the relationship falls apart.

You also may have noticed that it is far easier to be autonomy-supportive when we stop ourselves from responding in our typical, reactive ways, and instead emphasise that the relationship we share with our children comes first. We can then use that as a platform on which to build our teaching.

When we get our relationships right, and respond to our children in ways that teach, we find that traditional 'discipline' (in other words, punishment) is required far less.

A central element to effective discipline – that is, effective teaching and instruction – is that it cannot happen when emotions are high.

How to discipline in ways that teach

I recommend five central strategies to work with our children in constructive, positive ways as we discipline them, although there are probably countless gentle, compassionate and effective alternatives.

Modelling

One of psychology's classic experiments[76] was conducted at Stanford University by Albert Bandura. It spawned one of the most influential theories in social psychology – social learning theory[77] – which has had enormous impact on discipline for parents and children.

The experiment involved a Bobo doll – an inflatable plastic toy, usually about 150 centimetres high, with a weighted bottom. When you hit or push against the top of the doll, it sways over, but always lifts itself back to an upright position.

Bandura conducted several studies in which children watched adults who either behaved in aggressive ways towards the doll or who ignored the doll entirely. Once children had observed the adult either hitting or ignoring the doll, the children were left alone to play with it and their behaviour was observed. Those children who watched the adult behave aggressively were significantly more likely to be aggressive towards the doll than those who saw the passive adult. In other words, children consistently followed the examples they saw.

> When we get our relationships right, and respond to our children in ways that teach, we find that traditional 'discipline' is required far less.

While there is some criticism of the study[78] (specifically that Bobo dolls are designed to be hit), the concept of social learning theory has been resoundingly supported through the decades in a vast array of alternative studies and contexts. Children see what we do, and they copy it in spite of everything we say to convince them to do otherwise.

If we wish to discipline our children effectively, we must practise what we preach. We cannot lift our children to greater heights if we are not standing on higher ground ourselves. The model we set for our children will be the most powerful form of discipline they experience.

> If we wish to discipline our children effectively, we must practise what we preach. We cannot lift our children to greater heights if we are not standing on higher ground ourselves.

Understanding development

I speak to many parents who are concerned that their two-year-old isn't sharing, or that their three-year-old is defiant, or that their six-year-old still struggles with big emotions, has outbursts, or cries a lot. It is natural to be frustrated by this, but what we often fail to appreciate is that it is normal for our children to be unable to manage these challenges at these ages. Thinking our children need to be punished for these behaviours is akin to being mad at our 12-year-old for not knowing how to drive, or getting frustrated that our 15-year-old can't complete an income tax return for the family. Our children need to develop, and certain abilities take longer to develop than others.

Just as newborns can't walk (and we're okay with that), toddlers and preschoolers struggle with sharing and taking perspective. Young children who have just started school are still learning to regulate their emotions, particularly when they are hungry, angry, lonely, tired, stressed or sick. Teens are learning to balance relationships and other life priorities. And even our spouses and partners experience challenge and difficulty as they develop throughout their adult life.

When we approach our children's challenging behaviour with an understanding of their development, we tend to discipline in more patient, compassionate ways. Understanding development is helpful for good discipline because it keeps us focused more on teaching, guiding and instructing, and less on punishing our children for being inconvenient and getting things wrong.

Simon, a concerned father and a nurse of 12 years, described an experience where his sister-in-law, Ruth, tried to 'discipline' her three-week-old twin baby girls. Ruth had very little experience with babies. She had complained to Simon and his wife that the babies were crying a lot at night. When Simon asked if his sister-in-law was feeding them every time they woke crying, the reply was, 'I'm not feeding them between scheduled feeds because I don't want to reward all that crying.'

Aside from the fact that babies less than six-weeks-old (and perhaps that could be extended to babies less than 6-years-old!) are usually best fed on demand (schedules can and should wait), there is a mismatch in terms of expectations and the babies' development.

Simon asked his sister-in-law what sort of alternatives she thought the babies might come up with to let her know that they were hungry or cold or needed a cuddle. Their discussion led to Ruth's realisation that babies are not able to find alternative solutions to manage their hunger – it's just not developmentally possible.

In fact, I believe the only thing children under the age of two should be taught is that we love them unconditionally. There may be no more important message for them, particularly at this age.

Induction

The most effective form of discipline will often be induction – which means giving specific and explicit instructions to our children about how we want them to behave. This is what happens when adults commence a new job. Most workplaces have a formal induction process. They give us a tour, introduce us to key personnel, and give us video presentations and manuals that outline policies, procedures and processes.

In spite of this training, we typically retain very little of what we were taught at our induction. We show up on Day 2 and have forgotten people's names, if we remembered them at all to begin with. Our eyes glaze over as we read the grievance and harassment policy. We struggle to remember where the bathrooms were. And we usually have to be shown how to complete our electronic pay-sheet at least a few times, in spite of how important it is.

As parents we spend a great deal of time teaching our children what not to do. But our children learn better when we help them to understand what they *should* do. Instead of yelling, 'Would you all stop shouting?!' (which is, ironically, lousy modelling), we can softly ask, 'Would you mind speaking quietly? Our house is a soft-speaking home.'

When inducting children, it may help to keep in mind that because of their relatively limited cognitive development (compared to ours), they often take a much longer time than adults to retain things they are taught. And most children are like us when it comes to reading the manual – we don't do it, and they don't either. The problem we struggle with is that we're the manual, and they often don't listen to us because we're so boring – and we go on and on.

So explain what you require briefly. Then provide a clear rationale (autonomy support). If you do this, you have inducted your child. Then, be prepared to do it again when they get excited, distracted, frustrated or forgetful.

Asking questions

Perhaps the most valuable form of teaching, guiding, instructing or disciplining our children is going through a process of careful questioning. You may have noticed that in my discussions with my eldest daughter about her disobedience and her deception, I led our conversation with questions. I asked things like, 'How did what happened this morning affect how much I can trust you?' I asked her to restate the rules. I asked her if she could please explain *why* those rules exist. I asked her how we might move forward in a positive and constructive way.

When adults talk, we tend to talk too much. Our lectures seem altogether rehearsed, and our children roll their eyes and start thinking about other things. We have a wonderful time expounding all of the rules. However, we really only have an audience of one – our self. The children have zoned out.

It is far more effective to engage them with questions. When they won't answer or if they grow defensive, we can acknowledge their feelings and let them know we can talk later, when they're feeling a little more open.

> When adults talk, we tend to talk too much. Our lectures seem altogether rehearsed, and our children roll their eyes and start thinking about other things.

Asking questions helps our children think through their position. And it helps us understand how much they know and understand, which enables us to fill the gaps in their understanding without giving them long lectures on what they already know. Asking questions engages them far more than our talking. And as they talk, they will do far better at internalising the rules than through listening to our boring lectures.

Gentle reminders

Most of the time our children know the rules, but their impulsiveness, excitement or distractedness gets the better of them and they momentarily forget. When we give our children gentle reminders, we are giving them credit for having a brain. It's also an invitation to use that brain in a way that requires very little of us.

Giving a gentle reminder is a technique that helps our children do the right thing with minimal fuss or effort, and maximum calm. To do it, call your child by their name. When they show you they are listening, say what you would like them to do in as few words as possible. For example:

'*Caseyany, your ironing.*'
'*Josh, the rubbish bins.*'
'*Jasmine, soft words, please.*'
'*Lachie, your dinner plate.*'

Parents regularly tell me that gentle reminders have led to immediate and significant changes in the atmosphere of their homes. Mums and dads stop yelling. Children apologetically jump up and do what they were asked, or find ways to follow their parents' gentle instructions. Gentle reminders teach children what is expected, and they model kind ways of being assertive and clear in order to get things done.

Take-home message

When we misunderstand what discipline is, we are at risk of disciplining poorly. Effective discipline is centred on finding appropriate, respectful and understanding ways to teach our children good ways to act. When we focus on problem-solving, collaborating, understanding perspectives, helping our children internalise values by thinking for themselves, and supporting autonomy and choice, we achieve far better outcomes for children's behaviour, and for family happiness and wellbeing.

Happy family focus:
Practise talking, not punishing

When you are faced with a challenge today, move away from punishment and towards talking.

Consider, am I best off using induction or gentle reminders? Should I ask more questions? Is this developmentally appropriate for my child – and even if it is, is it worth a battle now?

Ask yourself if what you are about to do is going to hurt your child or teach your child. It is rare that hurting them teaches them anything worthwhile. Your family will be happier as you focus on teaching and working *with* them, rather than doing things *to* them.

CHAPTER 12

NO YELLING HERE!

If you're yelling, you're the one who's lost control of the conversation.

Taylor Swift

I don't remember what the yelling was all about – it was many years and many moves ago. I only remember that it was All. The. Time. There was considerable distance – and bushland – between our houses. But the loud screaming still carried from their living room to ours on most days. It was shrill. It was angry. It seemed to me that it was constant. But I can't believe for a moment that it was ever really deserved.

Why do we yell?

Yelling is a habit. Our 'shouty' neighbour had probably developed the habit of yelling because it got her a quick result. While I will never know the reason this mother yelled at her children, she seemed to flare up at the slightest provocation. She was my model 'puffer-fish' parent, using her size and power to intimidate her children for every infraction, or whenever she felt challenged or threatened.

Research tells us that parents dislike yelling. Surveyed parents indicate that they see yelling, along with spanking, as being the least acceptable disciplinary techniques, but those same parents also acknowledge that they yell as much as they use time-out[79] (which is used at a surprisingly high rate – especially for something that is generally ineffective). Despite the fact that we don't like yelling, we do it – and we do it a lot.

The question is 'why'? Why are we so quick to yell at our children at home? We seem capable of controlling our volume (and aggression) in public – it is rare that we see a parent start shouting at his children in public, and it is rarer still to see an adult shout at another adult. If you worked in an office where the boss summonsed you to her office by shouting out your name, you'd probably look for ways to avoid her, even if you weren't in trouble. And if you were shouted at when you were in trouble, you'd probably start looking for a new employer.

Why yelling doesn't work

Based on what I've said in the previous chapters, it is probably obvious that I'd think yelling is a terrible way to make our families happier. Firstly, it is highly authoritarian, which is an ineffective parenting style – it is lacking in warmth, and is all about demands, coercion and power. Secondly, it undermines our attempts at getting our relationships right – when we yell, we aren't demonstrating much mindfulness, emotional availability or gratitude, nor are we giving our children much to look forward to. It is not like we are shouting, 'Hey, children, I've got hugs and tickles for the first one to clean up their room!'

Being shouted at undoes all the good things that make families happy. And, sadly, yelling is an indication that it is us – the grown-ups – who are out of control. In yelling we have made a decision to stop regulating our behaviour maturely, and determined that our anger should rule. As Ralph Waldo Emerson said, 'Anger is never without a reason, but seldom a good one.'

Yelling and shouting are all-too-typical reactive responses to challenging situations, and while we yell and shout, we are ignoring

148

the needs of our children and failing to see them as real people with feelings that can be hurt through harsh words. Yelling does not teach good ways to act, either. In fact, yelling is a poor teaching strategy. When our children are yelled at, they get scared. They only think of escape (or fighting back if they're older and feeling feisty). They do not take in anything we are trying to 'teach' them. Instead they consolidate feelings of resentment and defensiveness.

Ultimately, we push our children away when we yell. And once they are into their teens, they will have perfectly internalised our strategies for dealing with difficult situations, and they will typically be only too happy to reciprocate when we yell at them.

Why won't they listen?

Many parents tell me, it's as if their children are deaf: 'I ask them and ask them and they either ignore me, or it's like they're deaf – they only listen when I yell.'

Of course, most typically developing children are in no way hard of hearing – watch what happens when your children are in earshot and you ask them quietly whether they would like a bowl of ice-cream ... or 20 dollars ... or just whisper the word 'chocolate'. Rest assured, they will hear you. Unless a child has a genuine physical hearing problem, he or she is choosing not to listen – perhaps for very good reasons.

I do not believe that children are being disobedient when they don't listen. So are they being rebellious? Troublemakers? Ratbags? Why are they ignoring us?

Well, perhaps our children choose not to respond to us because we have trained them to wait until we yell before they act – we ask them to do something in a nice, respectful way, but they choose not to act immediately, and notice that nothing happens. So we ask again, nicely, and still don't get a response. Then, finally, we yell. It's the same pattern I described while talking about parenting styles in Chapter 2, when our response moves dramatically from permissive to authoritarian.

There may also be a second reason our children are not responding – because of the way we speak to them. Think about it. When you're in the middle of doing something that matters to you, and someone asks you to stop doing it and pay attention to them, how do you feel? Are you inclined to respond immediately and willingly?

> Of course, most children are in no way hard of hearing – watch what happens when your children are in earshot and you ask them quietly whether they would like a bowl of ice-cream ... or 20 dollars ... or just whisper the word 'chocolate'. Rest assured, they will hear you.

Furthermore, what is the main reason we usually speak to our children? Most children will say when we call their name it means one of two things: I'm in trouble, or I'm going to be asked to do chores. So our children stop responding to us because our communication with them is typically only to correct or direct.

So the issue isn't really about getting our children to listen. They can hear us just fine – they just don't want to hear what we are constantly nagging them about. The issue is more about finding a way to invite our children to comply with basic requests in a timely manner – and keeping the volume down while we do it.

The effects of yelling

You may be surprised at the damage that can be done to your children when you yell. Researchers at the University of Pittsburgh and the University of Michigan in the US conducted a two-year study and found that 'severe verbal discipline' may have a profoundly negative impact on children's wellbeing.[80] They found that tweens and teens whose parents yelled for discipline experienced increased behavioural issues (including being violent or being vandals), and that the impact of being yelled at regularly was as serious as if the children were being hit. Watching a parent get in her child's face and scream at her while nose to nose is severe, especially when it is accompanied by name calling and other insults or threats.

Other research has shown that yelling at least 25 times in a 12-month period can have a negative impact on children's self-esteem, increase the likelihood of depression and promoting aggression in children.

Try tracking your yelling

Not sure you yell at your children *that* much? It's a good idea to track how often you raise your voice at your children, and what the reasons for yelling are. If you were to monitor yourself and record it in a spreadsheet, perhaps it might look like this:

Time of day	Who I yelled at	Why I yelled	Result (what got done, and how everyone felt)	Could I have done something different?
7.15am	Emily	Could not find school shoe	She cried. Still couldn't find shoe. Everyone felt lousy, stressed and helpless.	Gentle reminder, or walk around the house with her to find it.

There is power in creating a spreadsheet like this, regardless of the behaviour you wish to eliminate. Firstly, it helps to identify how often you act in a certain way, as well as the circumstances surrounding that behaviour. But the power comes in the fourth and fifth columns, as you consider the impact of your behaviour and look for alternative strategies to employ in the future. This cognitive rehearsal strengthens the foundations of your new habit and helps to literally re-wire your brain and establish new, more positive behaviour or thinking patterns.

> Tweens and teens whose parents yelled for discipline experienced increased behavioural issues (including being violent or being vandals), and the impact of being yelled at regularly was as serious as if the children were being hit.

Practical anti-yelling strategies

So let's get really practical for a moment. If you rely on yelling, screaming, shouting or 'speaking in an outdoors voice' more than you would like, the following strategies might help.

Go to your children

When you want your children's attention, walk to them. You would do it in an office with other adults or in nearly any context other than at home. This is respectful, mindful and a much better way to get a relationship right than by yelling. Speak to your children softly, calmly and kindly, and your children will be more likely to respond positively because you have shown them respect. They will also respond because they can't pretend not to have heard you – you're standing right in front of them.

> Speak to your children softly, calmly and kindly, and your children will be more likely to respond positively because

you have shown them respect. They will also respond because they can't pretend not to have heard you – you're standing right in front of them.

Look at the world through their eyes

Going to your children and calmly being with them will also allow you to see the world through their eyes. When we leave where we are and go to our children, we get to see precisely what they are doing. We might find that they are in the middle of drawing, playing a game, completing a school assignment or reading. Chances are that our yelling and demands have interrupted something else they really value. By being in their presence, we give ourselves an opportunity to see what matters to them.

I have regularly found that my children are quite happy to help when they've had an opportunity to 'just finish this page' or when I have respected the fact that they are working on some other important activity. It might be unimportant child's play to us, but to them it matters. When we see the world through their eyes and are respectful of what our children are doing, they are more likely to respond kindly to us.

I'll discuss this in far greater detail in the next chapter, but the key point is that if we see things from our children's perspective, we are less likely to yell at them, and more likely to work with them in kind and constructive ways in our quest to 'get things done'.

Timing is important

As a natural extension of being in our children's presence and seeing what they are doing, there may be times our requests might receive better responses if we give the children some advanced notice. If what they are doing matters to them (and you're not late for the airport) you could suggest: 'In the next few minutes I'll ask you to stop what you're doing to help me with a few things.'

Perhaps we might say, 'In 10 minutes' time, dinner will be ready. When I call you, I'd like you to come straight away so we can eat while the food is hot.'

As my children have grown, I have found that asking them when I can expect to have their input and contribution can be helpful. We might put a deadline on our request, such as, 'In the next 15 minutes I'll need your help in the kitchen,' but we give the children the freedom to choose when they will help. When we recognise our children's preferences, and allow them some autonomy in what is to occur in their lives, we are calmer, our children are happier, and there is less yelling.

Get softer

This is probably my favourite non-yelling strategy. From time to time, even when we are with our children and trying to see the world through their eyes, they can be unresponsive. Their eyes won't leave the screen. They don't look up at us. We get frustrated. The typical response is to make ourselves heard by getting bigger, louder and angrier; puffer-fish parenting. However, since we've discovered that our typical responses are usually the most unhelpful ways to respond, doing the opposite is often helpful.

If your children do not respond to your calm, kind and respectful requests for their attention, don't yell. Instead, speak more softly. If they still don't respond, quietly whisper their name and with peace in your heart and voice soft, hold their hand, look into their eyes and gently say, 'I've asked you to do something three times now. Have you got any idea what it was?'

If they respond that they have no idea what you previously said, you can softly repeat it. If you're looking into their eyes at the time, you'll know whether they've understood. And if they do know, then you can invite them to do it – either now, or when they've finished what they're presently doing.

The irony is that when we shout, people switch off because it's offensive and we have just demonstrated that we have lost control of the situation. We are now fighting for power – in the position of underdog. But when we speak softly they strain to take in every word we say.

Your message will get across with focused soft speaking.

> The irony is that when we shout, people switch off because it's offensive and we have just demonstrated that we have lost control of the situation.

Remember that emotions are contagious

A parent I once coached told me, 'I can be totally calm, but if my child is angry or yells at me I just lose it. It's like I've caught her emotions.'

Emotions are contagious. We can and do catch our children's emotions, and they can catch ours.

In the 1980s, scientists discovered something they called 'mirror neurons' in monkeys. They claimed that when a monkey observed another monkey use its hand, the brain of the observing monkey essentially lit up in the same region as the brain of the monkey who was actually performing the action.[81] Some researchers[82] believe that these mirror neurons work the same way with emotion as they do with action. In other words, mirror neurons may be the seeds of empathy – when we see someone experiencing an emotion, we 'catch' it because of our mirror neurons. (Which might explain why I get tear stains on my shirts when I see other people cry in movies.)

While there is some dispute about whether this is true,[83] most researchers acknowledge some kind of reciprocal neurological, behavioural, or emotional response that impacts on our interactions. So in order to stay calm, we may need to fight our mirror neurons. That means we need to mindfully recognise that our child is angry, and that the emotions flying our way are highly contagious. When we know we need to fight those usual reactions that form in our brain (arguably our mirror neurons), we can respond proactively, calmly and respectfully. If we fight this automatic, reciprocal response to these challenges and stay calm, our children may even catch our calmness.

It is a paradox that the more we have to rely on our power, the less power we really have. When we avoid yelling and stay calm and quiet, our children will respond to us in a more positive and appropriate way than if we yell at them, and power in the relationship will be retained, ironically, because we didn't need to use it.

> A parent I once coached told me, 'I can be totally calm, but if my child is angry or yells at me I just lose it. It's like I've caught her emotions.' Emotions are contagious. We can and do catch our children's emotions, and they can catch ours.

Call out to your children for other reasons

Parents spend a good deal of time communicating with children about things we don't like, or things that we don't like about them. We call out because bags have been left at the door, or clothes and shoes are still on the floor. We shout for our children's attention so we can delegate and dictate. Our relationships swing too far towards endless correction and direction. Instead, try engaging in relationship-building and making things go right a little more. In so doing, you may find your children become much more open to being influenced when it's time for correction and direction.

I love yelling out my children's names and then saying, 'I love you!' It means that it's okay to be loud sometimes, and even to yell. But the yelling is for good, rather than for my own convenience or frustration. My dad had a sign on our fridge when I was growing up that said, 'Only speak loudly if the house is on fire.'

The choice is yours

Dr John Gottman, one of the world's most celebrated relationship experts, has suggested that when our interactions start with harshness (such as when we yell at someone), the likelihood of a positive outcome from the interaction is very low. Instead, negative outcomes are likely.[84]

Every day, most of us will have many, many opportunities to decide whether or not to raise our voices or speak harshly. From tired, forgetful or obstinate children first thing in the morning, to busy, stressed and exhausted children in the evening, countless circumstances conspire against our best-laid plans for an efficiently executed routine and a happy family.

Even the other adults in our world exasperate us and leave us struggling to stay calm. Our own emotional baggage and stress adds fuel to the pile of emotional kindling that is ready to spontaneously combust over the slightest provocation. The choice to stay calm – or at least to speak quietly – requires discipline and effort. It is rarely easy. But experience will likely remind you that when you are yelled at, things rarely improve. Likewise, when you yell at others, the outcomes are often sub-optimal. Making the choice to remain softly spoken is the preferable option for a happy family.

Take-home message

Yelling and anger leave us feeling lousy, our children feeling worthless and our relationships damaged. Our children don't learn anything we want them to when we yell. What they learn, instead, is that yelling and puffer-fish impersonations are a sure-fire way of getting what we want in life *and* upsetting everyone at the same time. There are many other ways we can provide effective discipline to our children – with the volume kept down – that we will feel good about and that work.

Happy family focus:
Next time you are inclined to yell …

Go to your child, see the world through their eyes, consider your timing, and speak with a softer voice. And find reasons to speak with them other than to give them correction and direction.

CHAPTER 13

Seeing the world through their eyes

To speak to a child's heart, we must know a child's needs.

Rosemary Wixom[85]

In my work I use the expression 'see the world through your child's eyes' a lot. This is the concept of empathy, and it may be at the very heart of what makes our families happy. Indeed, one of the most influential human relationships experts of the past several decades, Dr Stephen R. Covey, says, 'The greatest human need is to be understood.'[86]

The following story from one of my parenting-coaching clients, describes how showing empathy and understanding, while often the opposite of what we feel like doing, can have a great impact on the relationship outcomes we experience.

She explained to me that she was using different strategies to help her daughter, Cecilia, think of how to handle challenges. This is an exchange between her and Cecilia in the car:

Annette: How was ballet? Did you have fun?

Cecilia: No.

Annette: Oh dear, what happened?

Cecilia: We played musical statues and I got out and I didn't want to be out. [Holding back tears.]

Annette: Did you feel sad because you couldn't keep playing?

Cecilia: Yes.

Annette: I'm sorry you felt sad. What do you do when you're out?

Cecilia: Sit on the floor near my teacher with my legs crossed.

Annette: Do you get to go back in?

Cecilia: Yes, but it takes ages and ages.

Annette: Can you think of anything you could do while you're waiting to make you feel happier – to make it more fun?

Cecilia: No. Can you Mummy?

Annette: Well what if you played pretend in your mind? Could you pretend to be a tree? Or a fairy?

Cecilia [sounding much chirpier]: Or a rabbit! Or a toadstool! Or a liriope! [A plant in our garden]

Annette: That sounds fun to me. Would that make it easier to wait to go back in the game do you think?

Cecilia: Yes.

Annette: Can you think of anything else you could do?

Cecilia: Like what?

Annette: Perhaps you could keep playing the statues game quietly while you're sitting on the floor. Maybe you could just let your fingers dance, or your head …

Cecilia: Or my ankles?

Annette: Sure. Dancing ankles sounds good. Do you think that would be helpful?

Cecelia: I think it would.

Annette: Great. Shall I remind you before your next lesson?

Cecilia: Yes.

Annette also told me that she would always have been sympathetic but, short of talking to her teacher, she'd have found it hard to know how to help Cecilia.

'This feels much more constructive and appropriate,' she said. 'Sometimes I have to get Cecilia started on the ideas like I did in this instance, but other times she comes up with them herself with a bit of questioning.'

About empathy

It can take many shapes, but empathy typically contains a short list of specific factors. Mark Brackett, from The Center for Emotional Intelligence at Yale University, suggests that empathy can be described and taught via the acronym RULER.[87]

Each letter represents a different emotional skill: Recognising an emotion, Understanding it, Labelling it, Expressing it and Regulating that emotion.

You might note that in the example above, this process was generally followed by a mother who was attuned to her daughter's emotional needs. This mum and her little girl both recognised an emotion and understood it. They showed this by labelling the emotion as sadness. Cecilia was allowed to express her emotion. Annette didn't get frustrated or annoyed. Cecilia was not told to get over it or cut it out, which would have been disapproving or turning-against behaviour. Cecilia was not told that it would all be better later, which would have been turning away or dismissal.

Instead, Annette leaned in to the emotion, turned towards it and explored it, and encouraged Cecilia to express it in constructive ways. She saw Cecilia's difficulty and challenge as an opportunity to connect and be intimate with her daughter, and as a chance to gently teach, guide and instruct – in other words, to discipline. Cecilia regulated her emotion, and discovered potential strategies to feel better in future.

Emotion coaching

Dr John Gottman calls this process 'emotion coaching'.[88] In a five-step process, Gottman suggests parents should:

1. Be aware of the child's emotion

2. Recognise the emotion as an opportunity for teaching and intimacy
3. Listen empathically and validate the child's feelings
4. Help the child label the emotions
5. Set limits while helping the child to problem-solve.

> Children who have adults in their lives who are empathic, and who coach them through the challenging emotions they feel, are less anxious, less depressed, less likely to abuse alcohol and other drugs, less likely to bully, and more likely to perform well at school.

Gottman's research, as well as that conducted at Yale and elsewhere, confirms that children who have adults in their lives who are empathic, and who coach them through the challenging emotions they feel, are less anxious, less depressed, less likely to abuse alcohol and other drugs, less likely to bully, and more likely to perform well at school. Their social connections are stronger, and their wellbeing is higher.

The great challenge we have with empathy and seeing the world through our children's eyes is twofold: firstly, it goes against our typical instinctive responses, and secondly, empathy is more about the condition of our heart – or our orientation towards our child – than it is about any technique.

While the research I have described distils different ways of helping our children manage their emotions into formulas, it doesn't work so well when we go through the motions. It can feel inauthentic, stilted, and rehearsed.

To show true empathy requires a strong foundation of love, compassion, respect, and a genuine charitable desire to guide our children through their challenges. The previous chapters have been designed to establish a strong foundation that helps things go right.

I'm scared of ghosts...

In my first book, *What Your Child Needs From You: Creating a Connected Family,* I shared the following story about how to show empathy:

> Some families enjoy watching movies together. One evening a family watched a movie that had some mildly scary themes and some of the characters in the film were ghosts. One of the children in the family was a 10-year-old girl. Watching the movie seemed like fun at the time. Unfortunately when the lights went out at the end of the evening, the little girl was scared.
>
> As her parents put her into bed, Emma resisted. She became clingy. She wanted cuddles, a story, a song, a drink, and so on. Her parents found her behaviour tedious, but they indulged her. Soon, however, it was beyond annoying. Emma's parents were tired. She was stringing her bedtime out, and ruining what had been a pleasant evening. It was long past her normal bedtime. This behaviour was foolish. Their plans for the evening did not include dealing with a scared 10-year-old girl who was refusing to sleep. Besides, they'd had a special family night. If this was how she was going to react from watching a silly movie, that's fine – 'We just won't do these movie nights anymore.'
>
> Emma's parents could have shown that they understood that she was scared, and dealt with it compassionately. But their agenda got in the way of their being understanding. At an intellectual level they understood. They could verbalise that, 'Yes, Emma. We know you're scared.' But recognising it and understanding it are two different things.
>
> As the little girl's fear and crying increased, the minutes turned into quarter-hours. Over an hour later, Emma's

parents had gone from annoyed, to exasperated, and now her dad was simply angry. Each parent had used all of the logic they could think of to help their daughter realise that no ghosts would be in their house. They had reasoned, bribed, threatened, yelled and demanded that she recognise how silly she was being, and calm down and go to sleep. Like most parents, they believed that they had done 'everything'.

At around 10pm Emma's father had finally had enough. It was past her bedtime by two hours. And it was past *his* bedtime too! He pulled his daughter from her bed, hostility evident. He set her on the floor, grabbed her by the hand and part walked her, part dragged her, around the outside perimeter of the house in the pitch dark of the late night. Through the front yard, along the path, down the side fence, out into the backyard, back down the other side of the house and inside the front door. All the while she cried, screaming that the ghosts would get her. He argued back. 'Where are the ghosts?' 'There are NO ghosts!'

Petrified, she was dragged back into her bedroom and told to go to sleep.

There are no ghosts!

As I consider this story, I can't help but wonder whether Emma may have felt that her dad was scarier than anything supernatural.

So what might the outcome of this experience have been for Emma? You can probably guess that she went to bed and didn't disturb her parents anymore that evening. Instead, she spent the time until she fell asleep sobbing into her pillow. But did that settle the problem in her mind? Did she feel any safer because her dad had proved that there were no ghosts around the house? Probably not – on both counts.

Because of the way the situation was handled, in some small way a dent was made in her relationship with her dad. Trust was reduced. Emotional pain was inflicted rather than healed.

If this experience were a one-off, then it probably would not have a significant impact on Emma's feelings of safety and security. But if it became the standard way that her father dealt with her emotional pain, then her relationship with her father would be strained, and her wellbeing would suffer.

Caring not scaring

This story is not meant to demonise Emma's father. He was a loving and devoted dad who had been good-natured and helpful at the beginning of the night: 'I know you're scared of the ghosts sweetheart, but look … there's no such thing as ghosts.' Isn't that what most well-meaning parents would say to their concerned child?

Unfortunately, his intellectual acknowledgement that he 'understood' was not the empathic response Emma needed to feel calm. Rather than feeling turned-towards, Emma felt dismissed, or turned-away-from. And by the night's end, she felt turned-against. Dad was now the enemy.

How differently the night may have been if Emma's dad had calmly responded to her fears with a statement such as, 'Sometimes movies can really frighten us, can't they?' This turning-towards would have meant he could identify, understand and label Emma's emotion. If you can name it, you can tame it. He may have then given her a hug and said, 'You feel worried, don't you. What do you think we can do to help you feel safe?' Emma would likely have suggested that Dad snuggle with her. Any kind-hearted father would agree to that request. They may have hugged for about two minutes and then, given that it was already well past bedtime, Emma would have been asleep.

If you can name it, you can tame it.

In this alternative scenario, Emma's understanding father would have strengthened the relationship with his daughter and left the bedroom feeling like the best dad in the world. No tantrums. No fuss. No tears. Just love, an emotionally intelligent father who could give his daughter's emotions a name, and a little girl who felt cared for and understood.

Don't fix me – understand me!

As parents, we generally see our children's emotions as problems we should fix. They come to us crying, hurt or frustrated – or we interrupt their sibling clashes, or other challenging behaviour – and we present a solution. We use our logic. And we believe that our superior reasoning and knowledge of how to make things better will actually make things better. But in most cases, what this approach does is it disempowers our children. They are left feeling helpless. They never learn to develop solutions to difficulties or implement those solutions to the challenges they face.

The idea I am suggesting here entails a significant shift in mindset – for us to move from fixing and finding solutions, to being less hands-on. We still care, deeply. But our focus is on naming emotions, coaching our children through emotions, and then giving them the space to develop their own solutions.

When we view our children's emotions as an opportunity for us to show compassion and empathy, our children learn to understand and regulate their emotions. As they do so, their emotions reduce from their climax, and our children's thinking becomes clearer. At this point, they can probably determine what they might do to resolve challenging circumstances by having us ask, 'What do you think is the best way forward?'

If they are particularly young, getting up off the floor is usually enough. A cuddle might be a bonus. If they are older, our children will develop strategies that work for them. Because we have supported them through their emotions, they will be more likely to be open to our suggestions, as was the case with Cecilia in the previous example.

Think back to Michelle's experience with her daughter in the Introduction to this book. Her little girl was upset. Both Michelle and her husband could identify the emotion their daughter was feeling. But while Michelle's husband wanted to get logical and tell his little girl to sort herself out – in a solution-focused way – Michelle realised that naming the emotion, helping regulate the emotion, offering compassion, and then letting her little girl develop solutions, would be more beneficial. And it was!

When parents focus less on *punishment* and more on *teaching* through considering their child's perspective – children learn more and behave better.

Take-home message

When we are mindful of our children's needs and responsive to them *at an emotional level*, we tend to approach them differently. Rather than attempting to coerce them into adhering to our agenda, we look into their hearts and respond to their feelings. This approach promotes safety and security, builds a sense that they are worthy, and empowers our children to regulate their emotions and develop their own solutions to their problems. It's all about stopping to look at the world through their eyes.

Happy family focus:
Empathy in action

When your child is experiencing challenging emotions, try the following specific steps as an exercise in empathising. You can do this with your spouse or partner, too.

1. Become aware of the child's emotion.
2. Become aware of your response to it, and recognise the emotion as an opportunity to connect, build intimacy and teach.
3. Listen carefully so you can see the world through your child's eyes.
4. Show you understand emotionally and not just intellectually by labelling the feelings in your child's heart and showing you really understand.
5. Problem-solve together once your child feels calm and safe.

CHAPTER 14

Making family meetings work

If you want to call a family meeting, just turn off the WiFi router and wait in the room in which it is located.

Anonymous

Bronwyn and Kurt's family was in trouble. I knew it as soon as I saw the look of broken-ness on Bronwyn's face as she talked about their children. By her own admission, the children were 'out of control'. Kurt chimed in with statements about their offensive behaviour, refusal to contribute in any way, addiction to screens, and unwillingness to even get out of bed and go to school.

As we discussed their habits I discovered that they had no routines at all. Bedtimes did not exist. There were no limits on behaviour. Kate was ultra-permissive with the children until she couldn't stand it, at which point she became authoritarian, yelling, lashing out and often hurting her children, if not with her hands ('They just laugh at me when I hit them'), then certainly with her acerbic tongue.

Kurt was reactive and hard on the children – hard-line authoritarian. His rule was, 'If I ask them once and they don't do it, that's it. They're in for it. I hit them, or I remove privileges. No second chances.'

The family climate was perpetually uncomfortable and pervasively angry. In addition to their ineffective parenting styles, their family structure was clearly working against them – Bronwyn and Kurt's family was a blend of Bronwyn's three children to her first husband, combined with the two children they'd had together. The children's ages ranged from six to 14 years. The toxicity of their parenting combined with the vitriol and hostility they felt towards Bronwyn's ex-husband had created a challenging environment that was poison to positivity.

The catalyst for their call to me occurred one recent night. As Kurt lay on the couch watching a movie in the parents' retreat – a small room just off the master bedroom – he overheard a conversation Bronwyn was having with her two youngest children from her first marriage. Kurt could hear the two boys, aged eight and 10 years, softly weeping and then openly crying as they described to their mother the pain they felt as they shifted between the two homes, where they felt unwanted in both places by the men who bore the title 'father'.

Kurt turned the volume down and listened as Bronwyn cried with them, attempting to soothe their sorrow. Kurt's eavesdropping left him feeling broken-hearted. He loved his wife. He loved their children. And he wanted his stepchildren to feel safe and loved, too.

Introducing the idea of family meetings

As I spoke with Kurt and Bronwyn, they each described the pain they knew their family was in, and their personal desire to do something to make things better. Their only wish – 'We just want our family to be happy.'

Our discussion was basic. With so many areas to focus on, it would be easy to create an impossibly long list that would be motivating for a moment, before reality reduced it to a responsibility far too heavy to lift. Instead we talked about the times they could remember when things were good. They described the early part of their relationship, and suggested that it had become harder as the new children had arrived. We spoke about what their vision of a happy family was. And that dream, or picture, led to some invigorating discussion.

Bronwyn and Kurt wanted order, structure and routine. They wanted soft voices and gentle tones. They wanted relaxation. (I did mention that they had five children, and suggested that relaxation and large families were probably mutually exclusive concepts, but they were focused on their vision, and it felt good for them.) Warm relationships were high on the list. So was some willing help from the older children – something that was almost non-existent without Kate and Kurt resorting to poisonous puffer-fish impersonations.

As Bronwyn and Kurt expanded on their dream, something interesting happened to them. They become enlivened. Their tone changed. The optimism they began to feel was tangible. I watched as they relaxed, looked at each other, smiled more. And then the serious discussion began. We talked about many of the things described throughout this book – the power of habits and patterns, the difficulties inherent in trying to break free from old, automatic ways of doing things. Strategies were discussed. Bronwyn and Kurt chose two things to work on: speaking calmly and respectfully, and getting a basic routine started.

I asked them, 'How are you going to get the children in on the new routine?'

They looked at each other, shrugged, laughed, and Kurt said, 'We'll just start.'

While anything is possible, I suggested that perhaps a family meeting might be helpful: 'What if you sit down with the children over a bowl of ice-cream or some other treat, and chat with them about changes? Keep it simple. Rather than telling them how it's going to be, let them know that things have been crazy lately and you feel as though some routine will be helpful in making the family happier. Ask *them* what *they* think. If they agree, ask *them* what changes *they* think would be helpful, and use their input. If their ideas stink, be gentle about it and ask for more ideas.'

Bronwyn and Kurt decided to give it a go. They called me shortly after their meeting. 'It was awesome! It worked! The children loved it. They came up with the routine, the bedtimes, the dinner times, everything!'

'Great!' I replied. 'Well done. It will be awesome to see how this works. But keep in mind there will be some teething issues – expect to get it wrong a few times.' Then I added, 'Now the trick is to do this each week. Keep everyone on track.'

'Every week?' They were incredulous. 'We thought we were done!'

> Family meetings work best when we include input from our children. Ask them what they think. Invite them to suggest ideas they think would be helpful, and engage with their suggestions.

Effective family meetings

I know that any discussion of having a family meeting is likely to be accompanied by a collective eye-roll and groan. Apart from being closely aligned with the mission statements and vision/values ideals (that so many people baulk at) we discussed back in Chapter 1, family meetings might simply seem a bit 'naff'. But – and it's a big but – the success of the meeting depends on how you run it.

Remember this too: the success of the *family* is more likely if we have *family meetings*. That's because family meetings are a tremendous way to bring everyone together to communicate 'policy decisions', stay focused on vision and values, spend a bit of quality time, and even have some fun. Holding meetings consistently with the family helps everyone stay focused on the big picture of what the family is about, helps to refine (and re-find) routines, gives us an opportunity to explicitly teach our children, and may even boost family unity.

> Family meetings are a tremendous way to bring everyone together to communicate 'policy decisions', stay focused on vision and values, spend a bit of quality time, and even have some fun.

I am not aware of any solid empirical research that tells us precisely how often this type of family meeting should occur to achieve optimum results, but I would typically recommend a weekly get-together to review agendas, work out issues, plan and play a little. Some families might like a five-minute meeting each morning or evening. Other families might function best with a monthly meeting that is turned into some kind of an occasion. But to keep people on the same page, you need to keep talking – and listening.

Our WFIs

When Kylie and I began having our meetings, I suggested we call it our weekly Family Council. Kylie's own family had used that term, and her memory of family councils was unpleasant. She remembered it as a time where her parents gave a lot of lectures, and meetings that regularly ended in tears. Uh oh. So we called it a Weekly Family Inventory (or WFI for short) briefly, but now the meeting has no name. It's just a family meeting. While it may not have a name, it does have some very clear guidelines:

1. The family meeting is a time for positive interaction, not discipline or being nit-picky.
2. Everyone is invited and everyone has a voice. No one *has to* participate, but everyone does need to be there.

3. As a general rule, the parents run the meeting. While both the mum and dad can do this, I think dads need to step up here. This is not about sexism or reinvigorating the patriarchy. Rather, it is a chance for dad to connect with the family. All too often mum is left with the weight of running the family while dad looks after himself and his agenda (even when mum is in paid employment outside the home). Data tell us that even though dads are more involved with family than in previous generations, they are still significantly less involved than are mums. When dad steps up and facilitates the family meeting, his family buy-in increases – he gets more involved and he is more likely to engage with the family right across the week. There is a small amount of research to support this approach as valuable for fathers and for families.[89] The meeting should be fun and future-focused.

The agenda

Each family will have different priorities for their family meeting but there are some agenda items that might be considered in regular family meetings.

Start with the mission or mantra

These first three questions keep the agenda focused on values and vision/mission, and move quickly toward a future focus:

- What went well this week?
- What did we do that was in line with our family principles or mission statement?
- If we were to pick one thing this week that we could work on, what would it be – individually and as a family?

In addition to these questions, the family meeting is a time to review routines, chores and commitments for the week. Take the time to calendar everyone's routines and correlate activities.

Next is teaching time

In our family we have found that taking between two and 10 minutes to explicitly teach our children specific values or principles is useful. Sometimes the values will be linked to our family mantra or mission. Other times, it will be something that we see as valuable for our children to understand.

We usually start with an object lesson and ask the children what that lesson might mean in relation to the principle we are discussing. For example, recently we did a cool experiment with fire. After I set fire to a piece of material one of the children was holding, the material floated off her hand and up into the air. The children were awestruck. My daughter had been fearful as the fire burned, but had trusted that I would not hurt her.

We then had a brief conversation about trust, telling the truth, and how dishonesty can lead to relationships being burned.

Over the years we have taught the principles of gratitude, honesty, service, kindness, respect, financial decisions, health and fitness, technology use, loyalty, determination, creativity, persistence, having a growth mindset, and many more things – sometimes many times.

If you are a family with a faith background, these meetings can be a tremendous time to bring in the principles of your faith. If you are a family without a faith background, the meeting is just as important for you to share your values with your children in structured, thoughtful ways. Your meetings might be inspired by your religious lessons, current events in the media, a book you are reading, or any other source of inspiration you stumble upon. What do you want to really teach your children? This is a great time to talk about it.

Ending on a positive note

To wrap up family meetings, some fun time might be scheduled. In our family this usually involves tickle games, card games, a family walk or ride, or a fun movie. We have also found that a treat can be remarkably helpful in ensuring the meeting is productive and ends on a positive note.

The best approach

Family meetings should be short, easy and light. When we start turning them into heavy lay-down-the-law sessions, we destroy the positive impact the meetings can have, and leave everyone feeling flat. Here's my rule: If you can't do it in under 10 minutes, pick the best fun things to do and concentrate on them. Do the hard, yucko stuff in quiet moments at an individual level so as not to reduce the family climate to 'frigid'. Keeping the formula simple, warm and fun gets great results. (It could even be a good time to talk about grateful things, or plan exciting family adventures to look forward to.) The family meeting is something that works in families regardless of their size. The key to their success is consistency.

> Family meetings should be short, easy and light. When we start turning them into heavy lay-down-the-law sessions, we destroy the positive impact the meetings can have, and leave everyone feeling flat.

A word on children's councils

Sometimes it can be great to simply let the children decide what needs to be done and when. Deferring to the children can reduce parent stress, offer opportunities for the children to be responsible, increase buy-in from the kids, and lead to some really interesting family policies! The idea of letting children 'govern' themselves is one that can cause some parents to become nervous. However, research on 'autonomy-supportive parenting'[90] suggests *that one of the best things we can do to teach our children to be responsible is to give them responsibility,* which I talked about in Chapter 2.

How does a children's council work? When major decisions need to be made, parents might invite their children to go to their room to talk about the best way to move forward. In some instances, the children may develop solutions or ideas that are ridiculous, self-serving and entirely out of the question. If that occurs, parents should smile, thank them for their ideas, and then ask, 'Can you convince us that this will work?' or 'What other ideas can you come up with?' But often children who are given a degree of self-determination will respond with responsible, well-considered plans for moving beyond an impasse, overcoming a challenge or making valuable improvements in the family.

> One of the best things we can do to teach our children to be responsible is to give them responsibility.

The children's council may not always work well. Children need to be mature enough to have a conversation with one another. The eldest child needs to be willing to put aside any manipulative tendencies. And sufficient instruction and rationale need to be shared with children to help them navigate their way through a children's council without adult input. When this is possible, giving our children a chance to be responsible can lead to surprisingly positive results.

Take-home message

Family meetings and children's councils provide regular opportunities for families to focus on how they can remain aligned to what matters most to them. They also give children a chance to be responsible, learn leadership and work together. Hold them regularly, keep them short, focus on what is going well and they can keep your family on track.

Happy family focus:
Schedule your first family meeting

Your first family meeting may or may not guarantee immediate happiness today, but talk with your family about getting the process started. Create an agenda or meeting outline that will work for your family and your unique needs. Then work hard to make sure the meeting is fun.

CHAPTER 15

Getting involved – in a good way

The evidence suggests that … when parents use techniques that exert pressure … they undermine their own goals. Children are less likely to take responsibility for their own behaviour, and are less likely to take on the parents' values.

Wendy Grolnick, *The Psychology of Parental Control*

I worked with one parent who shared an experience she'd had with a friend and her three-year-old son:

My friend Kerrie's son was refusing to eat dinner and she was getting frustrated. Kerrie told him he must be hungry and talked about when he last ate and how much he'd eaten all day. She threatened punishments. She ordered him to eat. She got more and more irritated, and he started to get upset. I was feeling concerned about both of them and looked at my daughter (who was eating happily) and thought, 'What do I do when this happens?' And it dawned on me – I assume she's too tired to feed herself and I feed her. I asked Kerrie if I could try. She said, 'Sure – good luck!' And threw her hands in the air and walked off.

I asked him if he needed some help and he nodded. I spoon-fed him and he ate the meal.

Opt for autonomy-supportive involvement

The very best parents seem to know when to step in, and they know when to step back. They are highly attuned to their children's needs, and only get involved at the right time and in ways that show they care. They step back at times as well, in a way that lets the children know they can always have their parents' support, but that they need to do things on their own. In other words, even when they step back, they are still turned towards their children.

These parents are attuned to what their children need to feel safe and loved. Wise parents also recognise that over-involvement and 'hot-house' parenting are rarely in their children's best interests – as those children get older such strategies can in fact drive a wedge in the parent–child relationship.

I'm going to suggest three different areas of our children's lives I think we should be involved in – but not too involved. They are chores, friendships and schoolwork. As we look at these three areas, you will see how autonomy-supportive parenting practices trump controlling or passive strategies every time – getting the balance just right by being involved and caring (and giving direction where necessary) while not being too controlling or intrusive. On the one hand, families are happier when we get the balance right, and on the other hand, families experience greater challenges when we misjudge and get the balance wrong. Use these three examples to guide your stepping in or stepping back as you interact with your children.

> The very best parents seem to know when to step in, and they know when to step back.

Approaching chores

Most children hate chores – it's a rare child who comes asking for opportunities to do more around the house. We ask our children to do chores, though, because we hope that they will become responsible. We want to teach them how to do those things because we believe that they matter for later in life, and we expect that they will make a contribution in our home. Sometimes we ask them to do chores for no other reason than we're over doing the work and we want them to pick up after themselves!

When our children are learning new chores, we take time to teach them. We get involved. We induct them. We spend time helping them as they learn. For some tasks this only takes a moment. For other tasks, it can take a number of days or weeks. However, as they develop greater competence, we step back and encourage them to do things on their own.

There are some days, however, when things don't go so well. Our children know how to do as we have asked, but rather than helping out, they go to ground. Either they disappear and find other things to do (like read or play games on their tablet – or vanish entirely by visiting their friends), or they whine and moan and complain that they can't do it, or they don't know how to do it. These situations give us a perfect opportunity to determine whether we should step in or step out.

Stepping in when it is typical to step out

Our eldest daughter was invited to play at her best friend's house. Casey, my daughter's friend, was about nine years old. When Kylie arrived to drop our daughter off, she found Casey in a fit! Her mum was trying to stay calm as she explained to Kylie that Casey had been sitting in her bedroom doorway for over two hours, refusing to tidy her room. Casey had been threatened. Stubborn refusal resulted. The play date seemed doomed. Casey dug her heels in further. No amount of yelling or threatening was enough to dislodge Casey and get her to do a simple chore – one that she routinely took care of. For some bizarre reason, today was the day that Casey was overwhelmed with the task.

Casey's mum was mad, and Casey had spent a good deal of the morning crying.

After listening to Casey's mum for a few minutes, Kylie asked if she could speak with Casey. She tentatively walked down the corridor and spent a few minutes labelling Casey's emotions and showing she understood. Quietly, she asked, 'Would you feel better if someone helped you a little? I could help you tidy things up.' Casey nodded. Then Kylie pointed to a few things on the 'floordrobe' and said, 'How about you do those things there while I help with the bed.' Kylie made the bed very slowly, and gently prodded Casey, guiding her as she picked up her mess. Within five minutes, things were clean enough to satisfy Casey's mum.

Sometimes our children should be left alone to do something. They are capable. They are responsible. They are able to do it. But other times, in spite of their capability, they struggle. In these instances it may be entirely appropriate (and compassionate) to step in and lovingly lift them. Whether that means being involved to the degree that we do something with them, for them, or that we simply stay near them and talk with them as they do their chores, is a matter to be decided by caring parents at the time.

Chores can make us all feel a little overwhelmed from time to time. This is especially so for our children. They are generally far less competent than we are, far less efficient, and have less capacity for regulating their feelings of overwhelm.

The group blitz approach

Chores are usually no fun, either, which only exacerbates the challenge. And the bigger the chore, the greater the chance of a meltdown – which means there is an increased likelihood that we may need to step in, even though we would rather step out.

In our home we often make cleaning easier for our children by doing a sweep of the house as a family. As many of us as possible converge on one room at a time and put everything away. Lounge rooms are clean in moments. The dining area is cleared in seconds. Bedrooms are sparkling in a minute or two. Bathrooms and the kitchen take a little longer, but having company makes it faster, easier and more fun. We call it the '10-minute tidy'. We choose three or four songs to listen to, crank up the volume, and do as much as we can to tidy up in 10 minutes.

Working as a team is energising – the work gets done quickly and it reduces the feeling of being overwhelmed that our children might feel if just we pointed at a room and commanded, 'Clean it.' And it actually makes the process more fun.

Also, when we get involved by stepping in to help with our children's chores rather than stepping out and making them do it so they can 'learn to be responsible', something interesting happens besides the productivity boost that comes from collaboration and cooperation. Relationships improve. It feels good to be together as we work side by side. And along the way, the children are developing the skills they will need to be independent and eventually make us redundant. They are becoming more responsible, and they are enjoying the process.

Managing friendships

Getting involved with our children's friendships is a tricky business. While stepping in is usually useful as standard practice with chores, the reverse may be true with friendships. If we overstep the mark by getting involved in their extra-familial relationships, we can push our children away by making them feel that we are judging their friends.

While this is not usually a problem with children in the preschool years, friendship dynamics begin to shift once school begins. By the time children are around third-grade age, relationships begin to become much trickier to navigate, and by fifth grade, children are highly socially attuned – girls especially.

At this point, if we begin intruding into friendships in a judgemental way, we can leave our children feeling disempowered and worthless, as though the decisions they make about their friends is a reflection on their own character. Comments like, 'He doesn't treat you very nicely. Why don't you play with someone else?' or 'How about we try and organise a play date with someone who knows how to be a nice friend ...' can leave our children questioning their judgement (which may in fact need to be questioned), and harm their relationships.

A woman I worked with, Rachael, disapproved of her young daughter Charlotte's friends. Rachael begged Charlotte to find nice friends – like the friends her twin sister chose. So Charlotte, only eight-years-old, felt judged. She felt as though her choices were not good enough for her mother. And she did not know how to make new friends. When she tried to talk and play with a different group of girls at school, they made her feel uncomfortable and asked why she was talking with them. Her old friends followed her, shadowing her as she attempted to shift allegiances, and making everyone uncomfortable in the process.

Charlotte felt like she could neither please her mum, her current (unpleasant) friends, or her desired friends. Rather than helping, Rachael's comments eventually only served to strengthen the relationship her daughter had with her friends.

Research on adolescent friendships shows the same process occurs as our children move into high school. In a three-year longitudinal study[91] involving 497 youth (starting when they were around 13-years-old), annual surveys were administered, not just to the youth, but to their parents, and also to their best friends. Findings indicated that where youth spent time with 'deviant' peers, they were at risk of engaging in delinquent behaviour. This is not surprising. Further, as time spent with challenging and deviant peers increased, the surveyed youth increased the degree to which they were acting in challenging ways themselves. Again, no real surprises there. Importantly, the research indicated that challenging behaviour did not promote time with deviant peers. Rather, it was the peers that influenced the youth's behaviour.

But the most important aspect of this research in relation to knowing when to step in and knowing when to step out – or gauging our involvement – was this: *The more parents prohibited their children from being in contact with deviant peers, the more their children spent time with those peers, and the more delinquent their behaviour became.*

The researchers argued that when parents became too involved, and specifically were being too controlling, forbidden friends became 'forbidden fruit', which led to unintended negative consequences on their children's behaviour.

Stepping in with friendships seems to create unwanted and unhappy results. It challenges the relationships we have with our children. It can leave them feeling isolated in the schoolyard. And on average it appears to solidify unwanted relationships and drive deviant behaviour. This is a long way away from what we need to make our families happier. So how do we work through our children's relationship challenges in autonomy-supportive ways? Clearly we want to (and should) be available to help if they are struggling with unhealthy relationships. Can we step in without causing more harm than good?

> The more parents prohibited their children from being in contact with deviant peers, the more their children spent time with those peers, and the more delinquent their behaviour became.

Stepping carefully, not stomping in

Autonomy-supportive processes will usually help us to be involved enough to show we care without becoming too controlling and perpetuating the problem. When we become aware of a challenge, we can choose a time when our child is able to talk without feeling pressured, and explain what we are concerned about. We might ask whether they are feeling challenged by friendships. Then we can listen as they tell us about how their relationships feel.

In some situations we may need to give clear directions, but it's more likely their need is for us to spend time asking questions, helping them understand what makes friendships positive, and empathising with their difficulties. Then we can ask, 'What do you think is the best thing to do?'

Such challenges tend to take some time to resolve. From time to time we may need to engage with the children's school, or with other families to promote new and positive relationships. But such an approach is more likely to yield beneficial outcomes because children are part of the process – developing solutions, feeling understood, and working with their parents – rather than being dictated to.

When stepping in is unavoidable

There are times when we must step in, and sometimes this can lead to short-term difficulties and animosity. If our children are being bullied, or if they are continuing to associate with peers who are causing harm to them physically, emotionally or in relation to the law, we should step in. This would always be our final step, after previous autonomy-supporting strategies have been unsuccessful.

At this point, stepping in might mean working with our children's school, sporting organisation or church group. It might mean stopping them from associating with certain peers. This course of action becomes more difficult as children get older.

If we want our children to be happy in their relationships with peers, judging the degree to which we should step in or step out of their friendships can be a key element that impacts our family climate. This is true at all ages, but is especially so as our children develop and make their way into high school. Being available to talk at any time about their relationships may be the most important way we can step in. Working with them on decisions but leaving the final result up to them (in most cases, except where it would be unsafe to do so) may be the most important way we can step out.

Schooling issues

Getting our relationship right with our children in regards to their schoolwork is difficult. We want our children to do well. In fact, many parents I speak with want their children to be exceptional! Some parents view their children's school success as a badge of honour – a symbol of high-quality parenting. Other parents are focused on doing all they can to give their children a solid start in life, hoping that this will lead to success and opportunity.

Being involved in our children's school experience is important. But by now you may be sensing a theme in this chapter. The way we involve ourselves matters, as does the degree to which we involve ourselves. For example, our involvement in our children's homework and schoolwork.

The homework conundrum

Many parents are of the mistaken belief that homework is necessary for their children's academic success. As such, homework takes up an enormous amount of space in far too many homes – time space and emotional space. This, in spite of the significant amount of research that indicates most homework has a *negative* impact on our children's desire to learn, motivation for school and grades until around age 14 – with the exception of reading and self-directed learning projects.[92]

Parents become easily over-involved in their children's homework, demanding it be done, spending time checking, assisting and, yes, even doing their children's homework for them. This over-involvement rarely leads to improved learning and life success for children – or happier families. Instead, children lose motivation and feel disempowered, and even incompetent. Parents experience frustration that their children are not able to do certain work to a given standard, or that they are spending their time monitoring their children's homework activities instead of doing all of the other things they might be doing. (Some parents get frustrated because they don't know how to do their children's homework! Oops, I mean 'help' their children with their homework.) Either way, homework impacts on our children's wellbeing, and our own parental wellbeing.

> Many parents are of the mistaken belief that homework is necessary for their children's academic success. This, in spite of the significant research that indicates most homework has a negative impact on our children's desire to learn, motivation for school and grades until around the age of 14.

Each year since around 2008, I have written a letter to my children's school thanking them for the wonderful work they do in educating my children, and inviting them to chat with me about why I would prefer my children not be asked to do homework until high school. I make it clear that I expect my children to read each night (but not for any given number of minutes or pages), and I encourage spelling in early years of school, as well as self-directed projects and speeches. However, we lead full lives, with extracurricular activities, friends, chores and family time, leaving zero room for pointless, even harmful, 'busy' work (homework). The letter has been received warmly and with remarkable acceptance in all but one situation over the years. And, consistent with the research, our children have done just fine at school, even without homework.

If this is of interest to you, you can find it at my blog – happyfamilies.com.au/blog or just search my name and 'homework letter' on the internet. Thousands of people across the world have used it and shared it via the power of social media – including school principals!

School involvement

Some parents become highly active in their children's school community, joining parents' and citizens' groups, volunteering in class, and so on. This may be positive. But it may not. It can be a fine line we walk. If we can do it and cope just fine, that's fantastic. However, when we 'lean in' too far with our children's school we can wear ourselves out. Trying to juggle time in the classroom, covering books with contact, helping out in the canteen and volunteering on sports days can be a bridge too far for some families. Balance and wisdom are required. It is also valuable to remember that our children like to have autonomy. Some children may love having a parent so close so often. Others might prefer to have their own space, free to be themselves. There are no hard and fast rules here. There is no science to say where the line ought to be drawn. But over-involvement can impact on how happy our family is, just as under-involvement can.

How hard should we be pushing our children to achieve straight As or gain admission to that competitive university degree at the best university?

There is also the perennial issue of parental involvement in the educational aspects of their children's schooling. How hard should we be pushing our children to achieve straight As or gain admission to that competitive university degree at the best university? Everyone has heard of 'tiger parents' – mothers and fathers who accept nothing but perfection from their children in their piano and violin, their Mandarin and French, as well as their schoolwork. Stories abound about mothers who sit beside their children as they play the piano, demanding that the child 'play it again' until it is perfect, as the child sobs, fusses and begs to be allowed to go out and play.

Does this level of involvement in school and other pursuits lead to better outcomes? While there is no doubt that children who experience this intense parental involvement are often high achievers, research suggests outcomes are poor for those children in other areas of their lives – wellbeing is low, and motivation to participate in the 'controlled' or 'over-involved' activity is low once parents have stopped making demands. The children often come to resent the activity, even if they excel. In short, tiger parenting does not make families happier.

A fascinating study from Brigham Young University in the US showed that adolescents whose parents were high in autonomy support – that is, parents who taught their children to determine their own values in relation to schoolwork and simultaneously encouraged high standards – had children who were more engaged at school and in their schoolwork.[93] These parents were not over-involved. They were not tiger parents. There was limited control. Instead, these parents talked about expectations and values, and then deferred decision-making to their teenagers. The same research showed that as parental involvement increased, student engagement and academic outcomes lowered.

As a counterpoint, researchers have found that for youth who exhibit 'world-class' talent in a particular area, parents are instrumental in all aspects of that talent development. Parents in such families are heavily involved – they create an environment where their children's talents are identified and strengthened early, and they arrange for expert coaching, facilitate intensive practice and sustain their children's motivation. While not dealing directly with schooling, this data (albeit with a small sample size of just 24 youth and their parents) indicates that children can achieve remarkable feats with parental involvement. What the research did not investigate was whether the involvement, control and ceaseless hard work came at a cost to wellbeing, and the family's happiness.

So, should we get involved in our children's schooling? Absolutely. Research clearly shows that when parents expect their children to do well at school and support them in that goal, children perform well.[94] And when our children perform well academically, they experience greater wellbeing. But it depends on the process they go through to become more academically successful – having involved parents can make them (and us) happier, but being too involved often only succeeds in adding pressure to everyone in the family, reducing motivation, engagement and even achievement, and damaging relationships.

Take-home message

As parents, we are *supposed* to be involved in our children's lives – involved, but not controlling. Ultimately the decision as to whether we step in or step out should be based on context. Sometimes we need to be involved to help, and to love. Other times we need to step back so our children can be challenged and grow. But being involved, whether it is with chores, school, friendships or *life*, will lead to happier families – so long as we get that balance right!

Happy family focus:
Think before you step in (or out)

Become more conscious about your decisions to step in or step out. Each time you choose to step in, pause and ask yourself whether you really need to be involved. Will giving your child more space help or hurt? Each time you choose to step out, pause and ask yourself whether your decision to step out will improve or undermine your relationship with your child.

CHAPTER 16

Making it fun

We don't stop playing because we grow old.
We grow old because we stop playing.
George Bernard Shaw

Upping the play factor

Hopefully the message in this chapter is the most obvious in this book – if we want our families to be happier, we need to find ways to make family life FUN! And fun is most likely to happen when we find ways to play.

We may choose to play in an organised way, or to bring a playful attitude to our family interactions. Either way, play makes families happier!

Unfortunately, it seems that play rarely feels like play – particularly for parents. More often than not it feels like hard work. A prominent Australian media commentator wrote an article that defended parents who do not like to play with their children.[95] Her view was that playing with her children was boring. She noted the way her children's demands for play distracted her from monitoring eBay, writing columns and other 'important' stuff. She was tired of playing games which she did not enjoy the first time, let alone the hundredth time. For many parents, there is no fun in child's play.

When play is no fun

There are two central reasons play is no fun for some parents, and the mum who wrote that article was experiencing both. First, it is hard to put ourselves in a fun mindset when the afternoon is late, dinner is not cooked, children need baths or showers, school assignments and reading aren't done, the house is a mess, and the dog has to be walked. We typically find fun is absent during evenings like that, or mornings where everyone starts slowly, children need to be dressed and out the door, and we are stressed about making it to wherever we have to be. And we, as parents, are no fun when work is all we can think about – whether it is housework or paid employment. Competing demands mean that we often perceive that there is a time for play and a time for work. Trying to do both things at once feels incompatible.

When play is boring

The second reason parents feel play is boring, is because they're doing it wrong! I watch parents play with their children and I see two classic scenarios.

The child becomes dictator

Picture a child playing with her mum, and telling her what to do, how to do it and when. (Note that it is usually the mum that gets told what to do.) It's a common scenario. Parents seem quite willing to be dictated to in playtime. Other children wouldn't take that behaviour, but a parent will keep on taking instructions, speaking when told, saying what she is told to say, and not moving outside the parameters their child has established without permission. If you watch your children play with other children, however, you will note that this kind of behaviour is rarely tolerated for long. Once a child becomes too bossy, the other children leave. They either give up entirely, or cry to their parents about the unequal power distribution in their play date.

The child asks mum or dad to do the same thing repeatedly

The second scenario occurs when the child keeps demanding mum or dad do the same thing again and again. Once again, this does not work in relationships children have with other children. Once a child has had enough, the play moves on, or a child moves on.

This is not play! Not for the parents, at least. It may be play for our children as they explore different dimensions of their personality, but for parents it is hard work.

I define play as doing something for enjoyment and recreation. It suggests doing something that has little purpose other than having fun. If we, as parents, are spending time in activities with our children and we are not enjoying, or recreating ourselves, then we are not playing. We are being used as a chattel, an object, a prop – but not a playmate. We are teaching our children that their agenda is the only agenda that matters. This is perfectly okay from time to time, or for a short time. But play should be reciprocal, mutually rewarding, and offer opportunities to move away from everyday demands.

> If we, as parents, are spending time in activities with our children and we are not enjoying, or recreating ourselves, then we are not playing. We are being used as a chattel, an object, a prop – but not a playmate.

The rise of the grown-up playmate

It may only be in the past 50 to 60 years that adults have felt a need to play with children. Indeed, playing with one's children may be a relatively unique Western societal development. David F. Lancy, who wrote *The Anthropology of Childhood*, argues that historically children played with other children much more than they played with adults.[96] Parents saw little need to play with their children because their play 'needs' were satisfied with other children in their community. It makes sense, too, that children would prefer to play with others closer to their own age. They have similar interests, abilities, appraisals of the world and, most importantly, similar amounts of energy!

Today, our culture and society has developed in such a way that opportunities for our children to wander the neighbourhood looking for playmates are extraordinarily limited. Between our busy agendas, and the devastating truth that so few of us really trust our neighbours, our children are left to play with us far more than (potentially) any other children in the history of the world. So how do we shift our mindset?

> Ensuring that play feels like play for parent and child is an essential way of making play work. That may mean that sometimes children get upset. That's fine. They do that with their friends, too.

Play tips for big people

Play is a critical learning tool for children. They develop socially, cognitively, psychologically and physically through playing, and it boosts wellbeing. What can we do to bring more fun and play into our families? I have already suggested a few things earlier in this book that can make family life more fun – looking forward to things together, doing a 10-minute tidy with music blaring or getting involved in life together. Having quality, meaningful interactions together is usually seen as fun, too.

Ensuring that play *feels like play* for parent and child is an essential way of making play work. That may mean that sometimes children get upset. That's fine. They do that with their friends, too. But as we explain that we do want to play with them, and then help them explore ways we can play happily together without repeating the same game 500 times and without being dictated to, we will find that play can and will become a source of joy and help make family life happier.

Below are five more ways we can make family life more fun – and *fun*-ctional.

Smile more

Think about how often you see your children smiling. And you? Who smiles more? And who has more fun? Chances are, it's the children.

Yes, I know. We've got responsibilities that the children don't. It's okay for them! They can go off and play, stare at a screen or read a book. But the fact is people who smile are happy and are generally having fun.

Before I began my parenting and psychology studies, I spent close to a decade as a radio announcer. The number one rule I followed before speaking into that microphone was that I smiled. I intentionally and mindfully created a great big cheesy grin on my face. It made a difference. I sounded like I was having fun. My audience appreciated that they were listening to someone who was happy.

Try it yourself. Look at someone nearby and smile when you talk to them. Make sure your grin is big and cheesy. It will change the way you interact. It will change the way people respond to you (and not because they think you're weird). It will change the way you feel.

There is fascinating research to support the claim that smiling can make us happier. In an experiment that had the potential to make participants feel remarkably foolish (and look a little funny), researchers placed their participants into one of two groups. Each group of participants was invited to hold a pencil in their mouth, but with a slight difference depending on the group they were randomly assigned to. Participants in one group were asked to place a pencil horizontally between their teeth (which forces a smile). Picture a dog holding a bone in its teeth. It was the same kind of idea.

If you have a pen, pop it horizontally between your teeth now and you will note that you are contracting the same muscles you might contract if you smiled. (It may look and feel a little like you are grimacing, but you are probably activating your smile muscles.)

The participants in the second group were instructed to place the pencil gently between their lips without the pencil touching their teeth, which forces a frown.[97] (As an aside, you can also hold the pencil between your top lip and your nose to force a frown, and the experiment works the same way.)

While the participants were either frowning or smiling with pencils in their mouths, the experimenters asked that they judge how funny a series of cartoons was. Those who were smiling thought the cartoons were significantly funnier than those who were frowning. Of course they did not realise that they were smiling or frowning – they were simply holding a pencil in their mouth while looking at cartoons. Experiments have replicated and expanded on this study and it appears to be robust – smiling makes life more fun. We judge cartoons and other situations as more pleasant and more humorous when we smile. Think of the last time you walked into a room to see your spouse, partner or a loved one, and they smiled at you. How did you feel? Did you feel welcome or did you feel like you were intruding?

Imagine a child whose every interaction with their parent is met with a look of serious concentration or contemplation. From time to time, the parent nods their head or raises the corner of their mouth gently. Every time the child asks a question, engages with a sibling, or plays with a toy, their parent looks in his direction with 'that' look. The child gazes out of the window, picks up a book or swipes at their tablet, always glancing at their parent to gauge the degree to which their behaviour is acceptable. Every time the child glances, they are met with the look of stern concentration.

The parent is not angry or annoyed – just simply concentrating or thinking about other things. The child is not really doing anything wrong – just seeking acknowledgement or occasional approval.

Now, imagine that same child spending some time with their other parent – the one who makes eye contact regularly and is generally attentive. When the child looks at this parent, they receive warm smiles and gentle, approving eye contact. The child plays in the room, colouring or drawing, and when they ask for their parent to pay attention or inspect a drawing, the parent offers reassuring smiles, asks questions, and gives hugs and other touch. Would a child's wellbeing be influenced differently by these two parents? Of course it would.

Smiles improve relationships, and they seem to make life more fun. Some people insist that they are happy but look like they are going to a funeral. Let your face know you feel great. Smile. Try it and it might make your family happier! And if it doesn't, stick a pencil between your teeth!

> Think of the last time you walked into a room to see your spouse, partner, or a loved one, and they smiled at you. How did you feel? Did you feel welcome or did you feel like you were intruding?

Take time out

There are times when family life is stressful. We get caught up in our lengthy to-do lists, we chase deadlines, and in no time we find ourselves detached from everyone that matters and attached to everything that doesn't.

If your children are demanding your attention, give it to them. Just stop, drop and play. It may only take five minutes, but taking time out for five minutes of fun (you could even call it that) can make a big difference in how happy your family is.

There may be other times when you choose to let go of the agenda entirely. Perhaps you might ring work because you are 'sick', ring school and let them know the children are 'sick', and then take the children for an outing all day. From time to time it can be fun to pretend that time is not an issue. This is obviously not practical as a regular occurrence, but if it happened once or twice a year, would the world really stop? Or would the world be just a little more fun?

While I was writing this book, my children would run in the door in the afternoon, eat their snacks, do their chores (usually), and then beg me to have a swim with them. On every afternoon that I could, I gave the children between five and 15 minutes of fun. They knew I had let go of the agenda and stopped, dropped and played. It was what I could give them, and it made our family happier. They were also forgiving when I resumed work after our fun time.

Time out could also include a walk around the block with your children, a quick trip to the park, or a visit to a café with a teenager who is struggling so that you can share a bowl of wedges or a hot chocolate. Time out could be as simple as a hug and a short but attentive conversation, or as long as an entire day with nothing but time together.

When we let go of the never-ending non-stop agenda and take time out with our children, family life is more likely to be fun.

Learn new things together

One of my favourite scholars is a guy who loves the gym, only wears black t-shirts and listens to lots of loud music by bands whose names I can't pronounce. Professor Todd Kashdan is a lifelong learner who shares his enthusiasm with his students at university, but also at home with his children. Todd's research has shown that of all the character strengths related to happiness, curiosity – the desire to learn and understand – is the attribute most strongly linked with happiness in our children. His research showed that learning new things makes people feel great, and it lasts for the long term. How do we make this happen? In an interview with *Success* magazine, Todd acknowledged that children are not usually forthcoming with information about their school day – particularly what they learned in class. He suggested,

> Instead of asking what your child learned, say, 'I read this article about a fish that has human-like teeth! Can you imagine?'[98] (It's a pacu fish, by the way. They live in the Amazon and are related to the piranha.)

Most children are naturally inquisitive and deeply curious. They love to learn new things. Unfortunately, distracted, inattentive or busy parents who cannot find the time to explore life with their children numb curiosity and drive that desire to learn away. In Susan Engel's book, *The Hungry Mind*, she describes the way we diminish our children's drive to learn by our non-responsiveness.

Think about the last time your child asked, 'Why?' and received a response like, 'Just because ... okay?' Would you suggest that a 'because' response left them feeling happier about life? Or more inquisitive? Can you imagine them walking away and thinking, 'Gee, I'm so glad that I understand that now. And I'm really pleased to know that when I have a question, my parents will let me know just how it is'? Many children will feel deflated, unhappy and less likely to ask questions of their parents again. Responding in such a destructive and passive manner leaves us feeling that we have failed to live up to our best as well.

Curiosity drives wellbeing – and fun. It is also often relational, particularly for children. Learning is also both fun and potentially profound when we do it together. In Chapter 14 I described a fun experiment our family did with some paper, a flame and a slight element of risk. The children learned, and it was fun. My wife enjoyed spending significant time with our children as her sixth pregnancy progressed, describing the development of our baby to our curious children. Helpful books with wonderful pictures of babies *in utero* have led to positive and happy family interactions.

Learning can be an adventure if we make it so, and most would agree that adventures are fun. We can plant a garden, breed mice or rabbits, collect eggs from a hen house, go to a strawberry farm and pick strawberries, learn new sports, and do crafts. Watch a family – children and adults – exploring rock pools at the beach or a pebbly creek bed at a campground. Exploration, learning and curiosity are fun and make families happy. It simply requires that we are willing to be creative, explore ideas, and respond to our children's questions with enthusiasm and interest.

Just add treats

I don't know any family activity that can't be enhanced with treats. If you are having a family meeting or sending the children to the playroom for a children' council, include popcorn. Ice-cream, brownies, or ice-cream and brownies ... treats are fun. If you're a family that does not do processed sugars, bring out a beautiful bowlfull of strawberries or freshly chopped pineapple.

Here's how one super dad I know uses treats for fun in his home. When a room is particularly messy, he hides some chocolate under some of the mess. He then saunters into the room where his children might be idly staring at nothing, and gently suggests that 'good things come to those who tidy their rooms'. It only took a couple of instances of this approach, and now his children dash to their rooms to tidy up.

Such an approach does come with some risks, though. For example, a canny child may simply ransack the room for the treat, leaving parents out of chocolate and still dealing with a big mess. Similarly, offering bribes can lead to children making a room look tidy by taking every shortcut known to get the job done fast.

Therefore, this approach is best used randomly and for fun, rather than as a motivator to promote an immaculately tidy and spotless environment.

The idea is simply that we make things fun. Treats can help us to do this – but they should be offered unconditionally and to everyone, rather than only on conditions being met and only to those who meet the conditions. Otherwise it stops being fun for everyone.

Celebrate – whatever!

Our lives are potentially *full* of reasons to celebrate. Our children experience some form of success regularly. To what extent do we celebrate with them? Does winning a swimming race or athletics event warrant a high five? Or a treat with mum or dad at the local ice-creamery? Psychological research shows that celebrations for success should be unexpected and it is usually best to let our children know that it's just a one-off treat because we were so excited to hear how well they did. We don't want them expecting treats *every* time they do something well, which can lead to motivation to get more treats, but can undermine motivation to learn or achieve for its own sake. (In other words, don't bribe.)

Mix it up and celebrate in different ways when your children experience success. It could be a hug, kiss and bowl of ice-cream for dessert on one occasion, a trip to the movies on a special date with mum or dad another time, or a family dinner at a favourite restaurant to celebrate the end of a school term. The celebration should not be used as a carrot to bribe certain behaviour.

Managing celebrations with multiple children need not be tricky, either. In some cases we might let the children know that a particular celebration is just for one child because of the remarkable accomplishment they have achieved. But, ideally, when one person succeeds, the entire family celebrates with them – as with most celebrations, the more the merrier!

If our children have not achieved anything particularly exciting, it could be time to celebrate something unusual. We can celebrate when they put their bag away without being asked. We can print a commendation for the remarkable effort of putting on a seatbelt. We might applaud our daughter's happy singing while she cleans her room, or stand to attention and honour our son when he brushes his teeth without having to be reminded a dozen times.

> If our children have not achieved anything particularly exciting, it could be time to celebrate something unusual. We can celebrate the fact that they put their bag away without being asked. We can print a commendation for the remarkable effort of putting on a seatbelt.

This spontaneity adds an element of extra fun and silliness, which is usually a big win with little children (not so much with teens), and can simultaneously gently reinforce particular principles our children need help with – although we should be cautious that they do not see our celebrations as insincere or manipulative.

We don't need to make our children's minor experiences into front-page news, but we can have fun when they do well. Enjoy it. Celebrate it. Do something more than nod 'well done' while chopping carrots for dinner. Pause. Get into the moment. Respond actively and constructively. Celebrate!

Make fun your way

Family life is busy and finding time to have fun can be hard. Being a fun parent requires a degree of proactivity and a playful attitude. Unfortunately fun, for many of us, stopped becoming spontaneous and automatic around the time we decided we had to be responsible adults. But fun can become a habit – we can get into the pattern of putting down our tools (or spatulas or devices, or whatever) and becoming engrossed in five minutes of fun with our children. These micro-moments of positive engagement show that we are involved and available to our children. They teach our children that they are worthy, and they promote a sense of family cohesion and togetherness. They give us moments to be grateful for, to reflect upon and to savour.

> Fun, for many of us, stopped becoming spontaneous and automatic around the time that we decided we had to be responsible adults.

Every family will have different ways of having fun. My children love to jump and wrestle with me. I love to tell them to go and do something, and then hug them tight so they can't get away, all the while playfully reprimanding them for not doing what they were asked and demanding all the more that they go and do it, even though they're entirely stuck in my arms. Some parents have fun with their children by playing online or TV games, other parents cook or do craft, and other parents tell stories. Have fun in your unique way.

There are other advantages to stopping for long enough to play. As we play games with our children, whether formalised or just rolling around on the floor, we model the behaviours we want them to learn. They develop an understanding of cooperative play, relationships, emotional regulation, following the rules and working things out. They learn how to take turns. They also learn to play games that they may otherwise not have understood (like Monopoly, Uno or chess). Once they have learned the games, they can play them independently – we are not always needed (and although that may sound like a relief right now, as they get older we might wish for the days our children invited us to play).

Take-home message

Taking time to smile, have time out (which is really time in), learning new things together, finding a reason (any reason) for treats and celebrating positive experiences with our children all give us opportunities for fun. And when we have fun, our families are happy.

Happy family focus:
Find a way to have fun today

Today, find more to smile about. Drop your agenda and have some fun. Find something new to learn about or explore with your children. Cook treats, buy treats or just eat treats. And find something – anything – to celebrate.

Then, do it again, maybe a little differently, tomorrow.

CHAPTER 17

Practising acceptance and making peace

God grant me the serenity to accept the things I cannot change, the courage to change the things I can, and the wisdom to know the difference.
Reinhold Niebuhr

Although the following story isn't one particular couple's, I put it together based on the combined experience of many families I have worked with. Their names are made up for the purposes of the story and do not represent anyone I have worked with specifically. Like so many couples I see, from the telling of their stories, you would be convinced that they lived in different worlds. But they are married and living in the same home.

David's story

Melissa is awesome. I love her. We have been married for about 12 years now. She has supported me incredibly as I've built my career. She is great with our three daughters.

The thing is, Melissa is not particularly goal-oriented. She's not that keen on working towards anything in particular, either on a personal level, or as a family. I've suggested that she start at the gym to lose some of the weight she's gained since having the girls, but I keep getting raked over the coals for being critical. If I suggest Mel start a uni degree, or anything at all, I get accused of attacking her. I feel like I can't win. To me, life is about improving yourself. Mel seems happy enough as she is.

The thing that has really been getting to me lately is the way she talks to the children, and to me. She sounds angry all the time. I'm not sure if she really is angry. I ask her and she says she's not, but the way that she says it sounds angry. And when I push a little bit to find out whether she is really mad or not, I seem to actually make her angry, and I really cop it.

I really want to connect with her, but our conversations lately are pretty non-existent. She doesn't talk. When I ask her why she's not talking, I get the cold shoulder or I get attacked for attacking her for not talking! I can't win.

The hardest part is that when she snaps at one of the girls, I don't feel as though I can say anything. If I politely ask that she speak softly or nicely to them, I get death stares.

To listen to David's story is to hear a man who is concerned about his relationship with his wife. It is easy to sympathise with David, and to see him as the victim of Melissa's poor emotional regulation. Perhaps one of the central reasons that family life becomes unhappy is that there is a gap between our expectations of how our family should be, and our experience of how our family actually is.

Before you start taking David's side on this, read what Melissa has to say.

Melissa's story

I am just so tired. David thinks that because he goes to work and earns the big bucks, he is doing something special or noble. And he seems to think that I have nothing to do all day except cook a meal, iron a shirt or two, and run the vacuum around the lounge room. It doesn't seem to matter how much I tell him I am struggling, he just doesn't get it.

I had PND after our third baby, and it has been hard to bounce back from that. So right now, with three young children, I'm not interested in setting goals. I just want to enjoy watching the children grow. With a toddler and a preschooler, my days are non-stop. I do craft with the girls, we go for walks, and have stories and playtime. There are meals to prepare, messes to tidy up, activities to schedule, and an entire house to run. It is really full on.

Each morning I wake up with David and help him get organised for work. We have a few minutes over breakfast as a family and he is out the door before 7am. The rest of the day, I'm juggling children, play dates, school, appointments, baby naps, and the endless cleaning, washing, ironing and cooking that every mum has to do.

David comes home around 7pm, if we are lucky. By then the children are pretty ratty, and I'm tired. He kind of expects that everything will be perfect when he walks in the door. He gets stroppy if dinner is late or the children have not had their bath and aren't in their pyjamas. And then he'll ask, 'What have you been doing all day?' It just feels so condescending.

Life is really intense. I don't have the headspace for anything else. So when David starts on about all the other things I should be doing, I feel like I'm not good enough – I don't measure up. No matter what I do, unless I have a degree and I'm earning money outside the home, and still doing everything else for him at home, plus raising the children, it's not enough. I try to tell him that I have a pretty full plate, but he is just obsessed with goals and achievement and looking good.

He points out our friends who are doing it all and thinks they're awesome. I think they're falling apart, but he doesn't see it.

I've kind of given up a bit on our conversations. I'm tired of being made to feel like nothing I do is good enough, and that I forever need to do more and be more so we can have more. When he starts up about it these days, I kind of switch off. But that just makes him mad.

If he would just understand that there is a time and season for things – and that I'm not in the season he wants me to be in – things would be so much easier. And if he could just see that I'm doing the best I can at home while he's at work.

The thing I'm struggling with most is that with all of my exhaustion, I am not inspired to exercise. I want to, but I'm too tired. David keeps at me to join the gym. He wants me to walk with him at night, which means leaving the children in bed alone. When I have gone along with him, he walks too fast for me and tells me to go faster or there's no point walking, and looks for the biggest hills. It's so demoralising. I can exercise in another year or two, once the baby isn't a baby anymore. But right now, I'd really just like some sleep.

How do you read this situation? Who is at fault? Is David right? Should Melissa pick up her game and get focused on achieving? Is Melissa right? Is she justified in wanting peace, quiet, and rest? David and Melissa are focused on self-justification. And when we look at their situation, it is useful to think about how each is assessing the challenges they face.

What would David think the problem is that is preventing them having a truly happy family? Ultimately, David thinks all would be better if Melissa would make a few simple changes. She just has to speak more kindly, do some study, and lose some weight. According to David, Melissa's lack of motivation and consistent complaints of exhaustion are making a happy family impossible. In his mind, Melissa is the problem.

Melissa, on the other hand would probably describe the issues they face in terms of David being the problem: 'The way he treats me is awful. It is not possible for me to measure up to his standards. I can't do it all. He makes me feel less motivated with all of his lecturing. David is the problem.'

And what is David's solution to the problem (of Melissa)? In his ideal world, what needs to happen for family life to be happy? That's simple. Melissa needs to change. She needs to do more. Exercise, study, speak differently. Meanwhile, Melissa's response would be something like: 'David needs to change. If he would just lay off I'd be more motivated to make my own decisions and do what I already know needs to be done.'

So the ideal solution for each is that the other person should change.

The concept of acceptance

Neither person here is thinking about their partner's situation and feelings – in other words, there is limited acceptance of the other person.

David is consistently hounding Melissa to change, Melissa has tried to tell David to lay off and be patient, but at no point has one looked at the other and said, 'Hey, good point. You know, I really do need to change. I can see your perspective, and I think you're right. I really appreciate you pointing out my failings. I'm surprised it's taken me so long, but I'll try what you've suggested. I'm sure it will make a difference.'

Attempts at fixing each other have backfired. David's solution (trying to reason and be logical with an exhausted wife) is actually Melissa's problem. And Melissa's solution (snapping at David and the children, or ignoring her husband when he speaks to her – or perhaps eating chocolate and other comfort food) is David's problem! In his mind, David *has* to prod Melissa or she'll take no action. In her mind, Melissa *has* to fight or withdraw or David won't lay off. She hates his pressure. But her attitude and behaviour *create his need to pressure.* And he hates her nasty attitude or stonewalling, but his attitude and behaviour *create these behaviours in Melissa.*

The way to a happier family is often not more pressure on others to change. Rather, families are happier when there is more acceptance and less controlling behaviour. If we want something to change, we should change ourselves, and not others.

Expectations vs experience

Perhaps one of the central reasons family life becomes unhappy is that there is a gap between our expectations of how our family *should* be, and our experience of how our family actually *is.* We know what it is that we want, but when we are not getting it, we sometimes have difficulty dealing with it. We dream of that perfect Sunday sleep-in, but our slumber is spoiled at 5.30am when our toddler wakes us to let us know that he has wet the bed. 'This is not how it was supposed to be!' we cry as our hopes of a relaxing morning are absorbed into our unplanned early start like the moisture in the mattress into the cleaning cloth.

In situations like this, something inside us resists accepting what has happened and going with it. We feel as though life – and our child – has dealt with us unfairly. We feel short-changed. And what often accompanies this lack of acceptance of things as they are is a strong desire to change things – and the way to change things is to get mad at whoever has caused this inconvenience, and try to fix them. We demand that our children stop wetting the bed, or we demand that they grow up and stop acting like children! These demands might seem justified, but they make no improvements in the happiness we feel, or the happiness our children feel.

> What often accompanies lack of acceptance is a strong desire to change things – to get mad at whoever has caused this inconvenience and try to fix them.

Sometimes our lack of acceptance of things as they are goes beyond the human context. For example, we hope that our weekend camping trip will be bliss, but it rains, the children don't sleep, the food gets spoiled, and there are noisy campers right next to our campsite. Returning home is tense, with feelings of frustration and disappointment destroying the drive. Our inability to accept that sometimes that's just how things go, impacts on our happiness.

Let me speak from personal experience for a moment. I am not a clean 'freak', but I do appreciate things when they are clean and tidy. And they usually are. But in a home where there are lots of children, a business to run, a multitude of extracurricular activities to coordinate, and occasional fun to fit in, there are times when the house does not look particularly tidy. As a result, we have sacrificed several Saturdays to serve the god of sparkling surfaces.

My inability to accept the reality that houses get messy has resulted in substantial cost to our family's happiness. Children are miserable. Parents are bothered. Jobs take longer than they should because of reluctant contributors. And how many hours of genuinely fun times are missed? How many magic moments outdoors, how many cuddles and moments of pure reward with our children do we never have an opportunity to grasp because we had to make things perfect around the house? A lack of acceptance has led to less, rather than more, happiness.

Does this mean we should accept the unacceptable? No. We'll come to that shortly. First, let's take a closer look at the concept of acceptance.

The power of acceptance

One of the more counterintuitive psychological discoveries in recent times is the power of acceptance. It is counterintuitive because we think that for things to improve, it is up to us to change something (or someone – usually one of our children or our spouse). If we accept things as they are, how will things improve?

Acceptance may in fact be the oil that keeps relationships healthy and moving smoothly. A growing body of research suggests that parental acceptance of children, where our children feel loved for being who they are, is a critical protective factor in their lives. Investigations have demonstrated that when children do not feel accepted, they are at greater risk of substance abuse, depression, behavioural problems and conduct disorder.[99]

> When children do not feel accepted, they are at greater risk of substance abuse, depression, behavioural problems and conduct disorder.

The issue is not whether children *are* accepted – most parents will argue that they accept their children. The issue relates to whether or not the children *feel* accepted. The same principle applies to spouses and partners. Each time we respond to another human being in a conditional way – with conditional positive regard – we reduce the extent to which they feel accepted by us. Shouting, criticising, punishing and withdrawing our presence can all contribute to these feelings in our children. Behaviours like those demonstrated by David and Melissa, even when coming from a 'good place', leave people feeling that they are not accepted, and that they are therefore not good enough. The outcome, invariably, is less happiness in our homes.

The research also clearly shows that when we accept our children through offering unconditional positive regard, they enjoy stronger psychological adjustment and higher levels of wellbeing.[100] And evidence suggests that paternal acceptance may be more important than maternal acceptance. Children need to know and feel that their dad loves and accepts them for who they are.[101]

It seems, too, that fathers are more rejecting of their children – more annoyed, frustrated and critical, and more likely to avoid them – than mothers, who tend to be more accepting, on average. (There are some who point to data suggesting that children actually seek acceptance from the parent who has greater power and prestige, which may explain the divergent findings. When mothers are high status and high power, children seem to seek their approval over father acceptance.[102]) And rejection, rather than acceptance, is more common in lower socio-economic settings where parents are less educated.[103]

Take the acceptance test

Consider the following statements about your relationship with your child. Would your child say yes or no to each statement? If you're brave enough, ask your child. Write their yes/no response next to each statement.

a. My parent says nice things about me
b. My parent pays no attention to me*
c. My parent makes it easy for me to tell him/her things that are important to me
d. My parent sees me as a big nuisance*
e. My parent is always telling me how I should behave*
f. My parent is always too busy to answer my questions*
g. My parent is really interested in what I do
h. My parent makes me feel wanted/needed
i. My parent forgets important things I think they should remember*

j. My parent lets me know I am loved

k. My parent treats me gently and with kindness

l. My parent pays no attention to me as long as I do nothing to bother them*

m. My parent wants to control whatever I do*[104]

Of the 13 statements, note that items with an asterisk (*) represent rejecting statements. Of those seven rejecting statements, how many 'Yes' responses did you receive? More 'Yes' responses for asterisked items indicates more rejection and control, and less acceptance. It's good for happiness and wellbeing for this number to be *low*.

The remaining six statements are accepting statements. The more 'Yes' responses you have to these, the more your child feels accepted. This is good for happiness and wellbeing.

How did you go?

Working through that questionnaire with your child may be something of a reality check, but even if the news is bad, that is good. It offers a chance to change. Remember, when our children feel rejected, they suffer. It is better to know that now and do something than to bury our heads in the sand and pretend that everything is okay.

That is why the principles outlined throughout this book are so critical in making families and children happy. Our children need our acceptance, along with our guidance and boundaries. But they need to receive that guidance in ways that show we still accept them in spite of their difficult and challenging behaviour.

The irony is that when we reject them because of their challenging ways of acting, we *get more* of those challenges. David and Melissa's story is evidence of that. Our ongoing efforts to 'fix' others leads to them feeling rejected and controlled, which promotes negative outcomes. But when we accept them *in spite of their challenging behaviour, we get less of those challenges.*

Our children need to receive guidance in ways that show we still accept them in spite of their difficult and challenging behaviour. The irony is that when we reject them because of their challenging ways of acting, we get more of those challenges.

The negative effects of rejection

As we have already seen with the white-bear phenomenon described in Chapter 9, trying to reject our thoughts is ineffective. What happened when participants in the thought-suppression study tried to avoid thinking about white bears? They couldn't stop thinking about them! Yet we do this all the time with others. We are consistently sending messages of rejection and a need to 'shape up' to our family members. Our children (or spouse) feel they are not good enough. They do not receive our affection or comfort. We seem to be grouchy, implacable, cold and unaffectionate, hostile and aggressive, or indifferent and neglecting.[105]

Science tells a compelling story: parental rejection is associated with adolescent psychological disorders, and parental acceptance is associated with better psychological adjustment. Accepting those around us is good for our relationships. It can make our families happier. But it is not easy. I'll describe the process of acceptance in a moment, but first we should also consider the need for acceptance of our own internal states, emotions and thoughts.

Acceptance in action

Imagine that you walk into the living room after asking your children to clean it up. You see them rumbling on the floor with mess strewn all around. You feel stress and anger inside you and you let it out. The family is unhappy and children run to their rooms crying. You go back to the study or kitchen feeling like a failure.

Now let's change it up. Imagine that you walk into the living room after asking your children to clean it up. You see them rumbling on the floor with mess strewn all around. You feel stress and anger inside you. You acknowledge those feelings to yourself, and accept that this is how you feel. Then you say to yourself, 'In spite of my anger and stress, I'm going to act in accordance with my values or guiding principles. I'm going to look for the good, and speak calmly.' At that point, you look at your children and tell them you want their attention.

'Children, I appreciate that you're having fun. But what did I ask you to do?'

The children respond with a dreary, 'Tidy up the living room.'

You smile and say, 'I'm glad you heard me. When can I expect you to take care of it?'

Acceptance of our children or other family members is not indulgence, permissiveness or laissez-faire parenting. This is because acceptance is about accepting what we are feeling and thinking *on the inside*. We cannot always control what happens around us, but we can control our response to it. By showing we accept the people around us unconditionally, and then working on solutions to the issues we face, we get better results with a happier family.

> We cannot always control what happens around us, but we can control our response to it.

I am not suggesting for a moment that such an approach is easy. But it can become so. The power of habit and practice can make it routine – it can become automatic.

In another scenario, you hear screams from the lounge room and race in to find your children attacking each other, fighting with fists, fingernails and feet. Intervention is required. You pull the children apart. If someone is hurt, you tend to them, whether they were the instigator of the fight or not. Next, rather than trying to 'fix' things, or reprimand and offer correction and direction, you then ask who needs some time to calm down.

Once things are calm, you approach each child individually and offer hugs and unconditional acceptance. When they feel safe, you no longer have to fix them. Instead, you can invite them to reflect on what happened and suggest their own solutions.

This kind of acceptance is the essence of what autonomy-supportive parenting looks like. We may make requests and explain why, but ultimately we are interested in collaborative dialogue and encouraging our children to develop their own solutions. Younger children may need more instruction and induction, but when prefaced with hugs and kindness, feelings of acceptance are higher, and better solutions are more likely.

The vicious circle

When our children behave in challenging ways, it is tempting to see *them* as *the problem*. It is normal to want to *fix* them. When we see them like this, they perceive us as not accepting them. They feel unworthy. They take our correction and direction as rejection, and they begin to see us as the enemy.

As we make increasing demands, or respond in punitive ways to the challenging behaviours they exhibit, we reinforce the rejection they perceive. Since they do not feel accepted, and since they see us as their enemy, they respond to us in ever more challenging ways. Power struggles ensue. A vicious circle is created.

Acceptance is a *way of being* that reduces tension, fosters openness and improves relationships. Acceptance is *not* about being a victim. Acceptance is *not* about passivity. Rather, acceptance is about unconditional positive regard for our family, irrespective of their behaviour. It is about recognising what we can and cannot change. And it is recognition that the more we force issues, the more resistance we experience.

When we accept our family members unconditionally *and they feel it*, we can work on positive solutions together because they feel our acceptance and love for being just the way they are.

Acceptance is the recognition that the more we force issues, the more resistance we experience.

Take-home message

Whether the issue is about getting on with siblings, keeping a room clean, keeping a curfew, or any significant parenting problem, our children thrive when they feel accepted. The same applies to our spouses or partners.

Showing acceptance of a person in the face of challenging or unacceptable behaviour is difficult. In these circumstances, it is helpful to remember that a lack of acceptance (and that's rejection) not only makes others feel resentful, it turns our solutions into their problems. Acceptance is an enlightened approach that can make our families happier.

Happy family focus:
Try acceptance for a day

When something happens, just stop and accept that it has happened. Then move on. Sometimes moving on may require stepping in and teaching our children better ways to act. In each situation, see what has happened as something almost detached from you. Take your time accepting and understanding it. Then, when you are calm, respond to it in a peaceful, clear way.

CHAPTER 18

Getting the screen-time balance right

I hate television.
I hate it as much as peanuts.
But I can't stop eating peanuts

Orson Welles

Will is 15. He is compelled to stare at his screen and play games. He doesn't just play the games, he dreams about them. He thinks about them while he eats. He contemplates them as he walks. He reflects on them almost constantly if he cannot play them – which is not very often, because he plays them between 8 and 16 hours each day. Will's compulsion to play impacts on his sleep (he doesn't get enough), his schooling (he refuses to go), his diet (he only eats when somebody brings him food, or when he finally pauses the game to take a bathroom break) and his relationships (they only exist online).

Facing the screen tsunami

'What kind of tablet should I get for my 16-month-old baby girl?'

This was the question from a mum on social media. I was agog. What was even more awful was that the 50 or more responses to this mother's question almost unanimously described how awesome the various tablets on the market were for infants and toddlers.

Today's parents are facing a screen tsunami that is changing the way we interact, learn and live. Children under a year old are swiping, scrolling and playing on screens. Tech has invaded our bedrooms, living rooms ... even our bathrooms! If a teen (or many parents) enter a bathroom with a phone, what once took a few minutes takes at least 10 minutes now. If the WiFi is on in the house, it could take as long as 20 minutes. And heaven help us if they have a charger in there as well – they may never come out!

Decades ago it was discovered that television had the capacity to influence the way in which families communicated and interacted. Because progress was slower than it is today, there was a lot of time for parents to make accommodations for television. With the exceptionally fast progress of more recent technology, phones, tablets, and super-fast internet have seen accessibility skyrocket, and families are struggling to establish limits on how tech can enhance, rather than detract from, family life.

While some parents claim that the only way their family can be happy is if the TV or computer are switched on (because then the children are quiet and parents are sane), we have good evidence that an unbalanced approach to screen time is unhealthy and promotes distress rather than wellbeing.

Screen-time recommendations

Current recommendations for the amount of screen time that is considered healthy and safe suggest that our children under the age of two years have absolutely no screen time at all, and children between two and five years should see less than an hour a day (at the time of writing, the American Academy of Pediatrics was reviewing these guidelines). This advice is clearly being ignored.

Research from the Women, Infants and Children program in

New York[106] found that in the USA 82 per cent of one-year-olds and 95 per cent of two-year-olds watched television and videos on a typical weekday. The research also pointed out that the average amount of screen time increased with age. One-year-olds spent an average of 10 hours per week watching screens, while two-year-olds spent approximately 15 hours per week watching screens. Additionally, of the total sample of two-year-olds in this study, 43 per cent watched more than two hours on a typical weekday. And none of that research includes time on mobile phones, tablets or other electronic devices. (Other research is even more damning, suggesting that more than 60 per cent of preschool-aged children get too much screen time.[107])

> An unbalanced approach to screen time is unhealthy and promotes distress rather than wellbeing.

Even more research tells us that at least 49 per cent of children are comfortably exceeding recommended guidelines,[108] and that it is having a negative impact on them.[109] In a 2013 review of 29 studies (carried out between 1999 and 2013) into the relationship between screen time and childhood outcomes,[110] the following associations related to children's screen time were found:

- Older children watch more TV than younger children
- As TV viewing increased, so too did the child's body mass index, used as a crude measure of overweight and obesity
- The amount of time mum watches TV is strongly linked to the amount of time children watch TV[111]
- The more cognitively stimulating activities that are available in the home, the less screen time children get (this can include things like educational toys and books)
- The more time parents spend reading with their children, the less screens they watch.

The data also show that TV viewing is not correlated with a particular gender, the birth-order of a child, a family's native language or maternal employment. Family structure is also not associated with screen time. Children with both parents at home, one parent, lots of siblings and no siblings all get about the same amount of exposure to screens.

Not all content is created equal

It is well established that there can be some positive educational (or recreational) outcomes from screen time. Unfortunately, however, most of the 'educational' apps, videos and TV programs that are available are not educational at all. Data from a 2015 analysis of educational apps available for phones and tablets showed that well over 90 per cent were the equivalent of fairy floss for the brain – fun now and then, but terribly unhealthy as a consistent part of our diet.

A serious impact on children and families

Some parents think family life is easier if we all just relax a little about screens. Unfortunately, the data would suggest otherwise. (And that's why I'm arguing in this chapter that changing our screen habits will make families happier.) In a National Longitudinal Panel study examining the effects of screen time on youth, researchers interviewed over 700 youths aged 14–24 years.[112] Their discoveries over the course of a year were as follows:

Academic issues

As TV viewing increases, grades drop. Our children's academic activity and achievement suffers when they are absorbed in passive television-watching and screen time. (As a comparison, the more time that children spent reading, the higher their grades were.)

223

Mental health

'Heavy' internet use was associated with increased depression and, conversely, higher levels of depression also predicted heavy internet use. The two seem inextricably intertwined.

Behaviour

Data indicate that increasing time in front of screens is related to a host of negative behavioural outcomes. Children have been shown to experience less behavioural regulation, less emotional regulation, more irritability, higher levels of anger and conflict, and increased violence.

Health

Screen time is inversely correlated with healthy sleep patterns and sleep duration. Our children have poorer sleep the more screen time they experience. Time on tablets, or in front of TV or playing on phones has been linked to diminished levels of physical activity, and increases in overweight and obesity, possibly because of the lack of activity and an inability to recognise satiation signals while snacking.

Consumerism

Data also link screen time with materialism, likely as a result of increased exposure to advertising. With the advent of online crazes like 'unboxing', where children watch unregulated commercial material of other children literally unboxing products for up to 15 minutes per video, there is little wonder that screen time drives materialistic desire. (Some of the children's unboxing videos have had over 50 million views!)

Harmful material

Research indicates that as time in front of screens increases, so too does the risk of our children finding content that may be damaging to them, including drug use, and violent, coarse and pornographic material.

The pornography issue

At least 92 per cent of boys and 61 per cent of girls aged 13 to 16 years have viewed pornography. This may occur inadvertently as children search innocently for G-rated children's videos like My Little Pony, only to discover that cartoon porn is all too accessible, or it may be sought out intentionally. Some children are shown pornography in the schoolyard, at sleepover parties or on the school bus. If there is a screen, there is a risk that inappropriate content will be accessed.

Most boys are consuming pornography regularly, with first exposure on average around age 11. For many, it becomes a habit that intrudes on relationships, schoolwork, sleep, psychological health and more. It is concerning that our children's primary source of sexual (mis)information is now the internet, and the supply is endless.

The content of pornographic imagery has worsened, leaving many researchers and those who work with youth or in health within our communities fearful that our children are being terribly affected by what they are exposed to. A tolerance for porn develops, just like a tolerance for alcohol and other drugs. Soon the 'basics' aren't enough. Common next steps from pictures of naked women are images and videos of intercourse, fellatio and other sex acts.

> Most boys are consuming pornography regularly, with first exposure on average around age 11.

Maree Crabbe, an Australian researcher and documentary-maker in the area of the effects of pornography on children and young people suggests that the usual progression is to violent pornography, followed by images and videos involving larger numbers of participants in those acts. In some instances, curious children may also seek out gay or child-oriented porn as they seek to satisfy their curiosity and the icky cravings they cannot seem to overcome.

Research supports this idea that tolerance is developed and that more extreme images and videos are sought by consumers – including children.[113] Maree Crabbe's Australian data analysis of popular pornography titles indicates that 88 per cent of sex scenes include physical aggression (choking, slapping), and 48 per cent depicted verbal aggression (intimidation, humiliation) with women the victims in 94 per cent of cases. Ironically, the women 'acted' as though they enjoyed the abuse.

While empirical studies cannot prove a causal link at present, some point to pornography as the cause of increased sexual crime, including among young people.[114] Reports indicate that indecent assaults in schools have increased by 60 per cent in the past 10 years (to 2014). Child sex assaults in schools are up 20 per cent. Senior law enforcement officials suggest that access to online pornography has caused sexual assaults by young men to almost double in five years. Family violence and sexual abuse are at epidemic proportions – particularly in remote and indigenous communities – and pornography has been named as contributing to the damage.

Journalist and TV presenter David Frost once said, '[Screens are] an invention that permit you to be entertained in your living room by people you wouldn't have in your home.'

All television and screen time is educational. The question is, what is it teaching?

'[Screens are] an invention that permits you to be entertained in your living room by people you wouldn't have in your home.'

Creating rules and guidelines

So what is the best thing to do about screen usage in our homes? Researchers have discovered a range of set-ups so that screens can be used for the right amount of time each day, and in the right way – in ways that don't lead to unhealthy outcomes, but that actually keep our families happy and help our children thrive.

One of the simplest strategies to improve our children's outcomes is to create family rules or guidelines related to screen time, and then be consistent in the way we stick to them. From the University of Derrr, one review of the research found that having rules around media consumption is linked to less media consumption.[115] Imagine that! While this finding should not be surprising at all, what is surprising is that around one third of preschoolers have parents who do not actually set screen-time limits at all.[116] In effect, one third of preschool children are being told (either explicitly or implicitly) that they can watch as much TV as they want. And 12 per cent of children do not even have limits on the programming they can view. Yikes! So perhaps the idea is not quite so elementary after all. In fact, the research here is even more surprising because some parents who had negative opinions about the effect of TV on their children's learning still didn't really have limits in place.

The research tells a clear story: family rules around screen time are related to lower levels of screen time.[117] The same research also showed that parents need to actually believe that they are capable of keeping children's rooms screen-free, have the skills to limit screen time, and influence their children's screen decisions. You can do it. It is worth the conversation.

If this is something you think would be useful, you may wish to consider creating discussion points for a family meeting and sharing your ideas with your children. The content of this chapter may be helpful. Provide a clear rationale for what you are requesting. Then invite your children to give their input. If they are old enough, a children's council may be appropriate. After they have discussed things, they may share a perspective that differs from yours. Problem-solve together, and make sure everyone is in agreement.

While autonomy-supportive parents minimise the use of controlling techniques, it may be helpful to discuss what the outcome will be if children violate expectations and rules.

Keep your personal viewing habits low

Our children model what we do. We saw this in the Bobo doll experiment described in Chapter 11, and social-learning theory has strong support in relation to the way our children follow our example in screen usage. We cannot be upset with our children for being hooked on screens if we are checking our social media pages, our email, or browsing the web every six minutes, or gaming or surfing cable TV channels for hour after hour. Yelling at the children to get off their bum and go play outside might work briefly, but our example is a critical element in our children's screen choices.

Eat meals together as a family without screens

Research shows that when families eat dinner together, they typically have their screens off, but screens tend to be on when families eat apart.[118] This is key to having a happy family, because research shows that families who eat their meals together have children who grow up to be significantly less likely to drink, smoke, take drugs, or experience internalising (depression and anxiety) or externalising (anger and delinquency) disorders. Conflict will be lower. Their wellbeing is higher – and their dietary intake is healthier!

It seems the thing that leads to these positive outcomes is *not* the meal, though. Instead, it is the time that families talk during the meal that acts as a protective factor in children's lives. Screens interrupt those conversations in dysfunctional ways, and reduce the protection that the family meal offers.

Keep screens out of bedrooms

This may be one of the most obvious yet compelling findings in the psychological research related to screen and device usage.[119] When screens are in bedrooms, children use them. They stare at the box or get busy swiping the screen.[120] They stay in bed but sleep poorly. They interact on social media or with networked online games but have few quality relationships. Their schooling suffers. Their health deteriorates.

Parents have little idea of what their children are being exposed to on their screens, and may find their relationships becoming uneasy as their children are influenced more by the strangers on their screens than their loved ones in their immediate environment.

Using all of the strategies outlined above will have a significant impact on the amount of screen time your family gets. When we don't follow these ideas, chances are that our children will end up well above the screen-time recommendations. And the negative findings apply to little children and big children.[121]

Take-home message

My bias is evident in this chapter – I do not like the extent to which screens dominate too many family agendas and priorities. Screens can be terrific tools, but we ought to remember that they exist to serve us – and not the other way around. We cannot afford for our families to become slaves to our screens, or the outcomes will all too often be negative. Setting clear limits, being a good example, keeping media out of bedrooms and spending time in wholesome recreational family activities are all useful strategies for making screens work for you rather than against you.

Happy family focus:
Organise a family meeting

Make screen-use the top item on your agenda at this family meeting. Share your rationale, invite perspectives, and then set up mutually agreed-upon screen-free times. Perhaps take a holiday from screens altogether and find appropriate activities to replace your screens, and see what it does for your family. Remember, when you remove something, you need to replace it with something, otherwise old habits return.

Don't be ridiculous about it, because sometimes screens can be important and useful. Just see how much screen time everyone thinks they need, and make your decisions from there.

CHAPTER 19

Balancing 'me time' and 'we time'

Investing financial and emotional resources in others is associated with greater happiness than investing in oneself. In short, when it comes to parental wellbeing, you reap what you sow.

Elizabeth Dunn and colleagues

This story comes from a mother I worked with, who had issues about the amount of 'me time' her husband was claiming.

My husband and I have been married for four-and-a-half years, have a two-and-a-half-year-old little man, and are due for baby number two to arrive in around five weeks.

When we got married, I learned that he hadn't taken the time to figure out who he was as a person. I have stepped back to allow him space to try and sort himself out. Unfortunately he has turned selfish. All he wants is time to do what he wants to do, but he never wants to be with us.

For example, when my toddler wakes up at 6am, the first thing my husband will do is turn the TV on for him and then go and sit behind a computer, doing his own thing. I try to go out on family outings, only to find that the atmosphere gets tense from him, as he doesn't want to be out and just wants to be at home – a family gathering to him is putting on a movie to watch together.

I've tried to chat to my husband about these things and why he feels the way he does, and he says it is because he doesn't want to deal with the toddler, or he doesn't want to be out. It is like he only wants time for himself. He recognises that he may be being slightly selfish, but when I push him to become involved, he becomes more stressed and annoyed.

The myth of 'me time'

A pervasive narrative exists in the parenting sphere that says 'me time' is necessary for parent sanity and wellbeing. Articles in parenting magazines and web pages promote this idea by claiming that 'parents feel ripped off because they don't get enough me time.'[122] We are reminded that if we take time out from family life and childrearing, we will be calmer and happier.[123] 'Me time' appears to be the panacea we all need to make our own lives, and the lives of our family members, happier. There is no doubt that the headwinds of work stress and exhaustion can blow us off course, away from that harbour that we have identified as ideal. Other issues related to fear, anxiety and depression can impact on our happiness. And the constant neediness of our children can leave us feeling like we would be more comfortable if the house came and sat on top of us.

For the father in the story at the start of this chapter, 'me time' is not about the classic 'me time' justification – fitting his oxygen mask so he can help another person in need – it is about playing his own game with his own agenda. It is an excuse for selfishness. This kind of 'me time' is ultimately destructive, leaving spouse and children questioning their value, and feeling turned-away-from or turned-against. There is limited emotional availability for family. Instead, the husband in this situation seeks 'me time' to make himself happy at the cost of his family's wellbeing. As we will see later in this chapter, his desire for this time is also likely to be having a negative effect on his personal wellbeing and happiness.

And in my years of working with parents, I have found a strong correlation between parents prioritising 'me time', and parents experiencing a corresponding slump in parenting performance.

What kind of 'me time' are we talking about?

There is no disputing that we need to look after ourselves by sleeping well, eating well and exercising. And, yes, some 'adult' time is helpful, too. Some research promotes meditative and mindfulness practices as beneficial for calming, focusing and centring ourselves. We are told that in an emergency on an aeroplane, adults should fit their own oxygen masks before helping others, including their children. This is logical – we cannot help others if we are dying. To draw the analogy to family life, we cannot be a safe, secure, predictable and happy resource for our children and partner if we are spiralling out of control. We need to take care of ourselves first or we will be no good to anyone else. Martyrdom in family life is typically destructive.

But the parents I all-too-often speak with in my work are usually wanting 'me time' to get time away from their children, full stop. In some instances, this is understandable. Trying to get the house clean while the children are around can be like trying to brush your teeth while you are eating chocolate biscuits – it is hard work. And it does not seem unreasonable to expect to use the bathroom or take a shower without intrusions.

However, the 'me time' I am referring to – and the type the husband in the story at the opening of the chapter seems to want – goes beyond the oxygen mask analogy (for exercise, craft, meditation or maybe a moment of indulgence) or the day-to-day practicalities of personal hygiene and cleanliness. Many parents expect 'me time' because they are sick of dealing with children. In such cases, a week of 'me time' will typically not be enough, nor a month, because at the end of that time we must return to our children and to all of the things that made us crave 'me time' in the first place.

> For some, 'me time' is not about fitting an oxygen mask so we can help another person in need. It is about playing our own game with our own agenda. It is an excuse for selfishness. This kind of me time is unhelpful in creating happy families.

'Me time' as a means of escape

Another mum I coached complained that she never had any time to herself. Her four children were running her ragged. They even had showers with her, and they thought her time on the toilet was exactly when they should try and have important conversations with her. This mum had begun to do whatever she could to shut her children out so she could have some time alone. She found that the resentment she felt towards her children was growing. But even after time out of the house, brief weekends away with her husband, and finding a variety of ways to get more 'me time', this mum found her resentment growing rather than dissipating. She described how she was viewing her children as *more* of a burden. Her thoughts were consistently on finding more opportunities for escape.

In so many cases, 'me time' seems to perpetuate ever-greater needs for more and more 'me time'. Time out from the children is never enough for some parents. Their 'me time' is not about filling their lungs with oxygen before going back to help their children but, instead, it is almost as though life is what happens when they get away from the children.

Many parents I have helped confess that they see their children as a burden, and as an impediment in their otherwise well-ordered life. They want 'me time' not to recharge so they can be better parents, but because they see their children as an obstacle to getting some time to themselves to do the things they want to do.

This narrative is increasingly dominant in the mainstream parenting-ideas world. Several authors have written high-profile books and articles arguing that if we make our own needs subservient to the needs of our children, we create a rod for our backs and ultimately undermine our wellbeing.[124] But such a selfish approach flies in the face of academic research, as well as experience, both ancient and modern.

Happiness is … not having the children

Research tells us, quite clearly, that our happiness drops when we have children.[125] It is not a socially desirable thing to say that our children make us unhappy[126] but in some ways it makes sense. Children get sick. They get tired and irritable. They need our endless help. We get so stressed out that we wash the same load of washing every day for three days because we haven't had time to take it out of the machine and dry it. We don't get any time to ourselves – including in the bathroom. We never get to keep sleeping until our body wakes up naturally – that concept has become a fantasy! And the variety of bodily fluids (not ours) that we have experience cleaning up is often literally breathtaking.

One of the most-cited studies supporting this idea (by Nobel laureate Daniel Kahneman) demonstrates that we typically see time with children as a burden. In this study (which was conducted in 2004, before we had smartphones), a little over 900 American working mums in Texas wore a pager that went off at random intervals. Each time it went off, they wrote down what they were doing and how they felt. At the end of the study, the results were analysed and the researchers found that the average mum was happier shopping, watching TV and talking with friends than she was when playing with the children![127] And that's playing – not even dealing with dramas, finding lost socks and doing all of the other stuff parents have to deal with. Of course, if we asked mum to rank all she had done in a day in order of what made her happiest, playing with children would be far higher on the list – it is socially desirable to say that, and we believe it. This clever study took away the comparison element in the minds of mothers, and their ideas and judgements were revealing.

> Research tells us, quite clearly, that our happiness drops when we have children.

Yes, it sounds jarring, and we should remember that this is only a general finding that doesn't apply to all of us. It's an average. And this is where we should be careful about overinterpreting psychological studies.[128] You see, there are some parents who fall at either end of the spectrum. Some parents really are miserable with their children – even when they play with them (we spoke about that in a previous chapter). Some, though, are exceptionally happy, and they are the ones we want to know more about. They are the ones who have figured out how to have a happier family.

Is 'me time' the best strategy?

So is 'me time' the best strategy? It depends ... but not usually. Recent research has suggested that the way we view our parenting role, and the degree to which we put our children first (child-centrism), is strongly linked with how happy we are as parents, and how happy our family is. The type of parent that I described at the start of the chapter align themselves with the dominant view that exists regarding children. They love their children. They are mostly glad to have had them. But, wow, do they see their children as a pain! Their parenting role is just one more thing they *have* to do. They feel as though parenting really interferes with what otherwise could be a neat, efficient and pleasurable life. That is why they clamour for 'me time' in the mistaken belief that it will refresh them and make them feel like a human again.

They feel as though having children is causing them to miss out on everything else they could be doing. So they take some time out for themselves to do everything that they cannot do because of the children. If our attitude towards our children is one of underlying resentment because they make us miss out on life, we will be unhappy. This is the reason 'me time' is not always healthy. It depends on why we want it, and our approach to it. If it is to get our oxygen mask on and keep ourselves on track, great! If it is an escape that follows on from a resentful sense of frustration toward our children, and a desire to 'just get away', 'me time' may not be the best strategy for creating a happy family.

'Me time' vs 'we time'

What if, instead of getting more 'me time', we focused more heavily on getting more 'we time'? It may seem paradoxical, but research suggests that a child-centric view of family life makes us happier than a self-focused view. Researchers are discovering, more and more, what ancient philosophers have proclaimed for millennia: time and effort given in service with an orientation focused on helping to improve life for others has a wellbeing ripple effect.[129] It impacts on us, those we help and others.

What does this mean for parents? Don't we do enough? Surely taking some time out is good for us.

It may be. I am not suggesting we should never have a moment to ourselves – in fact, we need to make sure we do set aside time for other important relationships, and keep ourselves alive and well. Perhaps that regular yoga class or a hot chocolate with friends is exactly what we need to keep ourselves aligned and on track. This chapter is *not* an argument that anything done for us is self-serving and out of place.

What the data does suggest, however, is that when we invest more time in our children and family – and we do so willingly – the effects are positive, and flow through each of us in ways that increase the happiness and wellbeing of everyone in the family.

In two studies carried out with over 300 participants,[130] researchers asked parents to complete a child-centrism survey that measured their dominant parenting style. They were also asked to complete a measure of happiness and meaning in life derived from having children. For example, they were asked to rate their agreement with statements like 'My children make my life meaningful.' The data demonstrated that more child-centric parents were significantly more likely to report higher happiness and a sense of purpose in life derived from having children. In the second study, respondents were asked to reconstruct the activities of the previous day, and rank the feelings they experienced during those activities. Parents who were more child-centric indicated significantly greater positive feelings, less negative feelings, and experienced more meaning in life during activities in which they were involved with their children. Furthermore, the wellbeing of more child-centric parents remained higher throughout the rest of the day. The researchers suggested that being child-centric does not diminish parental wellbeing, even when parents are engaged with other tasks that do not involve their children.

The authors noted: 'These findings suggest that the more care and attention people give to others, the more happiness and meaning they experience. From this perspective, the more invested parents are in their children's wellbeing—that is, the more "child-centric" parents are – the more happiness and meaning they will derive from parenting.'

238

I suspect that the parents I described at the beginning of this chapter had stopped looking at their children as people, and saw them as things, objects and problems. When we stop seeing our children as people, and instead see them as impediments to our personal preferences being accomplished, we feel stress, anger, frustration and any number of emotions that are unhelpful in getting relationships right. If other people matter to our happiness and wellbeing, and if our relationships predict our happiness more than nearly anything else (see the Introduction to this book), then it makes sense that we should invest in them more, rather than look at them as an obstruction or hindrance in us finding happiness.

> 'The more invested parents are in their children's wellbeing – that is, the more "child-centric" parents are – the more happiness and meaning they will derive from parenting.'

The child-centric stance

The researchers stated, 'Putting one's children at the centre of one's life (thus presumably incurring more costs overtime) does not just enhance parents' theories about how much enjoyment they derive from their children, but is associated with the actual enjoyment and meaning that parents derive from their children.'

This stands in clear contrast to the dominant messages we hear about parenting and who we ought to be looking after – *numero uno*. My own scholarly research, conducted with over 1000 Australian parents, has shown that when parents are oriented towards their childrearing role and see it as what they are supposed to do with their lives (that is, they see parenting as a central aspect of their identity), such parents enjoy greater wellbeing, and their children do too.[131]

Getting the balance right

Those who invest in self over children are unlikely to become selfish narcissists who are doomed to misery if their 'me time' is discerned wisely. We *do* need to give ourselves permission to have our own time. The challenge is that, as much as possible, we seem to be most likely to make our families (and ourselves) happiest when we do all we can to avoid having our 'me time' at the expense of our 'we time'.

How we find this balance will depend on family context. Some parents of young children grab some 'me time' once the children are in bed. (Most young children go to bed early ... don't they?)

Some parents of slightly older children arrange for a babysitter to watch the children once they are asleep, and then they go on a regular date to invest in their relationship. When we were younger, we couldn't afford babysitters, so we took it in turns with some friends, a week about, babysitting each other's children so the alternate couple could have a date.

Ironically, after we spend so much time seeking that 'me time' while they are little, many parents of older children and teenagers indicate they get plenty of time to themselves because they don't see their children enough, and have to work hard on inviting their children back into their lives for some me-time!

Take-home message

Family life *is* tiring, and it is natural and normal to want some time to ourselves, and we should schedule it. But it is worth remembering that the more we *willingly and happily* invest in our relationships with our children, the happier our family will typically be – and the happier we will be, too. Balancing 'me time' and 'we time' is a delicate and sensitive process, but with the scales tipped in favour of family, we will usually find that everyone is happier.

Happy family focus:
Balance up your 'me' and 'we' moments

Think about the 'me time' you have. Is it for restoring balance, or getting away from the family? Schedule 'me time' for when the children are at school, in bed, or away from the family. Schedule 'we time' to maximise positive time together.

Consider the quality of your 'we time' and invest more in 'we time' if that works, and take a look at the way your 'we time' impacts on your personal wellbeing and your family's happiness.

CHAPTER 20

Exploring the pathways to happiness

Enjoy the little things in life, for one day you will
look back and realise they were the big things.

Anonymous

Think back to things you loved the most about your childhood and
your relationship with your parents (or your most significant and
important caregiver). What are the things that stand out as being
the best times? Was it the exciting holidays or the enormously
anticipated birthday gifts? If you were fortunate enough to have
them, there is every chance that you will remember those moments
with joy and gratitude. Whether they were regular occasions or
rare treats, we remember those experiences for good reason – they
were fun and exciting.

Were your best times in your childhood the times when you
were entirely absorbed in an activity, completely engaged? Your
parents may have been playing basketball with you in the driveway
or soccer with you in the backyard. Perhaps they rode along a bike
track or quiet country road with you for hours. You lost track
of time, entirely caught up in the moment, sharing a morning or
afternoon with mum or dad.

Or perhaps it is that quiet moment you had with your mother
or father one day when you were struggling, sitting under a tree
or on a windswept headland. Or the regular Saturday mornings

you spent at hockey, netball or football games. Maybe one of your parents took you on bushwalks or overnight camps. The best times may have been the consistent nightly stories, hugs and kisses before being tucked in to bed.

Orientations to happiness

Researchers have identified that there are three pathways to happiness[132] – pleasure, engagement and meaning. As individuals, we often favour one of these pathways to happiness over the other two, but they could also be used to represent the way in which we seek happiness as a family.

We call this preference for one pathway over the others an orientation, or a way of seeking happiness in our lives. Each pathway, or orientation, is valid. Each contributes to our wellbeing. Each is essential if we want to truly make our families happy.

When we find ways to bring more pleasure, engagement and meaning into our family through routine, activities and our interactions, we boost wellbeing in ways that make our family happier – sometimes lastingly. Let's take a brief, closer look at each orientation to happiness.

Pleasure

The pleasurable orientation describes a person who primarily tries to find happiness in fun and enjoyment. At an individual level, this might mean becoming absorbed in a good book, having a big night out or gorging on a more-ish mud cake. The term 'hedonism' is often used to describe this kind of happiness.

It really means that we're doing whatever we can to maximise what feels good in the moment, and avoiding anything unpleasant. From a family perspective, we find happiness in this way by kicking back on a Friday night with movies and a pizza. It's about fun. The focus is on here and now. Running around and playing with the children is another easy example, or reading books together, or dancing or wrestling.

A pleasure orientation is terrific for happiness in our families in the short-term. When we focus on maximising good feelings, we are happy, engaged in relationships in positive ways and even healthier.[133] However, if pleasure is our only pathway to happiness, we will see our positivity come in fits and starts. We will feel great while we are having fun, then when the hard work starts again, we find that there is no joy.

Those who seek pleasure tend to struggle with discipline. They chafe against routine, prefer to not think about doing any of the work that needs to be done, and become terribly unhappy when the less pleasurable aspects of life demand attention. They are, of course, tremendously happy while things are easy and fun.

But there is limited pleasure to be found in cleaning dishes, tidying bedrooms and doing laundry. Happiness wanes and dissatisfaction ensues when pleasure is our only pathway to happiness. So by all means, take the family to the park, the beach or the movies. Live and have fun, enjoy the pleasures of family life, but remember that 'life isn't all beer and skittles', and expecting it to be so will become a source of disappointment.

Engagement

This is when we look for activities that absorb us – we get caught up in something that is challenging and essentially lose track of time. At an individual level, this may be a craft project, a form of exercise or sport, or doing puzzles or playing challenging games (including video games). At the family level, engagement can come in the same ways, but in doing these things together.

Engagement flows when we are working on a task that is at that perfect level of challenge – where it is not too easy that it is boring, and not so hard that it is dispiriting – and we focus on doing something, pushing ourselves, or enjoying ourselves to the point that we even forget that other things are happening around us. We get caught up in the activity and the moment and the people.

Meaning

Having purpose and finding things we value in our lives brings meaning. For both individuals and families, we find meaning by volunteering our time and serving others (and each other), planning and working towards significant goals we value, expressing gratitude or seeking forgiveness (through letters or meaningful conversations), listening and spending time in developing relationships, or spending time learning and developing. More about this later ...

There is considerable cross-over with these examples – engagement and meaning usually (though not always) involve a degree of pleasure. For example, a conversation might be deeply engaging or enormously meaningful. It may not be until the conversation is over that we realise just how pleasurable it was. And we often enjoy engaging or pleasurable activities and build meaningful relationships and memories. Meaning often (though again, not always) comes from participation in the pleasurable and engaging experiences we enjoy together. At an individual level this can occur, but it is even more likely at the family level because we do these things together.

But washing the dishes is not pleasurable, engaging or meaningful, you say.

Family life is full of activities that are not pleasurable. Picking up our toddler's wet or soiled undies from the carpet is an example; few parents find preparing school lunches engaging; and it can be challenging to find meaning and purpose in attempting to get our teenager to participate in a family meeting. Yet we can do little things to invite pleasure, engagement and meaning into our family activities, even when they are not obviously or inherently any of those things.

Doing the dishes or driving to dancing (or sport, or art class) can become a valuable time to talk with our children about the things that matter in their lives – or about nothing much at all. That is important, too. The mundane can become meaningful. Cleaning a bedroom or doing laundry can become pleasurable, and even fun, as we play creative games with the children or sing songs and talk about what they are learning while we work. Preparing a meal can be incredibly messy, but also wonderfully engaging as we spend time teaching our children how to crack eggs, chop vegetables safely or present a meal appealingly on a plate.

It really comes down to our orientation toward parenting. Are we child-centric and focused on meaningful, positive experiences? Or are we looking at every task involving parenting and family as a burden – something that comes at a cost?

> Doing the dishes or driving to dancing (or sport, or art class) can become a valuable time to talk with our children about the things that matter in their lives – or about nothing much at all. That is important, too. The mundane can become meaningful.

There's something special about engagement and meaning

One of the most interesting findings from research into the three different pathways and orientations to happiness is this: there is a differential effect on our wellbeing, depending on how we try to obtain it.

Pleasure and fun are like the fairly floss of life – light, fluffy and nice as a treat. But they don't seem to bring lasting happiness.

Our lives are a little less satisfying if that is all we have, and if that is all we aim for. The periodic bursts of hedonic happiness feel good in the moment, but are typically short-lived.

Instead, the research suggests we will find long-lasting happiness from engagement and meaning. It seems the things that are built around making small deposits into the emotional bank accounts of those who matter most[134] bring about the greatest levels of happiness, and the greatest long-term wellbeing.

> We make our families happy when we make our
> relationships meaningful.

This research finding is consistent with the dominant message of this book – we make our families happy when we make our relationships meaningful, and we do this by getting things in our relationships right, by engaging mindfully in the moment and being emotionally available, and by choosing peace rather than conflict and being 'right'. We do it by finding effective ways to teach values and principles rather than turning ourselves into our children's enemies. We do it by establishing routines, rituals and traditions that are not just fun, but that provide meaning. And we do it by working together towards an agreed-upon set of goals that we look forward to achieving.

Visit your happiest parent place

I began this chapter by asking you to reflect on the things that made you happiest as a child – times you spent with your parent or another important caregiver that made you feel happy. Take a moment now and reflect on the times that you have been genuinely happiest as a parent. Do you think back to the 'big' experiences you had with the children? Or is it the small moments – the tiny and almost insignificant experiences that could be easily overlooked?

The times I have been happiest as a parent are the times I have been deeply engaged in my relationship with my children – running around outside, catching waves at the beach, riding bikes along the bike track. I used to love watching my little baby crawl away from me before I reached out, grabbed her legs, and gently pulled her back to me, and she would slide along the carpet doing that delightfully contagious nine-month-old's giggle. I recall being at the finish line of one of my daughter's school cross-country races, and seeing flushed red faces sprinting for the line – one of them being hers. Or sitting around the table talking about grateful things, and hearing my two youngest children argue over who would get to ask what everyone was grateful for, because they loved the experience so much.

There are moments when one of my children falls into my arms with heaving sobs because of a heartbreak, and while I sorrow for her pain, I feel deep gratitude that she trusts me enough to come to me for help.

And those precious moments as we say goodnight to our children, and watch them fall asleep – the little ones in our arms, the big ones in their beds, while we pat their backs, sing them songs, and thank heaven for the pure joy they bring to our hearts.

There are countless more tiny reflections – moments in time that fill me with gratitude and a deep sense of happiness that seems as though it might just be everlasting. Some of them are pleasurable, some are engaging, but *all of them* are meaningful.

The meaning that leads to such a deep sense of joy, gratitude and – well – happiness, *only comes because of the absolute focus that I had for my children at that time.* I wasn't checking my social media status, tapping out an email, or thinking about my ever-expanding to-do list. *I was there. In the moment. Witnessing the happiness that my children felt, and experiencing it for myself.* I was being child-centric. The focus was on them. You may have felt the same.

Happiness is ...

This next statement may be the foundation on which this entire book rests:

The compounding effect of our parental presence and focus in all of those micro-moments that could be so easily missed, is what, ultimately, makes families happy. Let me repeat that for emphasis: What makes us happiest – as parents, and as families – is the compounded memories of all of the times we have been truly present in one another's lives, and focused on one another.

Many of our moments in family life lack pleasure, engagement or meaning for us, but that does not need to be so. We can make a decision to make those moments pleasurable. We can make a renewed effort to be more engaged with the moment, and with our children. As we do so, we build memories that provide meaning – and ultimately, happiness – that lasts the rest of our lives.

The compounding effect of our parental presence and focus in all of those micro-moments that could be so easily missed, is what, ultimately, makes families happy.

Take-home message

We can choose to find happiness in our family life through pleasure, engagement and meaning. All three work to make us happy, but engagement and meaning seem to be the most strongly associated with happiness and deep joy.

Happy family focus:
Make some lists and check they balance

Make a quick list of the things you do as a family that are pleasurable.

Now make a list of the things you do that are engaging.

Finally, make a list of the things you do that are meaningful.

How do the lists balance out? Do you have multiple activities in each list? If yes, that's great. If not, consider what you can do to increase the time you spend as a family on all three pathways, with particular emphasis on doing activities that are engaging and meaningful.

CHAPTER 21

Savouring your time together

*Dost thou love life? Then do not squander
time, for that is the stuff life is made of.*

Benjamin Franklin

Some years ago, Kylie and I decided to do something different
at Christmas. Rather than paying for gifts, we decided that we
would make heartfelt and creative homemade gifts. I would love
to say that it was because we are craft-loving, creative people, but
that would not be true – at least not for me. We were going with
the homemade theme because we were living on a student budget
with a mortgage and children – things were tight and Kylie is
remarkably resourceful and crafty.

Homemade gifts require time and a great deal of thought. And
perhaps the most thought of all went into what we might give to
my father. My dad's idea of a perfect gift is to have some time
with everyone, talking together and eating good food. He isn't
into 'presents' at all. This, of course, makes getting him a present
(or making one) nearly impossible. But Kylie had an idea.

At Kylie's urging, I contacted each of my five siblings. I asked
each of them to write out 10 memories, each of them about one
or two sentences long, describing some of their favourite personal
times with dad. They emailed them to me and I printed them on
coloured paper. Each memory was on its own piece of paper, with

a specific colour for each child. That meant we had 60 pieces of paper describing 60 unique and specific memories of time with dad. Each piece of paper was rolled up like a miniature scroll and placed into a glass jar. On Christmas morning we handed Dad his gift. He hefted it in its wrapping, trying to figure out what it might be. His curiosity gave way to bewilderment as he unwrapped the jar to see it full of coloured paper.

'What is this?' he wondered out loud. We watched with baited breath as he opened the jar and reached in, removing one of the coloured scrolls. His eyes scanned the writing, before he looked at one of my siblings and laughed about 'that time' they had together. He looked at the jar again and a look of peace and joy slowly flooded his face as he realised the jar was full of memories just like that one. Slowly, and with wonder and awe, he put his hand back into the jar, removed it and read. This time he wept. Tears of gratitude dropped from his eyes – joy that refused to be held back for even a moment. For the next two hours, this good man, who had given more than 30 years of love and service to his wife and six children, sat on a couch and celebrated the times he had shared with each of us, his children, with tears, laughter and many, many smiles.

Welcome to the practice of savouring

One strategy that makes us happy individually, and that can increase happiness in our families, is the practice of savouring. We savour something when we amplify, extend or magnify a positive experience. Savouring is very much part of the pleasure pathway or orientation to happiness. But it also demands engagement and promotes tremendous meaning.

We can savour things that are happening right now. This is, in some ways, very much like mindfulness. We are absorbed by the moment. We are captivated by it. We breathe it in, and savour it, trying to make it last forever. Savouring might occur as we sit at the table and watch our family talking and laughing together, or while watching our children swimming in a pool or collecting shells at the beach. We smile, soaking up the atmosphere and revelling in the peace we feel as we contemplate the incredible people we have created.

We can savour things that have happened. This is a past orientation to savouring, and it occurs when we remember and reminisce about experiences and memories with our families. This is pleasurable, of course, but it is also wonderfully meaningful as we construct narratives about our past that bind us together. Looking through old photos with our children is a way we can savour the past. Or we might share recollections of events, and talk about what we did, where and when, and how much it means to us now. We might call this form of savouring gratitude. We reflect on what has happened and continue to enjoy it now.

In our home, we have a tradition on birthdays of telling our children the story of their birth. They savour all of the details as we explain how excited we were to know they were coming to our family, how the birth proceeded (complete with Dad speeding to the hospital and hoping the police would catch him and escort him to the maternity ward with flashing lights – they never did), and how filled with love and joy we were when they were born.

You might savour holidays, outings, funny experiences or some other time together that was meaningful.

We can also savour things in the future, before they have even happened. This future orientation to savouring might be called 'hope' or optimism. We can savour our upcoming holiday, delighting in our children's excitement about where we are going and what we will be doing. We can savour a pending birthday, a scheduled graduation, or anything else that we are looking forward to.

About time

Our children are wired to want to be with us. It is a biological imperative that they attach themselves to us at birth, and that desire to remain emotionally attached continues throughout childhood and even into adulthood. If we want a happy family, there is no substitute for time. Time is the universal language of love. Happiness and wellbeing come from time spent in engaging and meaningful activities with our family, and time spent with no agenda at all with those same precious people. If we are engaged emotionally and are making ongoing small deposits into one another's emotional bank accounts (or memory jars) – deposits of kindness, attention, service, gratitude, hope, curiosity, attunement and guidance – we develop within our children a sense of resilience and security, and within our relationships with them, a sense of wellbeing and joy. And it is these times that we savour.

Saving space to savour

So how do we get to a point where we can give our children the time they need to feel loved, and to grow happy and resilient in the midst of the crazy schedules that we keep, with the incessant buzzes and beeps of phones and email, commitments that are necessary to keep the bills paid, and appointments to bolster the development and talents of our children? Where do we find the space to savour life with our family?

This whole book has been about finding time to build our relationships. The steps outlined in the book are really building blocks of time in connection with one another. Take time in communication, time in gratitude, time in guidance, time in fun, and time together in every activity. It has been said that when our children are in our arms, they cannot possibly be underfoot.

The time we spend investing in our relationships with our

children will rarely be the kind of moment that makes it into a 'memory jar'. In Chapter 4, which is about mindfulness, I mentioned that I had been putting self-assembly furniture together. The store where I bought the kit is a little over an hour's drive away, and one of my daughters came along to keep me company.

> When our children are in our arms, they cannot possibly be underfoot.

During the whole journey, I rarely spoke while my daughter told me every possible detail about her life's ambition to be an author. She explored the genres that most excited her, the kinds of characters she wanted to write about, and the people who would read her books. With minimal prompting, she switched from career aspirations to school life to friends, family, her favourite books and movies, her hopes for high school and more. That day is unlikely to be a 'remember when' moment for her. But it was another small deposit of love into our relationship – a deposit that promotes a sense of *amae*, or belonging; a deposit that says 'we are important to each other, we matter'. Abbie has probably forgotten that conversation and that day. But I savour it. And family life is full of experiences like this.

Flecks of gold

I end many of my seminars with the following story:

> A young man heard that the gold rush was on, and he joined the stampede. He staked his claim on a bend in the stream that others had called a river of gold. Day after day the young man placed his pan into the stream. He searched, panned and prayed, hour after hour, for one of those nuggets that would make him rich and fulfil all of his dreams.

255

As the days turned into weeks, and the weeks into months, the young man persevered. He would dip the pan into the water, collect stones and mud, examine each rock hopefully, and then place the stones in a pile at his side. The pile came to be large, until it was almost as big as the young man.

With savings all but gone, his hands wrinkled from being immersed in the water, and his skin sunburnt from day after day in the heat with the sun's rays reflecting off the stream, the young man was despondent. Depressed, he contemplated returning to his home town and asking his parents to take him in so he could start his life again.

While he sat, ruminating and feeling hopeless, a wealthy and successful prospector walked by. The man's face was weathered. He wore old clothes and boots, his hands covered in mud and callouses, and his grey beard hiding his mouth and chin.

'That's quite a pile of rocks you've accumulated there my boy,' he chuckled to the young man.

The young man responded with gentle but clear disdain. 'I've been here for months. Everyone says there are gold nuggets here, but I can't find any. They promised rivers of gold. It's just a river of mess.'

'Oh there's gold here, all right,' replied the old man. The prospector picked up a small handful of the rocks in the young man's pile, bouncing them in his palm. He crouched down and randomly selected one of them from the small pile resting in his hand. Picking up the young man's pan, the prospector split the rock open on the edge of the pan. Then he pointed to the tiny flecks of gold, glinting in the sunlight, surrounded by dirt and pebble. 'You're sitting on a pile of gold right here. Look at all of these flecks. It's right here, waiting for you.'

'I don't want little flecks of gold like that.' The young man was annoyed. 'I'm looking for the nuggets that everyone seems to be talking about, but that *I* don't seem to be able to find. I want nuggets like those ones in your pouch!'

At this, the young man gestured clearly at the pouch sagging heavily at the prospector's waist.

The prospector raised his eyebrow and smiled kindly, before slowly opening the top of his pouch to reveal no nuggets but, instead, thousands and thousands of gold flecks just like those in the rocks at the young man's side.

'My boy,' he began. 'There are nuggets in this stream – you mark my words. But they don't come along all too often. They do from time to time, to be sure, but if you live only for them, you will have a lot of poor days between occasional rich days.'

He paused, before softly continuing, 'It is the steady accumulation of these flecks of gold that has made me rich – and it can do the same for you if you treasure them for what they are. Real gold.'

There are wonderful gold nuggets of joy and delight that we experience in our families from time to time. However, more common are the overlooked gold flecks that are so easily hidden in the messy, rocky, dirty everyday work of family life. It is our work, as parents who wish to bring more joy and wellbeing into our families, to find those flecks of gold in the mundane, and to savour them as treasured miracles.

Take-home message

We strengthen relationships and build bonds by spending time with one another. Just as dollars are the currency of our economy, attention is the currency of our relationships. As we give time and attention to our children, we will make our family happy. And we will find that we have a wonderful past and present to savour, with the hope that good times are ahead.

Happy family focus:
Savour your experiences as a family

- Spend some time with your family looking through old photos and talking about memories.
- Focus more on being right here, in the moment, and observing the good experiences you have as a family.
- Have conversations with your children about the things you can't wait to happen. Share your ideas together.
- At dinner, or on a quiet Sunday afternoon, encourage everyone to talk about their favourite times as a family.

Creating your happy family

Families get stuck in patterns. Some of them are good, healthy, positive and functional patterns. These are patterns we can be grateful for, and these are patterns this book is all about helping you establish.

Unfortunately, however, some of patterns we get stuck in are unhealthy and dysfunctional. With insight and will, we discover which patterns are leading to poor outcomes for our children, and we decide it is time to change. Big decisions are made. Commitments are created that are aimed at massive shifts in behaviour, attitude and habit.

A friend on a fitness bender tweeted, 'Day two of my #12weekchallenge and just had pizza and champagne for dinner #dietfail'. Good intentions only go so far. Sometimes we slot right back into those old patterns and behaviours, just like the participants in the change activity in my presentations that I described in the Introduction to this book. Perhaps we decide that the best way to make change is to get out of our environment for a while, so we schedule a family holiday. But we come back. We need more than a break – we need strategies, skills and a heart that says, 'I am committed to making things better.'

The purpose of this book is to share 21 principles of parenting that can bring greater happiness to your family. As you have read through the book, hopefully you have already tried a couple of these ideas, and they're making a difference.

I know there is a long list of habits and ideas to implement, and hopefully you have not tried to implement them all at once, or else you'll fail – badly! It will be too much, too fast. Perhaps you've tried to get fit fast. You go to boot camp on Day One and work out with all you've got. On Day Two you wake up and can hardly move. Then it takes a week to recover, and you give up. Old habits are easier and they hurt less. Going too far too fast reminds of this. Instead, I'd suggest that you choose one or two of the ideas in the book and sit with them for a few weeks. Work on them daily. Make them a habit. Then come back and pick something else that feels right.

Start today. Do something small. Build on it. You can do it.

You may find that something which seemed impossible when you first read the book feels entirely reasonable and doable a few months later with some new habits, routines or ways of being towards your children in place.

Turning ideas into habits

Starting is often the hardest part. If you are unsure about how to start, let's take a moment and consider what research tells us about creating a new habit. Studies indicate that we should start small, find an anchor and celebrate our successes.

We will take a look at three examples from the book to illustrate how simple it can be to make this work.

Start small
   i.   Starting small might mean talking about grateful things.
   ii. Starting small might be creating one simple tradition.
   iii. Or starting small could be making yourself more child-centric and focused on the children.

Find an anchor
If we were to use these three small changes as examples, we would next find an anchor to tie the new behaviour to.

i. Grateful things might be anchored to dinner each night, or the drive home from school each afternoon.

ii. Starting a new tradition might mean that you notice on your calendar that every Saturday morning you do the grocery shopping or have children's sport – so you decide that you'll take the children with you and have a milkshake or ice-cream before or after the shopping or their sports activity. Or you might have your spouse or partner (if available) take the children for treats while you get your chores done! Either way, it is family time anchored to another behaviour.

iii. Making yourself more child-centric and focused on the children could be anchored to your children's challenging behaviour. Instead of getting uptight, annoyed and frustrated, perhaps you could use their challenges as a call to action – an anchor that drags you away from what you are doing and into their world for 10 minutes of absolute focused time.

Celebrate every success

If you succeed, even once, at acting out your desired behaviour by anchoring it to some pre-existing action (or as a stand-alone behaviour), acknowledge it to yourself. Celebrate it. Immediately.

You are on your way to doing something great for your family! Keep it up and it will be part of your routine before you know it.

It might be useful to understand that our brains are quite poor at recognising the difference between doing something seriously awesome and feeling good about it, and doing something tiny (but still awesome) and feeling good about it. When we feel awesome, we build momentum. We feel optimistic and hopeful. We create a sense of confidence and self-efficacy (or belief in ourselves), and the habit becomes cemented – potentially in less than 21 days.

Then ... it's onward and upward. Bigger habits. Tougher challenges. More opportunities to strengthen your family and be happier. And all along the way we are re-wiring our brain, creating new neural networks that can become dominant neural super-highways as we embed these habits into our every interaction with a member of our family. Our typical responses to situations change from what they are now, to what we want them to be and have begun to practice.

When are you happiest?

Some years ago a client sought help from me to make her family happier. With her husband, we began discussing strategies that might make an impact on how the family functioned, and how everyone related to one another. They determined that screen-free family dinners might help, and that discussing grateful and happy things was something small that they could implement immediately.

A week after our initial discussion we got together to talk about their progress. Success! Family dinners were working, and they felt their family was happier. They then shared the following experience.

> We were seated at dinner and talking about our grateful
> things. The children all shared their ideas and so did we.
> Then we asked about what had made us happiest that day.
> One of our daughters was quiet for a while as she thought.
> Then she looked up at us, and with tears in her eyes, said,
> 'Right now. Right now is the thing that has made me
> happiest today.'

Where do I start?

Let's take a look at where you might start on the road to a happier family. I have two questions that should guide you.

Firstly, what does your goal look like? The first chapter of this book is dedicated to knowing where you want to go as a family. Where is your safe harbour? What would a happier family be for you? What would it mean? What would you do?

Remember, we don't become a fully happy, fully functional, perfected family in 21 days. Our goal has to be realistic. We might not be perfectly happy, but we *can* be happier than we are today.

Secondly, if you want to be happier, what do you believe you can change? Start there.

Just choose one thing. Change it. You might make the change by anchoring your new habit to a pre-existing behaviour. You might just go cold turkey! Whatever you do, do it. Don't try and do it. There is no try. Just do it. And if (when) you fall short, acknowledge it, learn from it, apologise for it, and do it right next time.

If you have ever climbed a mountain you may have experienced that moment when you wondered if you would ever reach the summit. You may have been climbing for hours. From time to time you may have caught glimpses of the top of the mountain way up above, and each time you saw it, you may have groaned, wondering if you were making any progress at all. Every now and then, however, you may have turned around and looked back over where you came from. Each time you did that, you would have realised that while the summit was still quite a way off, looking back was a powerful way to see just how far you had come.

Making our families happy can be like that mountain. We need to see the top and keep focused on the ideal vision. But we need to stop, enjoy the view, savour the progress we have made, and enjoy the journey.

Where are we going?

I don't know that we will ever get things totally happy and completely 'right' in our families. Truthfully, I'm not convinced that we're supposed to. I suspect that family life is designed to test us and try us in order to refine our characters and teach us the life lessons and wisdom that cannot be acquired in any other context. If we let it, family life can make us far better people than we might ever have been otherwise.

The relentless and overwhelming demands that encroach on our lives are challenging, but when we see those challenges as an opportunity to grow in character, maturity and goodness, we are more likely to willingly surrender our self-centred focus and find greater joy in dedicating ourselves to the wellbeing of those we love the most.

And that will go a long way to making us happier – and our families happier.

Endnotes

1 Steger, M. F., Kashdan, T. B., & Oishi, S. (2008). Being good by doing good: Daily eudaimonic activity and wellbeing. *Journal of Research in Personality, 42*, 22–42.

2 This finding has been emphasised repeatedly by one of the fathers of the Positive Psychology movement, the late Christopher Peterson, who argued that the most important thing we've discovered about happiness in life is that 'other people matter'.

See also chqdaily.com/2013/07/23/putnam-strongest-predictors-of-happiness-are-social-relationships/ retrieved 20 February 2014.

3 Pascual-Leone, A., Amedi, A., Fregni, F., & Merabet, L. B. (2005). The plastic human brain cortex. *Annual Review of Neuroscience, 28*, 377–401. Rakic, P. (January 2002). Neurogenesis in adult primate neocortex: an evaluation of the evidence. *Nature Reviews Neuroscience, 3* (1): 65–71. Much of the science related to neuroplasticity was popularised by Norman Doidge is his bestselling book: Doidge, N. (2007). *The Brain that Changes Itself: Stories of personal triumph from the frontiers of brain science.* New York: Viking.

4 The quote is ascribed to Emerson, but the quote is not found in *The Works of Ralph Waldo Emerson.* See www.rwe.org/resources/search-rweorg for more information and to search his works.

5 Baumeister, R. F., & Tierney, J. (2011). *Willpower.* New York: Penguin.

6 Lally, P., Van Jaarsveld, C. H. M., Potts, H. W. W., & Wardle, J. (2010). How are habits formed: Modelling habit formation in the real world. *European Journal of Social Psychology, 40*, 998–1009.

7 Drucker, P. F. (1974). *Management: Tasks, responsibilities and practices.* New York, NY: Butterworth & Heinemann.

8 Covey, S. R. (2000). *The 7 Habits of Highly Effective People.* Melbourne, Australia: The Business Library.

9 Braun, S., Wesche, J. S., Frey, D., Weisweiler, S., & Peus, C. (2012). Effectiveness of mission statements in organizations: A review. *Journal of Management and Organization, 18.4*, 430–444.

See also Desmidt, S., Prinzie, A., & Decramer, A. (2011). Looking for the value of mission statements. A meta-analysis of 20 years of research. *Management Decision, 49*, 468–493.

10 Benveniste, J. (2011). *The Parent Manifesto.* Belair, South Australia: Parent Wellbeing.

11 Covey, S. R. (1997). *The 7 Habits of Highly Effective Families*. St Leonards, NSW: Allen & Unwin.

12 Grieger, R. (2011). Creating vision, mission, and values for couples in counseling. In H. G. Rosenthal (Ed.). *Favorite Counseling and Therapy Techniques*. 2nd Edition. New York: Routledge.

13 Locke, E. A., & Latham, G. P. (2002). Building a practically useful theory of goal setting and task motivation: A 35-year odyssey. *American Psychologist, 57,* 705–717.

14 All references to parenting style throughout this chapter are derived from the extensive work done on the subject by Baumrind, D. (1967). Child-care practices anteceding three patterns of preschool behaviour. *Genetic Psychology Monographs*, 43–88. This typology was added to in 1983 by Maccoby and Martin in this paper: Maccoby, E. E., & Martin, J. A. (1983). Socialization in the context of the family? Parent-child interaction. In P. H. Mussen & E. M. Hetherington, *Handbook of Child Psychology: Vol. 4. Socialization, personality, and social development* (4th ed.). New York: Wiley.

For references that deal more directly with the ways that parenting style can affect child outcomes, the following works can be helpful, but are not exhaustive:

Cablova, L., Pazderkova, K., & Miovsky, M. (2014). Parenting styles and alcohol use among children and adolescents: A systematic review. *Drugs: Education, Prevention and Policy, 21,* 1–13.

Darling, N., & Steinberg, L. (1993). Parenting style as context – an integrative model. *Psychological Bulletin, 113,* 487–196.

Dornbusch, S. M., Ritter, P. L., Leiderman, P. H., Roberts, D. F., & Fraleigh, M. J. (1987). The relation of parenting style to adolescent school performance. *Child Development, 58,* 1244–1257.

Huebner, A. J., & Howell, L. W. (2003). Examining the relationship between adolescent sexual risk-taking and perceptions of monitoring, communication, and parenting styles. *Journal of Adolescent Health, 33,* 71–78.

Radziszewska, B., Richardson, J. L., Dent, C. W., & Flay, B. R. (1996). Parenting style and adolescent depressive symptoms, smoking, and academic achievement: Ethnic, gender, and SES differences. *Journal of Behavioural Medicine, 19,* 289–305.

Smetana, J. G. (1995). Parenting styles and conceptions of parental authority during adolescence. *Child Development, 66,* 219–316.

15 Baumrind, D. (1966). Effects of authoritative parental control on child behaviour. *Child Development, 37,* 887–907.

16 Kohn, A. (2014). *The Myth of the Spoiled Child*. Boston, MA: Da Capo.

17 Baumrind, D. (1972). Some thoughts about childrearing. In U. Bronfenbrenner (Ed.). *Influences on Human Development*. Hinsdale, IL: Dryden Press.

18 There is a number of studies that support the argument in this paragraph and that provide important insight into the challenges associated with operationalising the various Baumrind parenting styles in the way that they are developed and defined. They also point to the controlling aspects of Baumrind's model as being unhelpful to raising happy, healthy children and instead suggest that these components undermine the positive outcomes that are experienced in families where parents are available, warm, and talk with their children about boundaries, deferring to them for decisions about their participation in certain activities or behaviours. These studies include, but are not restricted to:

Lamborn, S. D., Mounts, N. S., Steinberg, L., & Dornbusch, S. M. (1991). Patterns of competence and adjustment among adolescents from authoritative, authoritarian, indulgent, and neglectful families. *Child Development*, 62, 1049–1065.

Lewis, C. C. (1981). The effects of parental firm control: A re-interpretation of findings. *Psychological Bulletin*, 90, 547–563.

Strage, A., & Brandt, T. S. (1999). Authoritative parenting and college students' academic adjustment and success. *Journal of Educational Psychology*, 91, 145–156.

Weisee, L. H., & Schwarz, J. C. (1996). The relationship between parenting types and older adolescents' personality, academic achievement, adjustment, and substance use. *Child Development*, 67, 2101–2114.

19 Joussemet, M., Landry, R., & Koestner, R. (2008). A self-determination theory perspective on parenting. *Canadian Psychology*, 49, 194–200.

20 Grolnick, W. S., Frodi, A., & Bridges, L. (1984). Maternal control style and the mastery motivation of one-year-olds. *Infant Mental Health Journal*, 5, 72–82.

21 Frodi, A., Bridges, L., & Grolnick, W. S. (1985). Correlates of mastery related behavior: A short-term longitudinal study of infants in their second year. *Child Development*, 56, 1291–1298.

22 Joussemet, M., Landry, R., & Koestner, R. (2008). A self-determination theory perspective on parenting. *Canadian Psychology*, 49, 194–200.

23 Padilla-Walker, L. M., Fraser, A. M., & Harper, J. M. (2012). Walking the walk: The moderating role of proactive parenting on adolescents' value-congruent behaviour. *Journal of Adolescence*, 35, 1141–1152.

24 Nelson, L. J., Padilla-Walker, L. M., & Nielsen, M. G. (2015). Is hovering smothering or loving? An examination of parental warmth as a moderator of relations between helicopter parenting and emerging adults' indices of adjustment. *Emerging Adulthood*, published online March, 2015.

25 Boles, R. E., Reiter-Purtill, J., & Zeller, M. H. (2013). Persistently obese youth: Interactions between parenting styles and feeding practices with child temperament. *Clinical Pediatrics*, 52, 1098–1106.

26 Vollmer, R. L., & Mobley, A. R. (2013). Parenting styles, feeding styles, and their influence on child obesogenic behaviours and body weight. A review. *Appetite, 71*, 232–241.

Tata, P., Fox, J., & Cooper, J. (2001). An investigation into the influence of gender and parenting styles on excessive exercise and disordered eating. *European Eating Disorders Review, 9*, 194–206.

27 Goldstein, S., & Brooks, R. B. (2006). *Handbook of Resilience in Children.* New York: Springer.

28 Nelsen, J. (1987). *Positive Discipline.* New York: Ballantine Books.

29 Coulson, J. C., Oades, L. G., & Stoyles, G. J. (2012). Parents' subjective sense of calling in childrearing: Measurement, development and initial findings. *Journal of Positive Psychology, 7*, 83–94.

30 Kashdan, T. B., & Ciarrochi, J. (2013). *Mindfulness, Acceptance, and Positive Psychology: The seven foundations of well-being.* Oakland, California: Context Press.

31 Hafenbrack, A. C., Kinias, Z., & Barsade, S. G. (2014). Debiasing the mind through meditation: Mindfulness and the sunk-cost bias. *Psychological Science, 25*, 369–376.

32 Teper, R., Segal, Z. V., & Inzlicht, M. (2013). Inside the mindful mind: How mindfulness enhances emotion regulation through improvements in executive control. *Current Directions in Psychological Science, 22*, 449–454.

33 Williams, J. M. G., Crane, C., Barnhofer, T., Brennan, K., Duggan. D. S., Fennell, M. J. V., et al. (2014). Mindfulness-based cognitive therapy for preventing relapse in recurrent depression: A randomized dismantling trial. *Journal of Consulting and Clinical Psychology, 82*, 275–286.

34 Bowen, S., Witkiewitz, K., Clifasefi, S. L., Grow, J., Chawla, N., Hsu, S. H., et al. (2014). Relative efficacy of mindfulness-based relapse prevention, standard relapse prevention, and treatment as usual for substance use disorders: A randomized clinical trial. *JAMA Psychiatry,* Published online March 19 2014. doi:10.1001/jamapsychiatry.2013.4546

35 Killingsworth, M. A., & Gilbert, D. T. (2010). A wandering mind is an unhappy mind. *Science, 330*, 932.

36 Wilson, T. D. et al. (2014). Just think: The challenges of the disengaged mind. *Science, 345*, 75–77.

37 Wilson, T. D. et al. *Science, 345*, 75–77 (2014).

38 This research used observational and interview techniques with a relatively small sample. Therefore results should be treated with caution. Hiniker, A., Sobel, K., Suh, H., Sung, Y., Lee, C. P., & Kientz, J. A. (2015). *Texting while Parenting: How adults use mobile phones while caring for children at the playground.* University of Washington. dub.washington.edu/pubs/398

39 Kashdan, T. B., & Ciarrochi, J. (2013). *Mindfulness, Acceptance, and Positive Psychology: The seven foundations of well-being.* Oakland, California: Context Press.

40 Vaillant, G., & Mukamal K. (2001). Successful aging. *American Journal of Psychiatry, 158,* 839–847.

41 Retrieved from www.theatlantic.com/magazine/archive/2009/06/what-makes-us-happy/307439/ on 26 March 2014.

42 Vaillant, G. E. (2012). *Triumphs of Experience: The men of the Harvard Grant Study.* Cambridge, Mass: Belknap Press.

43 For examples (among many) that support the notion that parental care has a powerful impact on the resilience and wellbeing of children, see the following:

Cederblad, M. (1996). The children of the Lundby study as adults: A salutogenic perspective. *European Child & Adolescent Psychiatry, 5 (supp 1),* 38–43.

Fergusson, D. M., & Lynskey, M. T. (1996). Adolescent resiliency to family adversity. *Journal of Child Psychology and Psychiatry, 37,* 281–292.

Masten, A. S., & Coatsworth, J. D. (1998). The development of competence in favorable and unfavorable environments: Lessons from research on successful children. *American Psychologist, 532,* 205–220.

Werner, E. E. (2006). What can we learn about resilience from large-scale longitudinal studies? In S. Goldstein & R. B. Brooks (Eds.). *Handbook of Resilience in Children.* New York: Springer.

Werner, E. E., & Smith, R. S. (1992). *Overcoming the Odds: High-risk children from birth to adulthood.* New York: Cornell University Press.

44 Moullin, S., Waldfogel, J., & Washbrook, E. (2014). *Baby Bonds: Parenting, attachment and a secure bond for children.* London: The Sutton Trust.

45 Brooks, D. (2012). The heart grows smarter. *New York Times,* 5 November.

46 Gottman, J. M. & DeClaire, J. (2001). *The Relationship Cure: A 5-Step guide to strengthening your marriage, family, and friendships.* New York: Three Rivers Press.

47 Halfon, N. (2012). *Could texting while parenting harm baby's development?* Retrieved from blog.nj.com/njv_guest_blog/2012/06/could_texting_while_parenting.html on 26 March 2014.

48 Maher, K. (2014). The new ground rules for parenting. *The Times.* Retrieved from www.thetimes.co.uk/tto/life/article4040993.ece on 28 March 2014.

49 Williams, K. D. (2007). Ostracism. *Annual Review of Psychology, 58,* 425–452.

50 Williams, K. D., Cheung, C. K. T., & Choi, W. (2000). Cyberostracism: Effects of being ignored over the internet. *Journal of Personality and Social Psychology, 79,* 748–762.

Twenge, J. M., Baumeister, R. F., DeWall, C. N., Ciarocco, N. J., & Bartels, J. M. (2007). Social exclusion decreases prosocial behaviour. *Journal of Personality and Social Psychology, 92,* 56–66.

51 Rothbaum, F., Weisz, J., Pott, M., Miyake, K., & Morelli, G. (2000). Attachment and culture – security in the United States and Japan. *American Psychologist, 55,* 1093–1104.

52 The following references may be useful for those interested in the concept of 'mattering':

Demir, M., & Davidson, I. (2013). Toward a better understanding of the relationship between friendship and happiness: Perceived responses to capitalization attempts, feelings of mattering, and satisfaction of basic psychological needs in same-sex best friendships as predictors of happiness. *Journal of Happiness Studies, 14,* 525–550.

Demir, M., Özen, A., Dogan-Ates, A., Bilyk, N., & Tyrell, F. (2011). I matter to my friend, therefore I am happy: Friendship, mattering, and happiness. *Journal of Happiness Studies, 12,* 983–1005.

Marshall, S. K. (2001). Do I matter? Construct validation of adolescents' perceived mattering to parents and friends. *Journal of Adolescence, 24,* 473–490.

53 Froh, J. J., Emmons, R. A., Card, N. A., Bono, G., & Wilson, J. A. (2011). Gratitude and the reduced costs of materialism in adolescents. *Journal of Happiness Studies, 12,* 300.

54 Rather than listing dozens of these studies, I refer the reader to two of the more authoritative books on the subject, both by Robert Emmons. These books outline all of the research described and present even more correlates of gratitude than those listed in the chapter.

Emmons, R. A. (2007). *Thanks! How the New Science of Gratitude Can Make You Happier.* New York: Houghton Mifflin.

Emmons, R. A. (2013). *Gratitude works! A 21-day Program for Creating Emotional Prosperity.* San Francisco, CA: Jossey-Bass.

For an empirical review, see Wood, A. M., Froh, J. J., & Geraghty, A. W. A. (2010). Gratitude and well-being: A review and theoretical integration. *Clinical Psychology Review, 30,* 890–905.

55 Emmons, R. A., & McCullough, M. E. (2003). Counting blessings versus burdens: An experimental investigation of gratitude and subjective wellbeing in daily life. *Journal of Personality and Social Psychology, 84,* 377–389.

56 Emmons, R. A. (2007). *Thanks! How the new science of gratitude can make you happier.* New York: Houghton Mifflin.

57 Dunn, J. R., & Schweitzer, M. E. (2005). Feeling and believing: The influence of emotion on trust. *Journal of Personality and Social Psychology, 88,* 736–748.

58 Helgeson, V. S., Reynolds, K. A., & Tomich, P. L. C. (2006). A meta-analytic review of benefit finding and growth. *Journal of Consulting and Clinical Psychology, 74,* 797–816.

59 Hugo, V., & Wilbour, C. E. (1992). *Les Misérables.* New York: Modern Library.

60 Taylor, S. E., & Brown, J. D. (1988). Illusion and Well-being: A social psychological perspective on mental health. *Psychological Bulletin, 103,* 193–210.

61 Weinstein, N. D. (1980). Unrealistic optimism about future life events. *Journal of Personality and Social Psychology, 39,* 806–820.

62 Gallagher, M. W., Lopez, S. J., & Pressman, S. D. (2013). Optimism is universal: Exploring the presence and benefits of optimism in a representative sample of the world. *Journal of Personality, 81,* 429–440.

63 Khallad, Y. (2013). Dispositional optimism and physical wellbeing: The relevance of culture, gender, and socioeconomic status. *International Journal of Psychology, 48,* 978–985.

64 Seligman, M. E. P. (1995). *The Optimistic Child.* Sydney: Random House.

65 Lopez, S. J. (2012). The how of hope. *The Phi Delta Kappan, 93,* 72–73.

66 Bryant, F. B., & Veroff, J. (2007). *Savoring: A new nodel of positive experience.* New York: Lawrence Erlbaum Associates.

67 Cox, M. (2012). *The Book of New Family Traditions (Revised and updated): How to create great rituals for the holidays and every day.* Kindle edition.

68 Duke, M.P., Lazarus, A., & Fivush, R. (2008). Knowledge of family history as a clinically useful index of psychological well-being and prognosis: A brief report. *Psychotherapy Theory, Research, Practice, Training, 45,* 268–272.

69 Malaquias, S., Crespo, C., & Francisco, R. (2015). How do adolescents benefit from family rituals? Links to social connectedness, depression, and anxiety. *Journal of Child and Family Studies, 24,* 3009–3017.

70 Wegner, D. M., & Schneider, D. J. (2003). The white bear story. *Psychological Inquiry, 14,* 326–329.
Wegner, D. M., Schneider, D. J., Carter, S. R., & White, T. L. (1987) Paradoxical effects of thought suppression. *Journal of Personality and Social Psychology, 53,* 5–13.

71 Muiz, E. I., Silver, E. J., & Stein, R. E. K. (2014). Family routines and social-emotional school readiness among preschool-age children. *Journal of Developmental and Behavioral Pediatrics, 35,* 93–99.

72 Biggs, S. N., Lushington, K., van den Heuvel, C. J., Martin, A. J., & Kennedy, J. D. (2011). Inconsistent sleep schedules and daytime behavioral difficulties in school-aged children. *Sleep Medicine, 12,* 780–786.

73 Brotherson, S. E. (2012). Anger, puffer fish parenting, and love. *Meridian Magazine.* Retrieved from ldsmag.com/article-1-10067 on 29 March 2014.

74 Myron-Wilson, R. (1999). *Parental style and how it may influence a child's role in bullying.* Paper presented at the Biennial Conference of the Society for Research in Child Development (Albuquerque, NM, April 15–18).

Chang, L., Schwartz, D., Dodge, K. A., & McBride-Chang, C. (2003). Harsh parenting in relation to child emotion regulation and aggression. *Journal of Family Psychology, 17,* 598–606.

Duong, M. T., Schwartz, D., Chang, L., Kelly, B. M., & Tom, S. R. (2009). Associations between maternal physical discipline and peer victimization among Hong Kong Chinese children: The moderating role of child aggression. *Journal of Abnormal Child Psychology, 37,* 957–966.

75 Definitions accessed from Merriam-Webster dictionary online. Retrieved from www.merriam-webster.com/dictionary/discipline on 29 March 2014.

76 Bandura, A., Ross, D., & Ross, S. A. (1961). Transmission of aggression through the imitation of aggressive models. *Journal of Abnormal and Social Psychology, 63,* 575–582.

77 Grusec, J. (1992). Social learning theory and developmental psychology: The legacies of Robert Sears and Albert Bandura. *Developmental Psychology, 28,* 776–786.

78 Ferguson, C. J. (2010). Blazing angels or resident evil? Can violent video games be a force for good? *Review of General Psychology, 14,* 68–81.

79 Moses Passini, C., Pihet, S., & Favez, N. (2013). Assessing specific discipline techniques: A mixed-methods approach. *Journal of Child and Family Studies,* no pagination specified. DOI 10.1007/s10826-013-9796-0.

80 Ming-Te Wang, Sarah Kenny. Longitudinal Links Between Fathers' and Mothers' Harsh Verbal Discipline and Adolescents' Conduct Problems and Depressive Symptoms. *Child Development,* 2013; DOI:10.1111/cdev.12143

81 Kilner, J. M. & Lemon, R. N. (2013). What we know currently about mirror neurons. *Current Biology, 23,* R1057-R1062.

82 Iacoboni, M. (2008). *Mirroring People: The science of empathy and how we connect with others.* New York: Picador.

Siegel, D. J. (2007). *The Mindful Brain: Reflection and attunement in the cultivation of well-being.* New York: W. W. Norton and Co. Inc.

83 For more information on the disagreement in science over whether humans do indeed possess mirror neurons, and specifically whether those neurons are present in the empathic response, a very well-balanced and relatively simple reading can be found at Wikipedia simply by searching mirror neuron. Further helpful information can be found here: integral-options.blogspot.com.au/2010/04/mirror-neurons-deconstructing-promise.html

84 Gottman, J. M. (1999). *The seven principles for making marriage work.* New York: Three Rivers Press.

85 Wixom, R. M. (2013). The words we speak. General Conference of The Church of Jesus Christ of Latter-Day Saints, April.

86 Covey, S. R. (2000). *The 7 Habits of Highly Effective People*. Melbourne, Australia: The Business Library.

87 The RULER program can be retrieved from ei.yale.edu/ruler/ruler-overview/, accessed 31 March 2014.

88 Gottman, J. M., & Declaire, J. (1997). *Raising an Emotionally Intelligent Child: The Heart of Parenting*. New York: Fireside.

89 See Covey, S. R. (1997). *The 7 Habits of Highly Effective Families* (previously cited) for more details.

90 Joussemet, M., Landry, R., & Koestner, R. (2008). A self-determination theory perspective on parenting. *Canadian Psychology, 49,* 194–200.

91 Keijsers, L., Branje, S., Hawk, S. T., Schwartz, S. J., Frijns, T., Koot, H. M., van Lier, P., & Meeus, W. (2012). Forbidden friends as forbidden fruit: Parental supervision of friendships, contact with deviant peers, and adolescent delinquency. *Child Development, 83,* 651–666.

92 There are dozens of research articles on this topic that can be easily searched for online. Most tell a consistent story: homework is not related to grades, and often undermines motivation. As one example:

Maltese, A. V., Tai, R. H., & Fan, X. (2012). When is homework worth the time? Evaluating the association between homework and achievement in high school science and math. *High School Journal, 96,* 52–72. (This article finds no relationship between grades and homework, but suggests a positive relationship between standardised test scores and homework.)

The following two books provide a strong empirical overview of the homework literature. The first is a balanced and scholarly review. The second is quite polemic, but makes a strong case for abolishing homework until high school.

Horsley, M., & Walker, R. (2012). *Reforming Homework: Practices, learning and policy*. Melbourne, Australia: Palgrave Macmillan.

Kohn, A. (2006). *The Homework Myth: Why our kids get too much of a bad thing*. Cambridge, MA: Di Capo.

93 Padilla-Walker, L. M., Fraser, A. M., & Harper, J. M. (2012). Walking the walk: The moderating role of proactive parenting on adolescents' value-congruent behaviors. *Journal of Adolescence, 35,* 1141–1152.

94 Amatea, E. S., Smith-Adcock, S., & Villares, E. (2006). From family deficit to family strength: Viewing families' contributions to children's learning from a family resilience perspective. *Professional School Counseling, 9,* 177–189.

95 Freedman, M. (2011). No time for games. *Sydney Morning Herald*. Retrieved from www.smh.com.au/it-pro/no-time-for-games-20110130-1a9ys on 2 April 2014.

96 Lancy, D. F. (2008). *The anthropology of childhood: Cherubs, chattel, changelings*. 2nd edition. Cambridge University Press: Cambridge.

97 Strack, F., Martin, L. L., & Stepper, S. (1988). Inhibiting and facilitating conditions of the human smile: A nonobtrusive test of the facial feedback hypothesis. *Journal of Personality and Social Psychology, 54*, 768–777.

98 Onderko, P. (2014). Your happiest day ever. *Success.com*. Retrieved from www.success.com/article/your-happiest-day-ever on 2 April 2014.

99 Rohner, R. P., & Britner, P. A. (2002). Worldwide mental health correlates of parental acceptance-rejection: Review of cross-cultural and intracultural evidence. *Cross-Cultural Research, 36*, 16–47.

100 Rohner, R. P., & Veneziano, R. A. (2001). The importance of father love: History and contemporary evidence. *Review of General Psychology, 5*, 382–405.

101 Khaleque, A., & Rohner, R. P. (2011). Pancultural associations between perceived parental acceptance and psychological adjustment of children and adults: A meta-analytic review of worldwide research. *Journal of Cross-Cultural Psychology, 43*, 784–800.

102 Carrasco, M. A., & Rohner, R. P. (2013). Parental acceptance and children's psychological adjustment in the context of power and prestige. *Journal of Child and Family Studies, 22*, 1130–1137.

103 Dwairy, M. (2010). Parental acceptance-rejection: A fourth cross-cultural research on parenting and psychological adjustment of children. *Journal of Child and Family Studies, 19*, 30–35.

104 Rohner, R. P., & Khaleque, A. (Eds.). (2005). *Handbook for the study of parental acceptance and rejection* (4th ed.). Storrs, CT: Rohner Research Publications.

105 These questionnaire items come from the short version of the Parental Acceptance–Rejection Questionnaire (PARQ) found in Rohner & Khalique (2005) as previously cited, and also Rohner, R. P., & Khaleque, A. (2003). Reliability and validity of parental control scale: A meta-analysis of cross-cultural and intercultural studies. *Journal of Cross-Cultural Psychology, 34*, 643–649.

106 Dennison, B. A., Erb, T. A., & Jenkins, P. L. (2002). Television viewing and television in bedroom associated with overweight risk among low-income preschool children. *Pediatrics, 109*, 1028–1035.

107 Tandon P. S., Zhou C., Lozano P., & Christakis D. A. (2011). Preschoolers' total daily screen time at home and by type of child care. *Journal of Paediatrics, 158*, 297–300.

108 Gingold, J. A., Simon, A. E., & Schoendorf, K. C. (2014). Excess screen time in US children: Association with family rules and alternative activities. *Clinical Pediatrics, 53*, 41–50.

109 Jago, R., Stamatakis, E., Gama, A., Carvalhal, I. M., Nogueira, H., Rosado, V., & Padez, C. (2012). Parent and child screen-viewing time and home media environment. *American Journal of Preventive Medicine, 43*, 150–158.

110 Duch, H., Fisher, E. M., Ensari, I., & Harrington, A. (2013). Screen time use in children under 3 years old: A systematic review of correlates. *The International Journal of Behavioural Nutrition and Physical Activity, 10,* Article 102.

111 See also Jago et al. (2012).

112 Romer, D., Bagdasarov, Z., & More, E. (2013). Older versus newer media and the well-being of United States youth: Results from a national longitudinal panel. *Journal of Adolescent Health, 52,* 613–619.

113 For some staggering statements from one of the world's pioneers in the research on neuro-plasticity in the brain and the way the brain is literally re-wired as tolerance for pornographic content grows, see this website: yourbrainonporn.com/doidge-on-pornography-and-neuroplasticity. Norman Doidge, author of *The Brain That Wires Itself* writes compellingly of the issues surrounding tolerance and withdrawal from pornography.

114 See *The Daily Telegraph*, March 21, 2015. Article entitled Sexual and indecent assaults by children against other children are on the rise. Note, specifically, that 'Indecent assaults in schools jumped by 60 per cent in the past decade while child sexual assaults in schools have also risen by almost 20 per cent.' While it is true that baseline numbers are relatively low, these increases remain significant with most experts pointing directly to media, and specifically pornography, as part of the problem. While I do not believe it is as simple as that, I do believe that there is an important association between pornography viewing and behaviour – particularly among children.

115 Hoyos Cillero I., & Jago R. (2010). Systematic review of correlates of screen-viewing among young children. *Preventive Medicine, 51,* 3–10.

116 Vandewater, E. A., Park, S.-E., Huang X., & Wartella, E. A. (2005). 'No – you can't watch that': Parental rules and young children's media use. *American Behavioral Scientist, 48,* 608–623.

117 Lampard, A. M., Jurkowski, J. M., & Davison, K. K. (2012). Social-cognitive predictors of low-income parents' restriction of screen time among preschool-aged children. *Health Education & Behaviour, 40,* 526–530.

118 See Duch et al. (2013).

119 Schmidt, M. E., Haines, J., O'Brien, A., McDonald, J., Price, S., Sherry, B., & Taveras, E. M. (2012). Systematic review of effective strategies for reducing screen time among young children. *Obesity, 20,* 1338–1354.

120 See Duch et al. (2013).

121 Atkin, A. J., Corder, K., & van Sluijs, E. M. F. (2013). Bedroom media, sedentary time, and screen-time in children: A longitudinal analysis. *The International Journal of Behavioural Nutrition and Physical Activity, 10,* Article 137.

122 Retrieved from www.bubhub.com.au/info/articles/baby/get_more_from_ your_me_time.shtml on 4 April 2014.

123 Retrieved from life.gaiam.com/article/recharging-ahead-7-ways-take-guilt-free-me-time on 4 April 2014.

124 Perhaps the most high-profile recent example of this is Senior, J. (2014). *All Joy and No Fun*. New York: HarperCollins. See also Skenazy L. (2009). *Free-range Kids: Giving our children the freedom we had without going nuts with worry*. San Francisco, CA: Jossey-Bass.

125 There is an abundance of research reflecting this finding. A snapshot of references to support the argument include:

Angeles, L. (2010). Children and life satisfaction. *Journal of Happiness Studies, 11*, 523–538. (It is important to review the erratum to this study. A coding error led to incorrect conclusions that called into question all previous work in this area. When it was discovered, the data fell into alignment with previous research.)

Dolan, P., Peasgood, T., & White, M. (2008). Do we really know what makes us happy? A review of the economic literature on the factors associated with subjective wellbeing. *Journal of Economic Psychology, 29*, 94–122.

Glenn, N. D., & McLanahan, S. (1981). The effects of offspring on the psychological well-being of older adults. *Journal of Marriage and the Family, 43*, 409–421.

Glenn, N. D., & McLanahan, S. (1982). Children and marital happiness: A further specification of the relationship. *Journal of Marriage and the Family, 44*, 63–72.

Umberson, D., & Grove, W.R. (1989) Parenthood and psychological well-being: Theory, measurement, and stage in the family life course. *Journal of Family Issues, 10*, 440–462.

126 See Senior, J. (2014) for more on this point.

127 Kahneman, D., Krueger, A. B., Schkade, D. A., Schwarz, N., & Stone, A. A. (2004). A survey method for characterizing daily life experience: The day reconstruction method. *Science, 306*, 1776–1780.

128 See the video clip by Kelly McGonigal at Stanford University at www.youtube.com/watch?v=jSMYqc4CAZU accessed 4 April 2014.

129 Weinstein, N., & Ryan, R. M. (2010). When helping helps: Autonomous motivation for prosocial behaviour and its influence on wellbeing for the helper and recipient. *Journal of Personality and Social Psychology, 98*, 222–244.

130 Ashton-James, C. E., Kushlev, K., & Dunn, E. W. (2013). Parents reap what they sow: Child-centrism and parental well-being. *Social Psychological and Personality Science, 4*, 635–642.

131 This is based on my doctoral research at the University of Wollongong with over 1000 Australian parents. The results were published in the following journal articles:

Coulson, J. C., Oades, L. G., & Stoyles, G. J. (2010). Parent's conception and experience of calling in childrearing: A qualitative analysis. *Journal of Humanistic Psychology, 52,* 222–247.

Coulson, J. C., Oades, L. G., & Stoyles, G. J. (accepted September 2011). Parents' subjective sense of calling in childrearing: Measurement, development and preliminary findings. *Journal of Positive Psychology, 7,* 83–94.

For information about the wellbeing of children, see ro.uow.edu.au/theses/3514

132 Park, N., Peterson, C., & Ruch, W. (2009). Orientations to happiness and life satisfaction in twenty seven nations. *Journal of Positive Psychology, 4,* 273–279.

Schueller, S. M., & Seligman, M. E. P. (2010). Pursuit of pleasure, engagement, and meaning: Relationships to subjective and objective measures of well-being. *The Journal of Positive Psychology, 5,* 253–263.

Vella-Brodrick, D. A., Park, N., & Peterson, C. (2009). Three ways to be happy: Pleasure, engagement, and meaning – Findings from Australian and US samples. *Social Indicators Research, 90,* 165–179.

133 Lyubomirsky, S., King, L. A., & Diener, E. (2005). The benefits of frequent positive affect: Does happiness lead to success? *Psychological Bulletin, 131,* 803–855.

Pressman, S. D., & Cohen, S. (2005). Does positive affect influence health? *Psychological Bulletin, 131,* 925–971.

134 Steger, M. F., Kashdan, T. B. & Oishi, S. (2008). Being good by doing good: Daily eudaimonic activity and wellbeing. *Journal of Research in Personality, 42,* 22–42. (previously cited).

Acknowledgements

I always find it fascinating to read the acknowledgements of authors. There are so many people involved in bringing a book from the mind of a writer to the pages in front of you. These people work (often) tirelessly and with tremendous dedication to support people like me. They deserve acknowledgement.

Firstly, to Alex Brooks, former Editor-in-chief at kidspot. com.au, and to Jeni O'Dowd, editor of the *Kidspot* liftout in the Saturday NewsCorp papers, a heartfelt thanks. From day one of our respective meetings, I have had your generous support and been granted an opportunity to influence and reach into so many families around Australia and the world because of the kidspot. com.au platform. I do not take this privilege lightly. Additional thanks to so many other Kidspot staff who have worked with me in a variety of roles to get my articles out there for everyone to see – and who have supported me in my work. Thanks to Marg Rafferty, Ella Walsh, Lucy Kippist, Kim Wilson, Pru Cox, Bek Day, Donne Restom and the rest of the team.

Secondly, I am grateful to Nicole Sheffield. A chance meeting in the Holt Street NewsCorp offices was the real catalyst for this book being published. Nicole, our conversation that day was a game-changer. Thank you.

To all the good people in the various teams at ABC Books, I extend my appreciation. I love what you have done to turn my 'manuscript with potential' into the polished, fabulous-looking book we can now hold in our hands. Thank you to Katie Stackhouse, in particular, for the endless conversations about what the book might be and should be, and for putting up with my thought-bubbles, crazy ideas, and over-zealous enthusiasm. Your expert, gentle guidance can be felt throughout this finished book Katie, and I am so pleased we could work together on this project. I could not ask for a more understanding, patient, and wise editor.

There are many amazing parents who have shared their stories with me, and allowed me to share those stories with you in the pages of this book. I am grateful for their trust in me. I am appreciative of their willingness to be influenced by my ideas. I am thrilled with the happiness their families have experienced. I thank them for allowing me to share their stories in this book.

My children live with a father who is a parenting expert, but who, from time to time, still struggles to practice what he preaches. Their patience with me, and their forgiveness of me, is an undeserved blessing I can never repay except with greater attempts at love towards them. To acknowledge them and express my gratitude for them seems entirely inadequate. Chanel, Abbie, Ella, Annie, Lilli, and Emilie, I love you. This has all been for you.

Most of all, I express my deepest gratitude to Kylie, my wife and companion for the past 18 years and counting. I suspect that a more supportive wife could not be found in all the world. While I get the public credit for being the 'model' father to our six girls, it is Kylie who holds our family together and does the heavy lifting of day-to-day intensive parenting. While I am flying around the country (and the world) giving talks about how to make families happy, or while I am writing books and articles to help everyone else make their family happy, it is Kylie who is in the trenches day in and day out, working with our girls and raising them wonderfully. My girls have a world-class mum.

Index